ADVANCED
CATIA V5 Workbook

Release 16

Richard Cozzens
Southern Utah University

CAD/CAM
ENGINEERING
TECHNOLOGY
www.suu.edu/cadcam

ISBN: 978-1-58503-321-8

SDC
PUBLICATIONS

Schroff Development Corporation

www.SDCpublications.com

Preface

This workbook is intended to be a natural continuation of the **CATIA V5 Workbook** written by Richard Cozzens and published by the Schroff Development Corporation (www.schroff.com). The **Advanced CATIA V5 Workbook** covers a select group of advanced CATIA V5 work benches and tools. The work benches/tools used and covered in this workbook are Sketcher, Part Design, Assembly Design, Drafting, Generative Stress Analysis, Generative Sheet Metal Design, DMU Kinematics, Prismatic Machining and Knowledgeware Tools.

The **Advanced CATIA V5 Workbook** is not meant to be a CATIA V5 reference guide. It is intended to be an organized, planned process to learn a selected group of advanced CATIA V5 workbenches. The CATIA V5 Help Menu is a great reference and The CATIA Companion makes a good supplement to this workbook. The contents of this workbook are a combination of materials gathered and adapted from a variety of projects.

Workbook Revisions

This is the Third release of the **Advanced CATIA V5 Workbook**. The material has been updated an improved from the first release.

Schroff Development Corporation and I are dedicated to keeping this workbook current and accurate to the latest CATIA V5 release level. Additional work benches and applications will be added to later releases. Suggestions are not only welcome but requested. For workbook updates, additional information and sample models log onto **www.schroff1.com**.

For information on CATIA Training:
www.CATIAV5Workbook.com

About the Author

Richard Cozzens earned his Bachelor of Science degree from Brigham Young University and his Master's degree from Southern Utah University. Richard is currently working on his PhD in Engineering. Richard has worked seven years for Boeing as a Manufacturing Engineer, Tool Designer and Manufacturing Research and Development Engineer. Richard is a graduate of the Boeing Engineering In Training program, receiving training in the following areas: NC Programming, Producibility, Manufacturing Research & Development and Manufacturing Engineering.

Richard worked for MTI (Metalcraft Technologies, Inc.) for five years as an Engineering Manager and CATIA Specialist. As an Engineering Manager for MTI, he worked with engineering documents and manufacturing plans from most of the major aerospace and defense companies.

Richard now teaches full time at Southern Utah University in the Engineering and Technology Department. He still works as a CAD consultant for MTI and other manufacturing companies. He has conducted training seminars for numerous companies and colleges/universities around the world. He has authored a series of workbooks on Mastercam, CATIA V5, AutoCAD, SolidWorks and Inventor. He has developed a web based training tool to supplement these workbooks (www.catiav5workbook.com). He is an active participant in the IBM HEAT program and has given presentations at COE (CATIA Operators Exchange) and other related seminars. Richard's continuing close relationship with CATIA V5 users from all types of industries and CATIA V5 instructors/professors from colleges and universities provides an invaluable resource for continually improving this workbook.

Acknowledgments

The concept of this book has been driven from the popularity of the original **CATIA V5 Workbook**. I have received many requests to cover additional CATIA V5 work benches and applications.

I would like to thank the following:

You the User: For making the **CATIA V5 Workbook** and **Advanced CATIA V5 Workbook** so popular in the CATIA V5 training arena.

Daniel Heaton, SUU: development of Lesson 1 & 2.

Daniel Cozzens, BYU and Lockheed Design Engineer: development of Lesson 3.

Jared Mortensen, SUU: development of Lesson 4.

Sid England, SUU & Metalcraft Technologies, Inc.: development and consultation on Lesson 5.

Tracy Day, SUU, Arbor Press: model development used on the cover of the **Advanced CATIA V5 Workbook**.

Download Site

****

To access and download workbook CATParts, CATProducts, CATdrawings, updates, additional information and sample models, as well as the model required for workbook lessons.

www.schroff1.com

****

Related Sites

****

www.schroff.com

www.schroff1.com

www.catiav5workbook.com

www.suu.edu/cadcam

www.suu.edu

www.coe.org

www.CatiaSolutions.com

www.catia.com

****

TABLE OF CONTENTS

Introduction to Advanced CATIA V5

Lesson 1   Knowledgeware

Lesson 2   DMU Kinematics Workbench

Lesson 3   Generative Structural Analysis Workbench

| Lesson 4 | Generative Sheet Metal Design Workbench |

Lesson 5   Prismatic Machining Workbench

Terms and Definitions

Overview

Overview of Workbook Lessons

Introduction:
Reviewing CATIA V5 Standard Menus and Tools

This section reviews the CATIA V5 Standard Menu and Tools. This section is also good for referencing Standard Menus and Tools.

Lesson 1:
Introduction to CATIA V5 Knowledgeware

Introduction to the **CATIA V5 Knowledgeware Tools**; **Lesson 1** Objectives; screen layout, tools and toolbars; creating required sketches; assigning & naming variable; creating & applying spreadsheet; linking the spreadsheet; creating a **Macro**; Modifying using **VB Script**; Creating prompts; creating & checking standards; updating the production drawing; **Lesson 1 Review** and **Lesson 1 Practice Exercises**.

Lesson 2:
Introduction to the Kinematics Workbench

Introduction to the **Kinematics Workbench**; **Lesson 2** Objectives; screen layout, tools and toolbars; importing existing assembly; create joints; create a mechanism; simulate a mechanism; compile a simulation; create a replay; replay to analyze; **Lesson 2 Review** and **Lesson 2 Practice Exercises**.

Lesson 3:
Introduction to the Stress Analysis Workbench

Introduction to the **Generative Structural Analysis Workbench**; **Lesson 3** Objectives; screen layout, tools and toolbars; creating a cantilever beam; Analysis setup; customize the view; structural properties; create restraints and loads; apply loads; store the results; analysis results; mesh size and sag; create virtual parts; customization; incorporate Knowledge Advisor; generate a report; **Lesson 3 Review** and **Lesson 3 Practice Exercises**.

Lesson 4:
Introduction to the Generative Sheet Metal Design Workbench

Introduction to the **Sheet Metal Design Workbench** screen layout, tools and toolbars;
Flattening existing sheet metal parts; Creating sheet Metal parts; Defining parameters;
Creating flanges; Working with holes; Saving in DXF format; **Lesson 4 Review** and
Lesson 4 Practice Exercises.

Lesson 5:
Introduction to the Prismatic Machining Workbench

Introduction to the **Prismatic Machining Workbench** screen layout, tools and toolbars;
setting parameters; machine axis; defining geometry; setting up strategy; defining tools;
feeds and speeds; using Macros; Using replay; drilling; milling pockets; post processing;
Lesson 5 Review and **Lesson 5 Practice Exercises**.

Workbook/CATIA V5 Terms and Definition

This is another critical section, because it adds to your CATIA V5 foundation of
knowledge. This section will also help you navigate and understand the terms used in
this workbook.

Introduction

Introduction to CATIA V5

CATIA is one of the world's leading high-end CAD/CAM/CAE software packages. CATIA V5 takes the power of an industry and technology-leading legacy CAD/CAM/CAE program and updates the programming (a total rewrite) to take advantage of the new Windows technology. CATIA V5 programming also allows you the flexibility of using sketched and parametric based design. CATIA V5 is the power you expect from CATIA with a greatly reduced learning curve. CATIA V5 makes a lot of processes practically automatic. You, the user, define the variables and CATIA V5 creates it for you. If it isn't exactly what you wanted, you adjust your variables and CATIA V5 will update the creation. CATIA V5 is the program that does it all. It is the leading edge technology starting with its product concept, through design, assembly, testing, manufacturing and modeling, to its rendering capabilities. For more detail on CATIA V5, refer to the CATIA V5 home page on the Internet. The address is: www.catia.com.

Workbook Objectives

The term Advanced is in reference to the Workbenches covered in this workbook not necessarily the process and applications. The steps for the advanced workbenches are basic and step by step. It is assumed the user already has a good understanding of the following Workbenches: **Sketcher**, **Part Design**, **Drafting, and Assembly Design**. If this is not the case it is suggested that the user go through the **CATIA V5 Workbook** available at **www.schroff.com**.

The objective of this workbook is to instruct anyone who wants to learn CATIA V5 through organized, graphically rich, step-by-step instructions on some of CATIA V5 more advanced Workbenches namely: **Knowledgeware**, **Kinematics**, **Stress Analysis**, **Sheet Metal Design** and **Prismatic Machining**.

How to Use this Workbook

Although most of the steps are detailed, the steps and processes are numbered and bolded so the more experienced user can go directly to the subject and/or area of interest.

All of the lessons follow the same format:

Introduction: This section introduces the problem covered in the lesson and the CATIA V5 workbenches and tools used to solve the problem. This section is a quick overview of the problem, basic steps and completed results.

Objectives: This section provides the main concepts that will be covered in the lesson. The Review Questions and Practice Exercises are tied directly to the stated objectives.

Workbench and Toolbars: This section introduces the workbenches and tools with a brief definition of each tool. The tool icons are also displayed in this section.

Step-by-Step Instructions: The bulk of each lesson consists of step-by-step instructions on how to apply the newly introduced tools to solve the lesson problem. This section is designed for basic users and more advanced users. The beginner will want to read through each step while the more advanced user may want to skip to the bolded words, which for the most part are the actions required by each step. There are **Notes**, **Hints** and **Comments** along with links to all of the graphics for visual explanations.

Summary: This section brings together everything you have learned.

Review Questions: This section consists of 20 questions taken from the lesson. The purpose of the review is to help solidify the concepts and tools taught in the lesson. The questions tie directly back to the listed objectives.

Practice Exercises: Being able to answer questions is one thing, being able to create is another! The **Practice Exercises** are problems that require the use of the tools and processes covered in the lesson. Some of the **Practice Exercises** have helpful hints on how to create the part.

To get the most out of each lesson, it is suggested that you preview the entire lesson so you get an overview of what information is contained in each lesson. This overview will also give you an idea of what it will take to complete the lesson. Read through the **Lesson Review** questions before you begin, this way you can be searching for the answers as you go through the lesson. Preview the **Practice Exercises**, as you go through the lesson you can be looking for the tools and processes required to complete the **Practice Exercises**.

CATIA V5 Running on Windows XP

This book was developed with CATIA V5 running on **Microsoft XP Professional.** CATIA V5 running on UNIX is almost identical. The biggest difference is UNIX will not have all of the **Windows NT** functionality. The **Windows NT** functionality gives the user the flexibility of having several options in completing almost any task. For example, you have the **Cut/Copy** and **Paste** tools in the **Windows NT** pull down menu, you have the quick keys that accomplish the same thing (**Ctrl c** and **Ctrl v**) or you could use the CATIA V5 **Cut** and **Paste** tool found in the CATIA V5 **Standard** toolbar. Another example is that you have the choice to highlight an entity then select the tool to apply or you can reverse the choices and select the tool, then select the entity. Some of these options are not available on the UNIX operating system. This workbook assumes you have at minimum a basic knowledge of the different **Windows 2000/NT** and **XP Professional** functions.

Reviewing CATIA V5 Standard Menus and Tools

The following standard screen layout shows you where different tools and toolbars are located. The numbers coordinate with the following pages where the tool label is bolded. The tool label is followed by a brief explanation and, in some cases, steps on how to use and/or access the tool.

Figure I.1

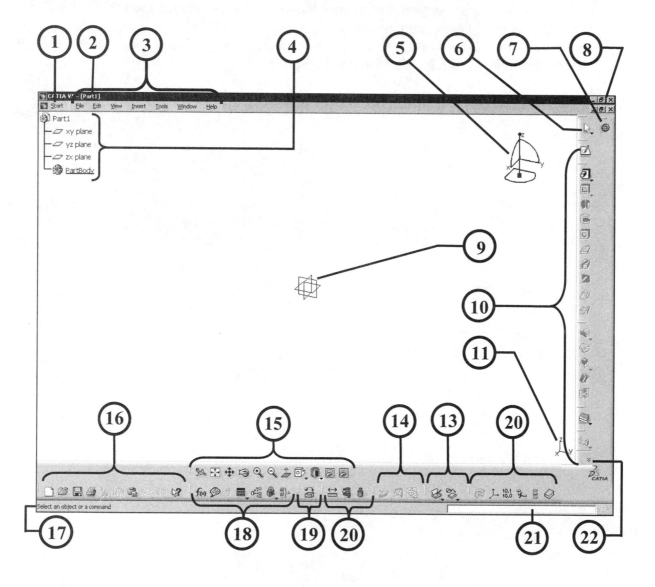

The following list of menus is not meant to be a comprehensive definition of every tool on the standard CATIA V5 screen. The purpose is to provide a quick reference and explanation. If more detailed information is needed and/or required, refer to the CATIA V5 **Help** menu and/or internet homepage.

The Start Menu

The **Start** pull down menu gives you access to all of the CATIA V5 Workbenches. The availability of the workbenches will depend on the CATIA V5 license's configuration; the one shown in Figure I.2 is the Educational Package (ED2) offered through the IBM HEAT Program. The workbenches used in this workbook will be found under the Mechanical Design, Shape, and Digital Mockup workbench categories. If you select the arrow to the right of the Workbench Category, the workbenches organized within that category will be displayed (reference Figure I.2). Figure I.2 shows the workbenches organized under the Mechanical Design Category; the Part Design Workbench is the highlighted workbench.

The second section of the Start menu displays the active (open) CATIA V5 documents. Figure I.2 shows that Part1 and Part2 documents are open; Part2 is the active document.

The third section of the Start menu displays the most recent active CATIA V5 documents. This allows you to quickly open recently active documents. For example, with the options shown in Figure I.2 the Analysis1.CATAnalysis document could be opened by selecting it from this menu rather than opening the browser window and browsing for it.

Figure I.2

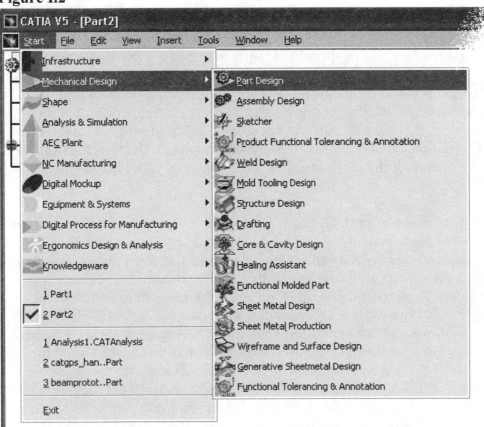

The Current Active CATIA V5 Document

This area of the screen displays the name of the current active CATIA V5 document. The active CATIA V5 document shown in Figure I.1 is the default name (Part1.CATPart) for a CATPart document. For a close up view with document circled, reference Figure I.3. Displaying the name of the current document is quite typical of MS Windows compatible software.

Figure I.3

③ **The Standard Windows Toolbar**

The Standard Windows toolbar contains your standard MS Windows pull down menus; reference Figure I.4. There are specific CATIA V5 tools found in the different pull down menus. The tools you will be required to use in this workbook will be defined in the lesson that they are used in. For detail information on the options found in the Standard Windows Toolbar reference Lesson 1 in the CATIA V5 Workbook.

Figure I.4

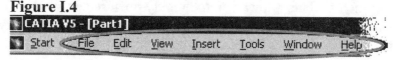

 The Specification Tree

The **Specification Tree** contains the history of tools and processes used to create a part. For example, you can look at a completed part and see that there were fillets and holes applied to it. At what point in the part creation were the fillets and holes added? Are there redundant processes and extra elements? Can the process for part creation be improved? Looking at the resulting part will not answer any of these questions. The **Specification Tree** on the other hand has all of this information. The **Specification Tree** contains the entire history of the part's creation. For a complex part, the **Specification Tree** could get large.

Select the **Tools**, **Options**, **General**, **Display**, **Tree** option to specify what you want the **Specification Tree** to show and how you want it to appear. The branches of the **Specification Tree** can be expanded and contracted by selecting the – and + symbols located on each branch. You can **Zoom In** and **Pan** the **Specification Tree** the same way you would a part. You must double click on a **Specification Tree** branch to make the workspace go dim. Once the workspace is dimmed (under-intensified), all of the screen manipulation tools will apply to the **Specification Tree** instead of the workspace. This means you can move and zoom the **Specification Tree** as you do the part in the workspace. Double clicking a **Specification Tree** branch will bring the part back to normal (the active workspace). The F3 key will hide the **Specification Tree** from view (a toggle key). CATIA V5 allows you to make modifications to the part by using the part itself and/or by using the **Specification Tree**. The **Specification Tree** is used in all the lessons. The **Specification Tree** is a very powerful tool, but you must know how to use it to your advantage. The **Specification Tree** shown in this section represents most of the branches and applications used in this workbook. The presentation of the tree will vary depending on installation and customization. The tree shown below was created with a standard installation. The tree was customized to show all branches such as **Relationships**, **Formulas** and **Applications** using the **Tools** > **Options** window. Figure I.5 displays a default Specification Tree, the Specification Tree has no geometry added to it. Figure I.6 displays all the geometrical elements that make up the part shown in the workspace. Notice the Hole.2 branch of the Specification Tree is highlighted, Hole.2 in the part is also highlighted. CATIA V5 allows you to select the elements using the Specification tree or the actual geometry in the workspace.

Figure I.5

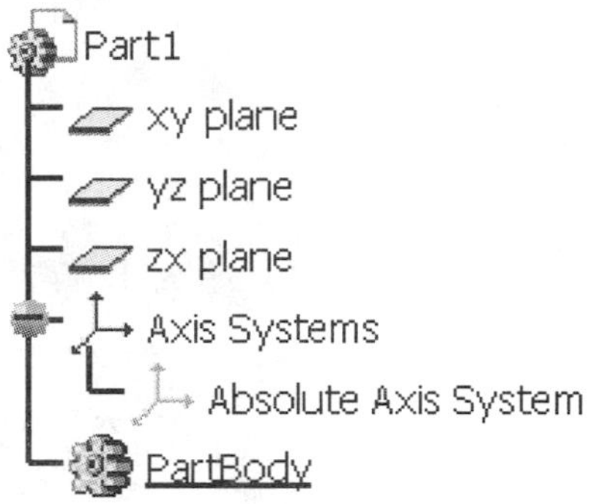

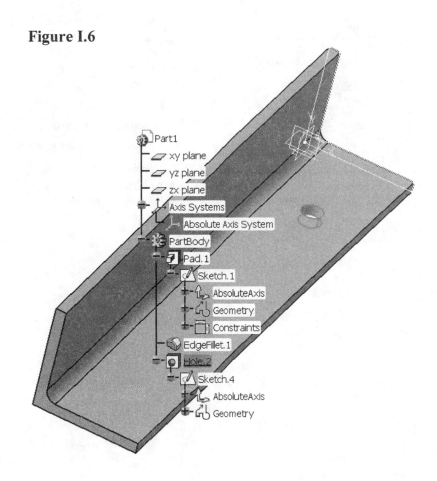

Figure I.6

You can control how and what is displayed in the Specification Tree by selecting **Tools** > **Options** > **Display** > and modifying the options found in the **Tree Appearance** and **Tree Manipulation** tabs. For the lesson in this workbook you will need to also go to **Tools** > **Options** > **Infrastructure** > **Part Infrastructure** and select the **Display** tab. Make sure the options are selected as shown in Figure I.7. For more detailed information reference the Lesson 1 of the CATIA V5 Workbook.

Figure I.7

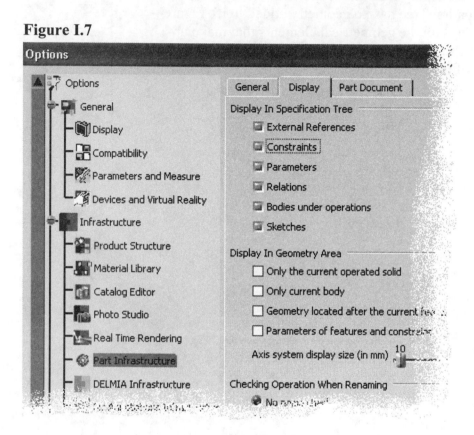

Figure I.8 provides a review for most of the possible types of information that can be viewed in the Specification Tree. The figure also provides a brief description of each branch of the Specification Tree.

Figure I.8

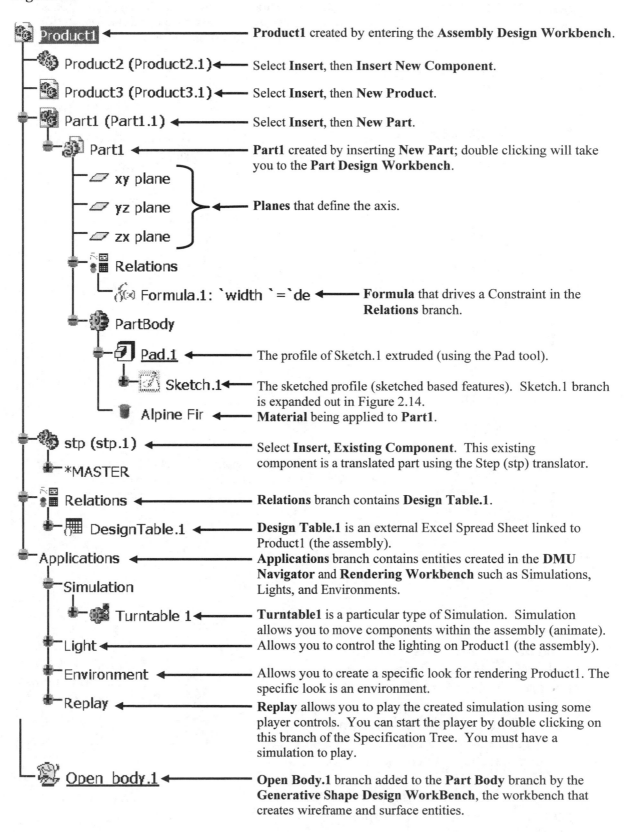

Product1 → **Product1** created by entering the **Assembly Design Workbench.**

Product2 (Product2.1) → Select **Insert,** then **Insert New Component.**

Product3 (Product3.1) → Select **Insert,** then **New Product.**

Part1 (Part1.1) → Select **Insert,** then **New Part.**

Part1 → **Part1** created by inserting **New Part**; double clicking will take you to the **Part Design Workbench.**

xy plane

yz plane → **Planes** that define the axis.

zx plane

Relations

Formula.1: `width `=`de → **Formula** that drives a Constraint in the **Relations** branch.

PartBody

Pad.1 → The profile of Sketch.1 extruded (using the Pad tool).

Sketch.1 → The sketched profile (sketched based features). Sketch.1 branch is expanded out in Figure 2.14.

Alpine Fir → **Material** being applied to **Part1.**

stp (stp.1) → Select **Insert, Existing Component.** This existing component is a translated part using the Step (stp) translator.

*MASTER

Relations → **Relations** branch contains **Design Table.1.**

DesignTable.1 → **Design Table.1** is an external Excel Spread Sheet linked to Product1 (the assembly).

Applications → **Applications** branch contains entities created in the **DMU Navigator** and **Rendering Workbench** such as Simulations, Lights, and Environments.

Simulation

Turntable 1 → **Turntable1** is a particular type of Simulation. Simulation allows you to move components within the assembly (animate).

Light → Allows you to control the lighting on Product1 (the assembly).

Environment → Allows you to create a specific look for rendering Product1. The specific look is an environment.

Replay → **Replay** allows you to play the created simulation using some player controls. You can start the player by double clicking on this branch of the Specification Tree. You must have a simulation to play.

Open body.1 → **Open Body.1** branch added to the **Part Body** branch by the **Generative Shape Design WorkBench**, the workbench that creates wireframe and surface entities.

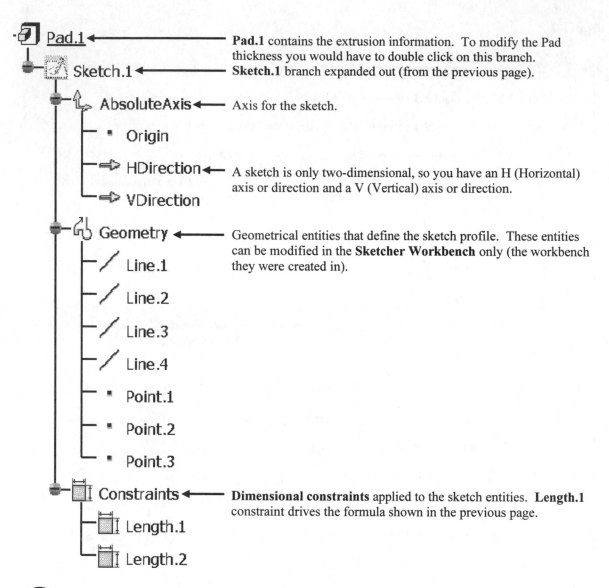

Pad.1 contains the extrusion information. To modify the Pad thickness you would have to double click on this branch.

Sketch.1 branch expanded out (from the previous page).

Axis for the sketch.

A sketch is only two-dimensional, so you have an H (Horizontal) axis or direction and a V (Vertical) axis or direction.

Geometrical entities that define the sketch profile. These entities can be modified in the **Sketcher Workbench** only (the workbench they were created in).

Dimensional constraints applied to the sketch entities. **Length.1** constraint drives the formula shown in the previous page.

⑤ The Compass

This tool allows you to modify the location and orientation of a part relative to the **XYZ** coordinates and/or relative to other parts if they are in an assembly. You can place the cursor over the center point of the axis and drag the compass and drop it on a surface. Once the compass is placed on a surface it will turn green. You can then use the cursor to manipulate the orientation of the part geometry by selecting the axis or direction on the compass that you want the geometry modified in. To restore the location and orientation of the compass select **View** > **Reset compass**.

Figure I.9

Select and hold to rotate geometry about the Z axis.

Select and hold to move the compass onto geometry.

The Select Tool and Toolbar

This tool allows you to select entities in the workspace and Specification Tree as well as the other areas of the CATIA V5 screen shown in Figure I.1. The default selector is the **Select Arrow**, which allows single point and left click selections. If you select the small arrow to the right of the icon, it will reveal the other selection tools, they are shown below.

Figure I.10

The **Select** Tool		
Toolbar	**Tool Name**	**Tool Definition**
	Select	This is the default tool; point and click (left mouse button) to select the desired entity. Multiple entity selection can be done by holding down the Ctrl key while selecting.
	Selection Trap	This allows you to draw a box around the entities that you want to select. The box is exclusive to entities that intersect with the selection box. This is a quick and easy multi-select tool.
	Intersecting Trap	This allows you to draw a box around the entities, but will also select the entities that are intersected with the box. The selection box is inclusive.
	Polygon Trap	This selection is similar to the box selection trap, but allows you to sketch a more defined area of inclusion and exclusion of entities. This selection tool is quick, and allows you to be more exclusive in the multi-selection process.
	Paint Stroke Selection	This selection tool allows you to paint a line across the screen and any entity that the paint stroke crosses is selected.

⑦ **The Current Workbench**

The side bar will be filled with toolbars and tools associated with the current workbench. As you select a different workbench you will notice the toolbars and tools will change (reference area 10 in Figure I.1). Figure I.11 shows the Part Design Workbench. This is especially critical when you have several windows open with different workbenches. If you have them displayed on a split screen, the active window will be the one with the blue border.

Figure I.11

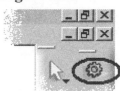

⑧ Window Maximize and Minimize

These options are the same as most other MS Windows programs.
The top row of tools control CATIA V5 Program as a whole. The
■ sign will minimize the program window. The ✕ (last tool)
will close the program. The tools in the second row control the
active window within CATIA V5. If you have several CATIA V5
documents open you can minimize one or each of the windows
within the CATIA V5 program. You can resize 🗗 each of the
windows. The last tool ✕ allows you to close an individual
window.

Figure I.12

⑨ Plane Representation (xy, yz and xz)

The intersecting planes represent the 0,0,0 point of the
workspace. Each plane is graphically represented in the
workspace and also in the Specification Tree as shown in
Figure I.13. If you select the YZ plane from the
Specification Tree the YZ plane in the workspace will also
highlight, as shown in Figure I.13. If you would rather have
the 0,0,0 point be represented as an axis as shown in Figure
I.14 you can customize the workspace representation by
selecting the **Tools** > **Options**. Expand the Infrastructure
branch of the Options Tree. Select the Part Infrastructure
branch. Select the Part Document tab. Under the new part
section select the box to "Create an Axis System when
creating a new part." Select **OK** to complete the
customization. Create a new CATIA V5 Document. The
new document will have an axis similar to the one shown in
Figure 1.14

Figure I.13

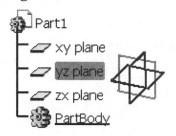

Figure I.14

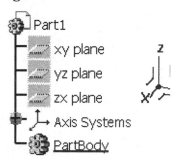

The Current Workbench Tools and Toolbars

This side bar will be filled with toolbars and tools associated with the current workbench. If you select a different workbench, the tools and toolbars will update to the newly selected workbench. Each lesson covers a specific workbench; the tools and toolbars specific to that workbench will be covered in that particular lesson. The following is a list of things you can do with the tools and toolbars.

Figure I.15

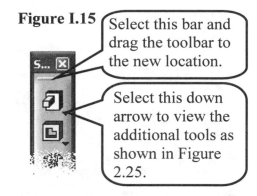

Select this bar and drag the toolbar to the new location.

Select this down arrow to view the additional tools as shown in Figure 2.25.

➢ All the toolbars are tear away toolbars meaning that you can select the top bar of each tool as shown in figure I.15 and drag it to a new location.

➢ If you do not know the name of the tool, you can hold the cursor over the tool and the tool name will be displayed as shown in Figure I.16.

Figure I.16

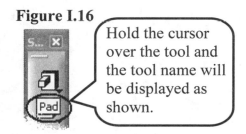

Hold the cursor over the tool and the tool name will be displayed as shown.

➢ To close the toolbar you can select the red ⊠ at the top of the toolbar.

➢ To reopen the toolbar you can drag the cursor over the side toolbar area and left mouse click. This will bring up the contextual window shown in Figure I.17. Notice some tools are already selected and some are not; each tool can be toggled on or off just by selecting it. Figure I.17 only represents a few of the 35+ toolbars.

Figure I.17

➢ You can create your own customized workbench with your own favorite tools. To complete this you would select the **Tools** > **Customize** > **Toolbars** options.

Axis Orientation

This tool shows the orientation of the Axis within the workspace. The orientation will change as you rotate the part or workspace around.

Figure I.18

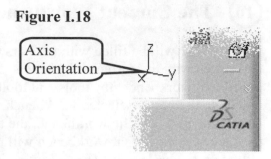

 The Tools Toolbars

This toolbar changes depending on which workbench you are in. The three tools that are consistently in this toolbar are listed below.

Toolbar	Tool Name	Tool Definition
	Update All	This tool will be under-intensified unless there is an entity in the document that requires updating. If the tool is colored (not under-intensified) it is signifying that some entity requires updating. Selecting the tool will update all of the entities. This tool is used most when revisions/changes are made to existing constraints whether it is part design changes and/or assembly changes. If you make a change and the part/assembly does not reflect the change, check this tool; it may require you to select it to force an update.
	Axis System	This tool allows you to create multiple local axis systems. The Surfacing Lesson gives detailed instructions on how to create and orient new axis systems.
10,1 10,0	Mean Dimensions	This tool only works if you have previously defined a tolerance to the entity. When tolerances have been applied, this tool will compute the actual (mean) dimensions of the entity being reviewed.
	Create Datum	This tool deactivates the history mode. The entities used to create it will not be linked. The tool is a toggle tool; if you select it you must unselect it to turn it off.
	Only Current Operated Solid	This tool gives you the option to display only the current operated solid.
	Open catalog	This tool allows access to the user-defined catalog. Reference the **Help** menu for detailed instruction and application.

13 The Product Knowledge Template Toolbar

 This toolbar allows you to create Power Copies and document the places the Power Copies are instantiated.

Toolbar	Tool Name	Tool Definition
	**Power Copy Creation**	This tool allows you to create Power Copies. The Power Copies can be applied to similar parts or parts with similar features. The Power Copies can also be saved to the Catalog.
	Instantiate From Document	This tool allows you apply a previously saved Power Copy.

14 The Analysis Toolbar

This is another toolbar that is dependant on the active workbench.

Toolbar	Tool Name	Tool Definition
	Draft Analysis	This tool allows you to analyze draft angles and distances. This tool is particularly helpful when the angles and distances are too small to visually inspect.
	Curvature Analysis	This tool allows you to analyze the curvature of a surface. This is particularly helpful when you have a max and min curvature radius.
	Tap – Thread Analysis	This tool provides the ability to analyze the current part for thread and tap information.

⑮ The View Toolbar

This toolbar contains CATIA V5 specific functions. This workbook will have you use most of them in one lesson or another. Most of the tools apply to all of the workbenches.

Toolbar	Tool Name	Tool Definition
	Fly mode	Sets the fly mode. This is a very powerful and fun tool. Reference lessons covering the DMU Workbenches on how to use this tool.
	Fit All In	This tool will show the extent of all the graphics currently on the screen. It is a quick way to see what elements are on the screen and where they are in relationship to one another.
	Pan	This tool allows you to move the part around on the screen. The part does not change its location in the XYZ coordinate system, only in relationship to the screen. Every time you want to **Pan** the part you must select this tool first, unless you have a three-button mouse. **Quick Key**: With a three-button mouse you can press the middle mouse button down and drag the part to the desired location on the screen.
	Rotate	This tool allows you to rotate the part in three-dimensional space. It will place a representation of a space ball (sphere) in the center of the screen. There is a three-dimensional X on the space ball; you drag the X to where you want on the space ball and the part will rotate accordingly. This tool is critical to part manipulation. It is important that you get the hang of rotating the part to the orientation you want. This tool must be selected every time you want to rotate the part. This process is explained and shown step-by-step in Lesson 4, Step 7. **Quick Key:** A quicker method is using the mouse. Press the middle mouse button first. While holding the middle button down, press the left mouse button and drag the mouse around on the sphere. This brings up the space ball (sphere). Another method is to press the CTRL key while pressing the middle mouse button and dragging the mouse around the screen.

	Zoom In	This is similar to other graphics programs. This allows you to get a closer look at finer detail. **Quick Key**: Press the middle mouse button, hold it down as you press the left mouse button and release it. Now use the mouse to drag the cursor up the screen and the part will **Zoom In**. Using the mouse to **Zoom In** is a much smoother zooming method; you have more control.
	Zoom Out	This is similar to other graphics programs. This allows you to get the big picture, making the part smaller. **Quick Key**: Press the middle mouse button, hold it down as you press the left mouse button and release it. Now drag the mouse down the screen and the part will **Zoom Out**.
	Normal View	This tool allows you to view a particular plane/surface in a true length view. You specify the plane/surface and CATIA V5 will rotate the plane/surface 90 degrees to your screen view. This will make the geometry on that plane/surface true length. This is a very useful tool. You could try to rotate a plane using the space ball so it is normal to your point of view, but you could only get it "close." This tool gets it "exact." This tool can also be used to flip the direction in which you view a sketch. If in any of the lessons you go into the Sketcher Workbench and your view is from the wrong direction, use this tool to flip your view 180 degrees. It will switch your point of view from looking down on a part to looking up from the bottom.
	Hide/Show	This tool allows you to select any entity or multiple entities and place them in "no show space." This removes the selected entity/entities from the "working space." Sometimes there are entities that you want to keep for future references but do not want them visually in the way. You can pull the entities back into the "working space" when you are ready for them.
	Swap Visible Space	This tool works hand in hand with the **Hide/Show** tool. Selecting this tool will take you out of the "working space" window and into the "no show space." To pull an element from the "no show space" you would select the **Swap Visible Space** tool icon. This would show the "no show space." You could select the entity you want back in the "working space," and then select the **Hide/Show** tool icon. This would take the entity back to the "working space." You would then need to select the **Swap Visible Space** tool icon to get back to the "working space." This can be confusing; try bringing a part back and forth until you get control of the two tools.

Quick View Mode:

Quick view ⊠		This tool icon has the arrow to the bottom right of it, as explained in toolbar 5. The tool options are all of the orthographic view options. **NOTE:** the view projection is dependant on the plane the body was created on.
	Isometric View	Select this tool and CATIA V5 will rotate your part to an isometric view.
	Front View	Select this tool and CATIA V5 will rotate your part to a front view.
	Back View	Select this tool and CATIA V5 will rotate your part to a back view.
	Left View	Select this tool and CATIA V5 will rotate your part to a left view.
	Right View	Select this tool and CATIA V5 will rotate your part to a right view.
	Top View	Select this tool and CATIA V5 will rotate your part to a top view.
	Bottom View	Select this tool and CATIA V5 will rotate your part to a bottom view.

View Mode:

View mode ⊠		This tool icon has the arrow to the bottom right of it, as explained in toolbar 5. There are six different options associated with this tool; they are listed below.
	Wireframe (NHR)	This shows the part as a wireframe (no solid, no shading). The (NHR) means "No Hidden Line Removal." With no hidden lines removed, all edges of the part will be visible at all times. This can be confusing at times; you could lose track of which is the front side and which is the back side of a part.
	Dynamic Hidden Line Removal	This is very similar to the **Hidden Line Removal** tool except as you rotate the part, the hidden line removal is in real time, whereas the **Hidden Line Removal** tool will only update the hidden line removal after the rotating process is complete.
	Shading (SHD)	This tool shows the solid shaded without any edge line representation.
	Shading With Edges	This tool allows you to control how your part is going to be represented, how it looks on the screen. This tool shows the solid shaded and with the edge line representation. The majority of the graphics in this workbook are represented in this format.

	**Shading with Edges and Hidden Edges**:	This tool shows the solid shaded and the edge line hidden.
	Applies Customized View Parameters:	This tool will bring up a "**Custom View Modes**" window that gives you many different parameters to choose from. If you apply material to your solid you will not see the material represented unless you select the material option in the "**Custom View Modes**" window.

⑯ The CATIA V5 Standard Toolbar

Standard	This toolbar has nine tools in it, some offer an alternative method of accomplishing a similar task found in the **Standard MS Windows** toolbar. The tools are listed below with a brief description.

Toolbar	Tool Name	Tool Definition
	New	Creates a new file (document).
	Open	Opens an existing file (document).
	Save	Saves the active file (document).
	Quick Print	Prints the active file (document).
	Cut	Deletes the selected element and/or elements. This tool has the **Windows NT** functionality of select, drag and drop.
	Copy	Another method of copying a selected element and/or elements. The tool places the copied element and/or elements onto the Windows NT clipboard.
	Paste	Another method of pasting an element and/or elements from the Windows NT clip board.
	Undo	The greatest OOPS tool developed since the invention of the computer! This tool allows you to step backwards one mistake (function) at a time!
	Redo	Make that a double OOPS! This tool allows you to undo your undo! If your last operations weren't so bad and you don't remember all of the parameters you entered, this tool is for you.

![What's This icon]	**What's This?**	Direct link to the help file. Select the item you have a question about then select this tool. CATIAV5 will search the help files for information on the selected item.

⑰ The Prompt Zone

The Prompt Zone (bottom left of the screen) prompts the user for the information and/or input required to complete the process. A good rule of thumb: When in doubt, read the Prompt!

Figure I.19

Select a plane, a planar face or a sketch

> Prompts the user for the information required to complete the process.

⑱ The Knowledge Toolbar

This toolbar allows you to use formulas and spread sheets to parameterize your sketches, parts and assemblies.

Toolbar	Tool Name	Tool Definition
$f(x)$	**Formula**	This tool allows you to use a formula to drive parameters.
💬	**Comment & URLs**	This tool provides access to the Comment and URLs editor.
	Check Analysis Toolbox	This tool allows the user to define design standards and check parts against the standards.
▦	**Design Table**	This tool allows you to use data from an existing spread sheet to drive assigned parameters within a design.
fog	**Law**	This tool allows you access the law editor.
	Knowledge Inspector	This tool allows you to preview a design change prior to committing to the change. This is an advanced tool.
🔒	**Lock Selected Parameters**	This tool allows the user to lock selected parameters.
	Unlock Selected Parameters	This tool allows the user to unlock selected parameters.
▦}=	**Equivalent Dimensions Head**	This tool allows the user to make two parameters equal to each other. This tool applies to most dimensional (length) type parameters.

⑲ The Apply Material Tool

This tool allows you to apply a material to your solid. Applying a material will give it the properties of the material, such as the density, so CATIA V5 can calculate weight, volume and other part analysis information. Applying material also gives the solid the texture and color of the selected material. CATIA V5 has a library of materials. The use of this tool is covered in the Part Design Lesson. Remember, to see the material applied to the solid, you must select **Apply Material** in the **Applies Customized View Parameters**.

Figure I.20

CATIA V5 allows you to create your own material using the Material Library Workbench found in the Infrastructure Workbench category.

⑳ The Measure Tool

 There are three analysis type tools; they are listed below:

Toolbar	Tool Name	Tool Definition
	**Measure Between**	This tool allows you to measure the distance between two different entities. You can measure the distance between surfaces, planes, lines, points, etc. Select the **Measure Between** tool and then the two entities. This will bring up the **Measure Between** window. This window has more information than most designers would want. In most cases, the dimension created between the two selected entities is enough information.
	**Measure Item**	This tool is very similar to the **Measure Between** tool except that it measures the length of an individual entity. Select the **Measure Item** tool and then select the item to be measured. This will bring up the **Measure Item** window. As in 11.1, in most cases, the dimension created on the selected entity is all that is needed.
	**Measure Inertia**	This measures the physical attributes of the selected solid such as volume, mass, centroid, etc.

㉑ The Power Input Mode

This input window is for more advanced uses. You will notice as you select a tool, the tool command will appear in this window. In advanced uses, this window can be used similarly to quick keys and scripting. For detailed information, reference the **Help** menu. This tool is not used in this workbook.

Figure I.21

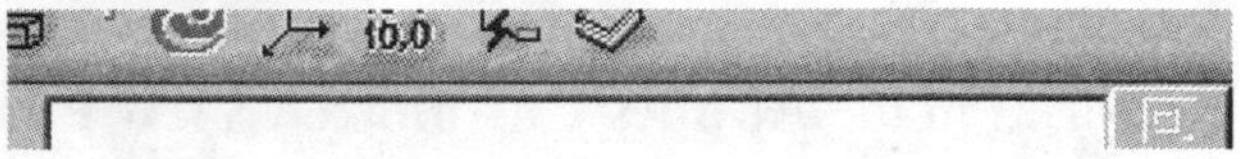

㉒ The Double Chevron Symbols

When the workbench toolbars show these arrows at the bottom or end of the toolbar, it signifies there are additional tools belonging to that particular workbench. CATIA V5 gives you an indication of this when you see the small double chevrons at the bottom of the side bar as shown in Figure I.22. To make all tools and toolbars visible select the small bar as shown in Figure I.22 and drag it to an open area in the workspace. If the double chevron symbols are still there that means you still have additional toolbars, continue the process until the symbol disappears.

Figure I.22

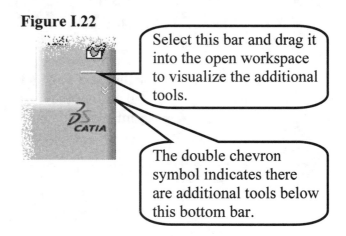

Select this bar and drag it into the open workspace to visualize the additional tools.

The double chevron symbol indicates there are additional tools below this bottom bar.

Additional Tools: The additional tools are not shown in this Introduction. There are other tools that appear depending on the current workbench.

Lesson 1
Knowledgeware

Introduction

Knowledgeware is not one specific CATIA V5 workbench but several workbenches. Some of the tools can be accessed in the **Standard** toolbar in the **Part Design** workbench. Simply put, **Knowledgeware** is a group of tools that allow you to create, manipulate and check your CATIA V5 creations.

Figure 1.1

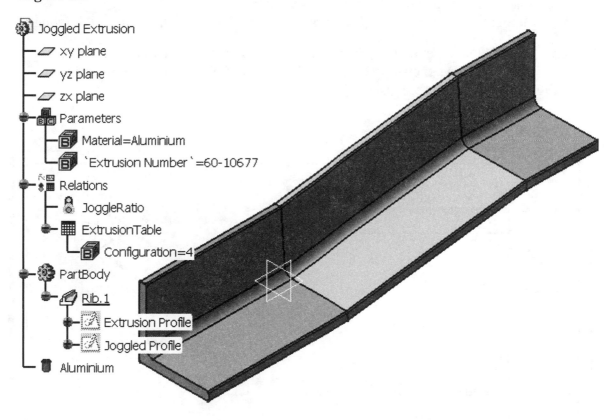

Objectives

This lesson will take you through the process of automating the creation of joggled extrusions as shown in Figure 1.1. At the end of the lesson you should be able to do the following:

1. Create the **Extrusion Profile Sketch** and **Joggle Profile Sketch**.
2. Assign variable names to the required constraints.
3. Create the **Joggled Extrusion.CATPart** using the **Rib** tool.
4. Create a spreadsheet with aluminum extrusion dimensions.
5. Link the spreadsheet to the **Joggled Extrusion.CATPart**.
6. Apply the spreadsheet to update the **Joggled Extrusion.CATPart**.
7. Create a **Macro**.
8. Modify the **Macro** using **VB Script**.
9. Create prompt windows for input using **VB Script**.
10. Check for company/industry standards using the **Check** tool.
11. Implement the updated **Joggled Extrusion.CATPart** in a dimensioned drawing.

Figures 1.1 and 1.2 show examples of the **Joggled Extrusion** you will create in this lesson. Figure 1.1 shows the standard **Joggled Extrusion** along with its **Specification Tree**. Figure 1.2 shows a spreadsheet with the resultant dimensioned drawing.

Figure 1.2

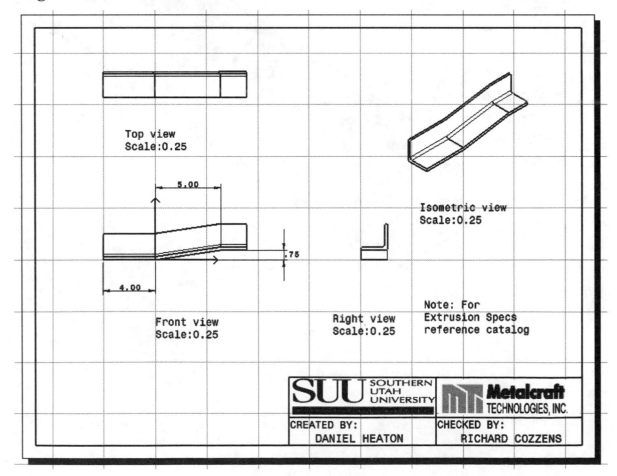

Top view
Scale:0.25

5.00

Isometric view
Scale:0.25

.75

4.00

Front view
Scale:0.25

Right view
Scale:0.25

Note: For
Extrusion Specs
reference catalog

SUU SOUTHERN UTAH UNIVERSITY

Metalcraft
TECHNOLOGIES, INC.

CREATED BY:
DANIEL HEATON

CHECKED BY:
RICHARD COZZENS

Workbench Tools and Toolbars

A combination of six toolbars is used in this lesson from the **Knowledgware Product**. The **Knowledgeware Product** is made up of the following workbenches; **Knowledge Advisor, Knowledge Expert, Product Engineering Optimizer, Product Knowledge Template, Product Function Optimization** and **Product Functional Definition**. Each of these workbenches has a different combination of tools in each toolbar. If you switch between any of these workbenches you may see the same tool in a different toolbar. For example the **Formula** and **Design Table** tools are accessible from many workbenches in the bottom toolbar.

The <u>Set of Equations</u> Toolbar
This toolbar contains only one tool.

TOOL ICON	TOOL NAME	TOOL DEFINITION
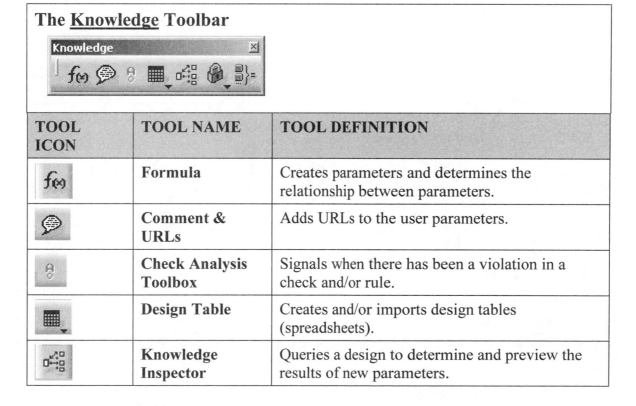	**Set Of Equations**	Solves a set of equations.

The <u>Knowledge</u> Toolbar

TOOL ICON	TOOL NAME	TOOL DEFINITION
	Formula	Creates parameters and determines the relationship between parameters.
	Comment & URLs	Adds URLs to the user parameters.
	Check Analysis Toolbox	Signals when there has been a violation in a check and/or rule.
	Design Table	Creates and/or imports design tables (spreadsheets).
	Knowledge Inspector	Queries a design to determine and preview the results of new parameters.

The <u>Reactive Features</u> Toolbar

TOOL ICON	TOOL NAME	TOOL DEFINITION
	Select	Highlights the element you want to select.
	Rule	Creates a rule and applies it to your document.
	Check	Creates a check and applies it to your document.
	Reactions	Creates a script that will change feature attributes.

The <u>Tools</u> Toolbar

TOOL ICON	TOOL NAME	TOOL DEFINITION
	Measure Update	Updates relationships.
	Update	Updates the CATPart and/or CATProduct.

The <u>Actions</u> Toolbar

TOOL ICON	TOOL NAME	TOOL DEFINITION
	Macro with Arguments	Opens a macro with arguments.
	Actions	Creates a script.

The <u>Organize Knowledge</u> Toolbar

TOOL ICON	TOOL NAME	TOOL DEFINITION
	Add Set of Parameters	Creates a set of parameters.
	Add Set of Relations	Creates a set of relations.
	Parameters Explorer	Adds new parameters to a feature.
	Comment & URLs	Adds URLs to the user parameters.

The <u>Control Features</u> Toolbar

TOOL ICON	TOOL NAME	TOOL DEFINITION
	List	Manage the objects you want to add to the list you are creating.
	Loop	Interactively apply a loop to an existing document.

The Problem:

One of the many Metalcraft Technologies Inc. (MTI) fabrication processes is fabricating a joggle in standard and non-standard extrusions. Most of the extrusion requirements are contained in large assembly Mylar sheets. Most of the drawings (Mylars) were created in the early 1970s. It is difficult for the engineer/planner to read and/or measure the Mylar accurately. It may take the engineer/planner 10 to 30 minutes to verify he/she has found and applied the correct dimensions. It is not productive for the fabricator to also have to go through the same time consuming process. Having the drawing interpreted so many times by so many different people will inevitably introduce more chances for error. It is MTI's policy that the engineer/planner creates an individual drawing for each joggled extrusion to avoid such confusion. MTI has minimized the time required to create the individual drawings by setting up templates and standards. Yet, even with templates and standards this process is still time consuming. Each drawing is basically the same but has to be re-created because of a few simple dimensional differences and/or a different type of extrusion. The goal was to cut this time down by capturing the engineer's knowledge using the CATIA V5 Knowledgeware tools. This captured knowledge will be applied to standardize and automate the process. This process will save time and reduce the potential for errors.

The Solution:

CATIA V5 **Knowledgeware** tools allow the user to capture and use the intelligence contained within the standard **Joggled Extrusion.CATPart**. CATIA V5 macro and scripting capabilities allow the user to be prompted for the critical dimensions. CATIA V5 then takes the information and updates the **Joggled Extrusion.CATPart** according to the supplied input. CATIA V5 also automatically updates the standard dimensioned drawing (CATDrawing). The dimensioned drawing is ready to be released to the production floor in a matter of minutes instead of 30 to 60 minutes.

An additional advantage to this process is adding dimensional checks. If the dimensional values do not match the company and /or industry standards the user will get a warning.

The following instructions will take you through the steps of creating the standard **Joggled Extrusion.CATPart** and then implementing the **Knowledgeware** solution described above.

The Knowledgeware Solution

A parameterized sketch/solid is a basic form of **Knowledgeware**; it contains intelligence. Prior to parametric applications you would have to create each variation of the extrusion from scratch. Parametric applications allow you to modify one constraint and the extrusion (solid) will update to that constraint.

1. Determine the Requirements

The general problem solving skills apply to implementing the **Knowledgeware** solution. You need to list all that is known and unknown and you need to list all of the variables, for example, what is known.

If you are not sure at first, manually go through the process. You must be able to create the process manually.

2. Creating the Extrusion Profile Sketch

Create an **Extrusion Profile** sketch on the **ZX Plane** as shown in Figure 1.3. The 0,0 point is located at the lower left corner of the extrusion. This sketch will be used as the standard; all other extrusions will be derived from this basic sketch. When you complete the sketch, exit the **Sketcher** workbench but do not use the **Pad** tool to create a solid. The solid will be created in Step 8 using a different tool.

Figure 1.3

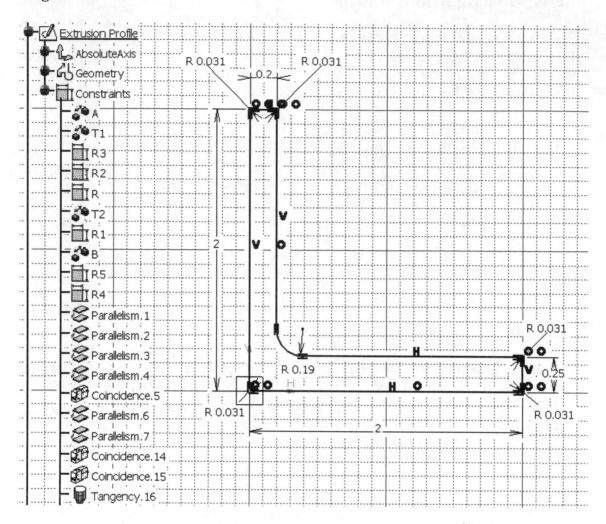

3. Constraining the Extrusion Profile Sketch

After completing the rough sketch of the **Extrusion Profile** sketch as shown in Figure 1.3 you must constrain it similar to the constrains shown in Figure 1.3.

4. Modifying the Constraint Names

In this particular step it is critical that you rename the constraints. Understand that it is not absolutely necessary, but it will make this process a lot easier if you rename the constraints with a name that signifies what it is constraining. If you have problems remembering what the constraint name is, write it down; the names will be required to create the spreadsheet later in this lesson. It is suggested that you use the constraint names shown in Figure 1.4 so your information matches what you will see throughout the remaining steps into this lesson. Also, change the branch name **Sketch.1** to **Extrusion Profile**. Once you have successfully completed this lesson it is suggested that you try different variations of this process.

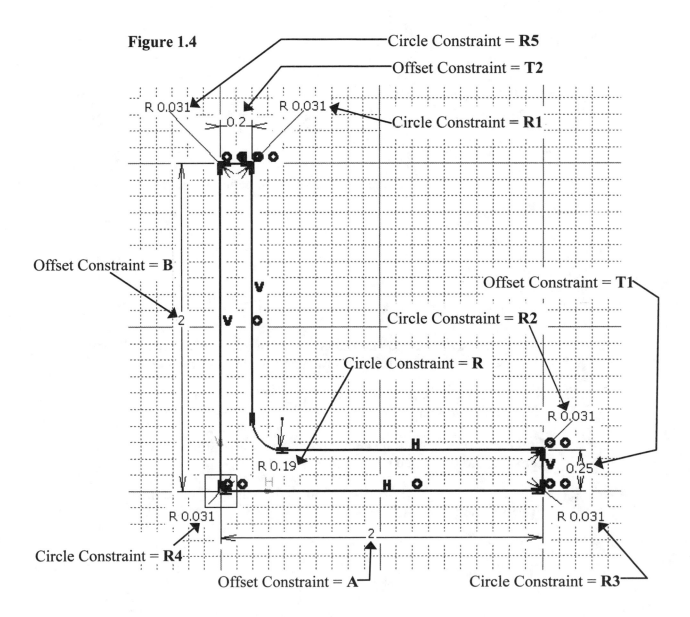

Figure 1.4

Circle Constraint = **R5**

Offset Constraint = **T2**

Circle Constraint = **R1**

Offset Constraint = **B**

Offset Constraint = **T1**

Circle Constraint = **R2**

Circle Constraint = **R**

Offset Constraint = **A**

Circle Constraint = **R4**

Circle Constraint = **R3**

Figure 1.3 shows the constraints in the **Specification Tree** already renamed. CATIA V5 will automatically give it a name as shown in Figure 1.5 below.

Figure 1.5

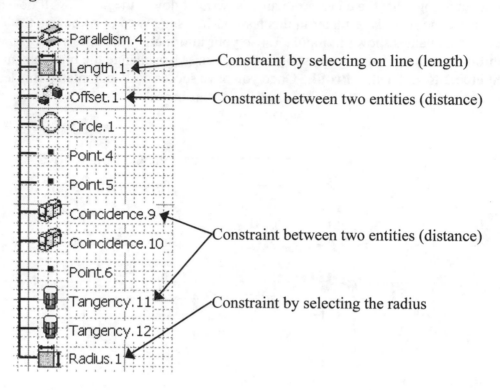

Complete the following steps to rename the constraints.

4.1   Double click on the constraint that you want to rename. This will bring up the **Constraint Definition** window with the constraint value in it.

4.2   Select the **More** button. This will bring up a **Constraint Definition** window as shown in Figure 1.6.

4.3   Edit the current constraint name in the **Name** box to what you want the new constraint to be named.

4.4   Select **OK**. The newly renamed constraint will show up in the **Specification Tree**.

Figure 1.6

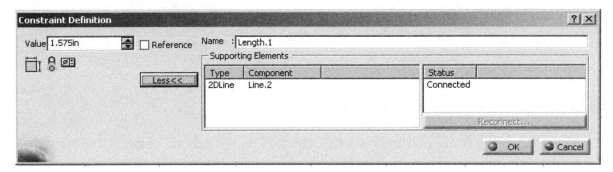

5. Creating the Profile Sketch of the Joggle

This step, like Step 2, requires you to create another sketch. This sketch is created on the **YZ Plane** in the negative direction (notice where the is located in relation to the sketch in Figure 1.7). Use the information in Figure 1.7 to create the **Joggle Profile** sketch.

Figure 1.7

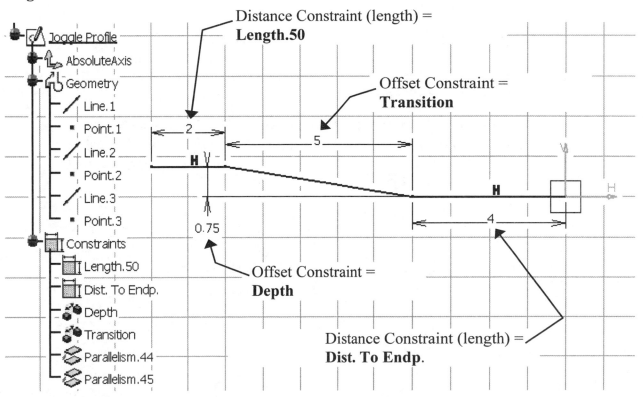

6. Constraining the Joggle Profile Sketch

Create constraints for the **Joggle Profile** sketch similar to the ones shown in Figure 1.7.

7. Modifying the Constraint Names

Modify the constraint names you created in Step 6 to match the constraint names shown in Figure 1.7. Step 4 describes the process of renaming constraints.

NOTE: It is important that the constraint names be consistent throughout this lesson. The names will be used to link the information to a table in the next few steps. If you deviate from the naming convention used in this lesson, the remaining steps will not work as described.

8. Creating a Solid of the Joggled Extrusion

Now that both sketches are created you are ready to create the solid. This will be accomplished by using the **Rib** tool found in the **Part Design** workbench. Complete the following steps to create the solid

   8.1   Select the **Extrusion Profile** sketch created in Step 2. Make sure it is highlighted.

   8.2   Select the **Rib** tool found in the **Part Design** workbench. This will bring up the **Rib Definition** window as shown in Figure 1.8. The prompt zone will prompt you to **Define the center curve**. The **Extrusion Profile** will be listed in the **Profile** box.

   8.3   The **Center Curve** box should be highlighted. Select the **Joggle Profile** either from the geometry or the **Specification Tree**. CATIA V5 will give you a preview of the **Extrusion Profile** being extruded along lines that define the **Joggle Profile** sketch.

Figure 1.8

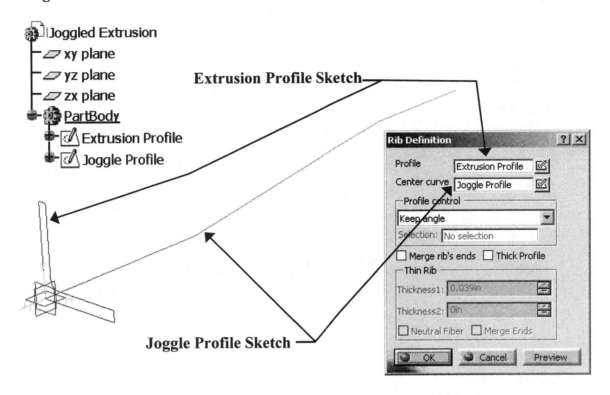

8.4   If the preview looks similar to the joggled extrusion that is shown in Figure 1.9, select the **OK** button to complete the operation. The **Joggled Extrusion** will be made into a solid.

Now that you have created a solid "Joggled Extrusion," you are ready to go on to the next step: creating a table of different types of extrusions.

Figure 1.9

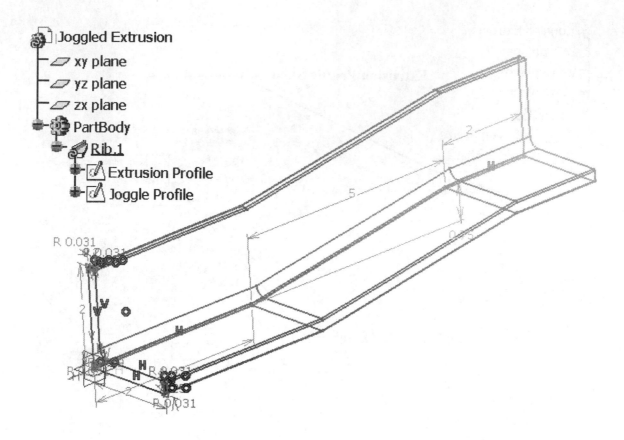

9. Creating an Extrusion Table

Figure 1.10 is an Excel (Spreadsheet) that contains the dimensions to four different types of aluminum extrusions. The extrusions and their dimensions were taken from the Tierany Metals Catalog. You might recognize the extrusion on row 5; it is the one you created in the previous steps. If you wanted to create the extrusion in row 2 you would have to start from step one again or you could go back to the **Extrusion Profile** sketch and revise the constraints. Obviously revising the constraints would be the quickest and easiest method to creating the new extrusion. CATIA V5 Knowledgeware tools can make this process even quicker and easier. This is accomplished by linking the Excel File to the CATPart.

Figure 1.10

	A	B	C	D	E	F	G	H	I	J	K
1	Extrusion Number	A (in)	B (in)	T1 (in)	T2 (in)	R (in)	R1 (in)	R2 (in)	R3 (in)	R4 (in)	R5 (in)
2	60-10677	2	2	0.25	0.2	0.19	0.031	0.031	0.031	0.031	0.031
3	60-4921	1.25	1.25	0.2	0.065	0.12	0.03	0.03	0.03	0.03	0.03
4	60-1490	1.5	0.0812	0.109	0.14	0.125	0.062	0.062	0.016	0.031	0.016
5	60-13028	6.06	1.8	0.19	0.61	0.188	0.094	0.094	0.016	0.016	0.016
6											

You can use an existing spreadsheet if it is available. If it is not available, you will have to create your own. The spreadsheet does not have to be an Excel program; any spreadsheet program will work. Each column requires a header. The header will be used as a variable link later in the lesson. Notice the column headers used in Figure 1.10 match the constraint names used in the previous steps to create the **Extrusion Profile** sketch. This is not absolutely necessary, but it does make the linking process much more intuitive.

To complete this step, go into the spreadsheet program of your choice and enter the information in as shown in Figure 1.10. Save the file; preferably in the same directory that your CATPart file exists. Remember the file name and where it exists as you will need that information in the following step.

10. Importing the Extrusion Table

CATIA V5 allows you to create a design table inside CATIA V5 or import an existing design table. This step will show you how to import the design table created in Step 9. As you go through the process of importing a design table, you will be able to observe how CATIA V5 allows you the opportunity to create and modify a design table inside of CATIA V5. To import a design table, complete the following steps.

10.1 In the **Part Design** workbench, double click on the **Design Table** tool. The **Design Table** tool is located in the **Standard** toolbar at the bottom of the CATIA V5 screen. The **Design Table** tool icon is shown in Figure 1.11. This will bring up the **Creation of a Design Table** window as shown in Figure 1.12.

Figure 1.11

10.2 Name the design table "**Extrusion Table**" using the **Name** box as shown in Figure 1.12.

Figure 1.12

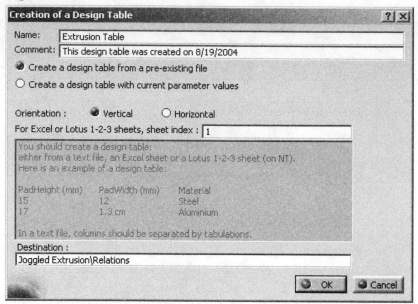

10.3   The **Comment** box will automatically place the date of creation. You can modify this box to any text that might help. This is just a comment box and will not have any effect on the following steps.

10.4   Select **Create a design table from a pre-existing file**. Although you will not use the other choice in this lesson it is important that you know that the other choice is available. The other choice is **Create a design table with current parameter values**. This choice allows you to create a design table inside CATIA V5.

10.5   Select the **OK** button. This will bring up browser window labeled **File Selection**. This is the standard Windows file browser. Reference Figure 1.13.

10.6   Select the directory and the file that you want to import. For this step, you will want to select the **Extrusion Table** created in the previous steps, as shown in Figure 1.13.

10.7   Select the **Open** button. This will bring up an **Automatic associations?** Window, as shown in Figure 1.13. The prompt window asks if you want to automatically associate the parameters.

10.8   Select **Yes**. This will bring up the **Extrusion Table Active** window as shown in Figure 1.14. Note that Figure 1.14 is shown with the **Associations** tab selected, not the **Configurations** tab. If there are no associations listed in the **Configurations** box, CATIA V5 was not able to automatically associate any of the **Constraint Parameters** or **Extrusion Table Column Headings**.

Figure 1.13

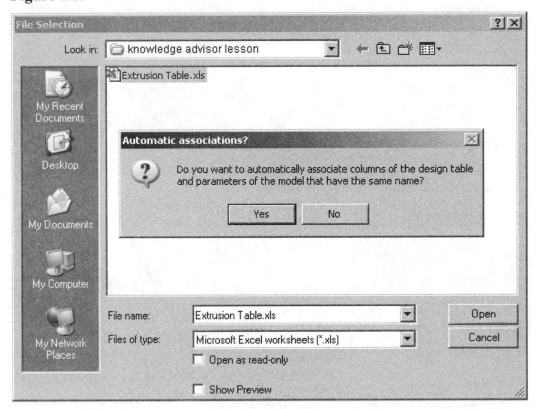

10.9   When CATIA V5 is not able to automatically associate the two together, you will have to manually associate them. To do this, select the **Associations** tab in the **Extrusion Table Active** window as shown in Figure 1.14.

10.10   The **Parameters** box lists all the parameters CATIA V5 created in the **Extrusion Profile** sketch. A CATIA V5 sketch contains a lot of parameters that the users are not usually aware of. What makes it more difficult, is the CATIA V5 naming convention. It is difficult to identify a CATIA V5 parameter listed in this box to an actual parameter in the **Extrusion Profile** sketch. This is where renaming the constraints in the previous steps will prove to be beneficial. You should be able to scroll through the **Parameters** box and identify the constraints you renamed. All the parameters are represented on two separate lines. For this lesson you will use the line that ends with a type of measurement such as **Radius**, **Offset** or **Length**. You will not use the line ending in **Activity**. For this step, scroll through the **Parameters** list; verify the constraints you renamed in Step 4 are listed.

Figure 1.14

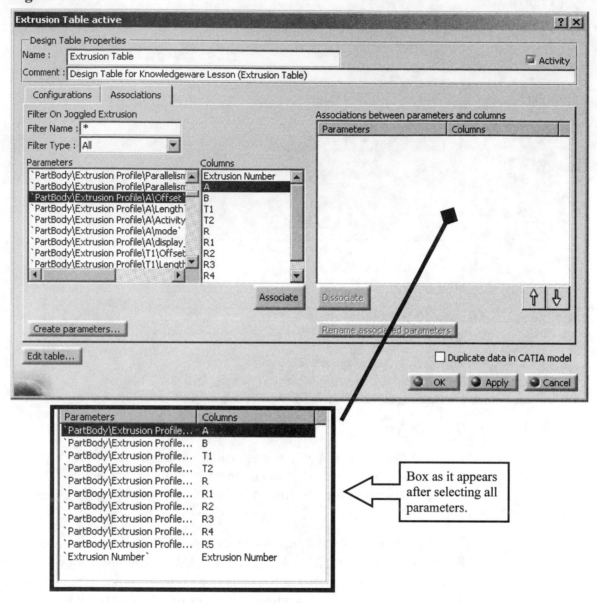

10.11   Select **A** from the **Columns** box.

10.12   From the **Parameters** box, find and select the line "**PartBody\Extrusion Profile\A\Length**".

10.13   Select the **Associate** button. Your two selections from the **Parameters** and **Columns** boxes will show up in the **Associations between parameters and columns** box. This means that they were successfully associated.

10.14   Continue this process until all the variables in the **Columns** box, except for **Extrusion Number,** is matched up to the appropriate parameter. (**R, R1**, etc. will of course be a **Radius** rather than a **Length**).

10.15   Now you can take care of the **Extrusion Number** column heading. The **Extrusion Profile** sketch has no associative value to the **Extrusion Number** that was created in the **Extrusion Table**. You can assign it one by selecting the **Extrusion Number** in the **Columns** box.

10.16   Select the **Create Parameters...** button. This will bring up the **OK Creates Parameters for Selected Lines** window as shown in Figure 1.15.

Figure 1.15

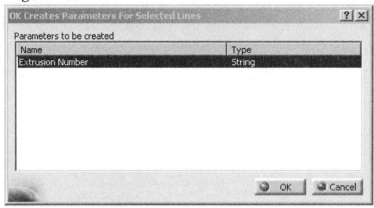

10.17   Make sure **Extrusion Number** is selected/highlighted.

10.18   Select the **OK** button. This will create an association of a string type to the **Extrusion Number** heading. The association will be displayed in the **Extrusion Table Active** window under the **Associations** tab along with all the other associations you created in this step. What this really does for you is allows the **Specification Tree** to show the **Extrusion Number**. Figure 1.16, under the **Parameters** branch, displays "**Extrusion Number**" =**60-10677**. The string of numbers **60-10677** is linked from the specific row in the **Extrusion Table**. If you select another row (extrusion) from the **Extrusion Table** the **Specification Tree** will reflect the change just as the solid does.

NOTE: In order for the parameters to show up in the **Specification Tree** you must have the **Options** set correctly. The selection steps are: Tools, Options, Infrastructure, Part Infrastructure, Display tab, and then select the Parameters box. Select **OK** and reference the Specification Tree.

10.19   Select the **Configurations** tab in the **Extrusion Table Active** window. If you correctly associated the **Parameters** and **Columns**. If your window looks similar to the one shown in Figure 1.16, select the **OK** button to complete the association process.

10.20   Doing this will make the window disappear and **Extrusion Table.1** shows up on your **Relations** branch of the **Specification Tree**. You may wonder what else is different. What did you just accomplish? Step 11 will show you the advantages of what you just accomplished.

11. Applying the Extrusion Table to the Joggled Extrusion

The purpose for linking a design table to the CATPart file is to update the part without having to redraw and/or revise the constraints manually. (Keep in mind that if you move your saved table, it will break the link and you will need to re-link it.) To test this, complete the following steps.

11.1   Double click on **Extrusion Table** in the **Specification Tree**. This will bring up the **Extrusion Table Active** window as shown in Figure 1.16. The data in row 1 is currently the active row. There are several methods to tell which row of data is active.

Figure 1.16

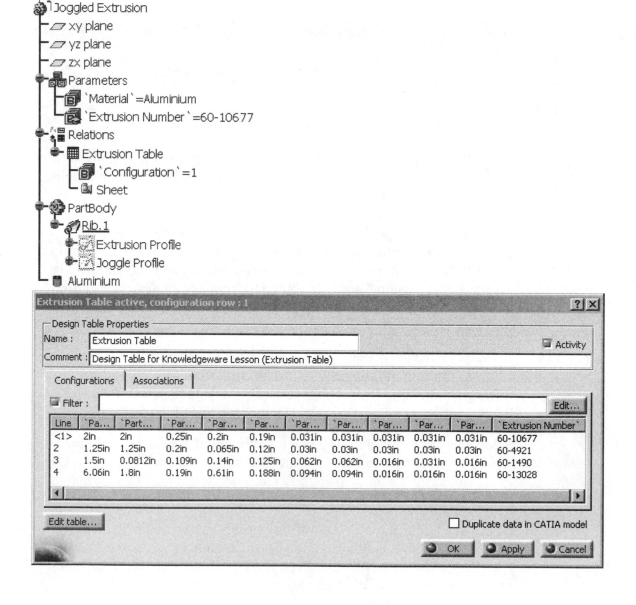

11.1.1   The window label contains the information: **Extrusion Table active, configuration row: 1**.

11.1.2   Row 1 has brackets around it [**<1>**]. The inactive lines do not have the brackets around it.

11.1.3   One other method is to check the data against actual extrusion dimensions. Figure 1.16 and the entire product in the previous steps represent the data that is contained in row 1.

11.2   To make row 4 (Extrusion Number 60-13028) active, select the row. The existing extrusion will turn red signifying it needs to be updated.

11.3   Select the **OK** button. This will update your active extrusion to the data contained in row 4. Figure 1.17 shows the row 4 extrusion. Compare the differences between the extrusion represented in Figure 1.16 and 1.17. Verify the extrusions with the dimensions in the **Extrusion Table** (design table).

NOTE: If your extrusion does not automatically update you will have to select the **Update** button in the **Standard** toolbar section to force the solid to update. If you want CATIA V5 to automatically update select **Tools**, **Options**, **Infrastructure** branch, **Part Infrastructure** branch, **General** tab, **Update** section and select the **Automatic** button.

Once you link your **Extrusion Table** to your CATPart, updating is quite simple. Click on the **Extrusion Table** in the **Specification Tree** to bring up the design table. Select the row of data you want to apply to the CATPart and select **OK**. Be sure to select row 1 (Extrusion Number 60-10677) again before moving on to the next step.

Figure 1.17

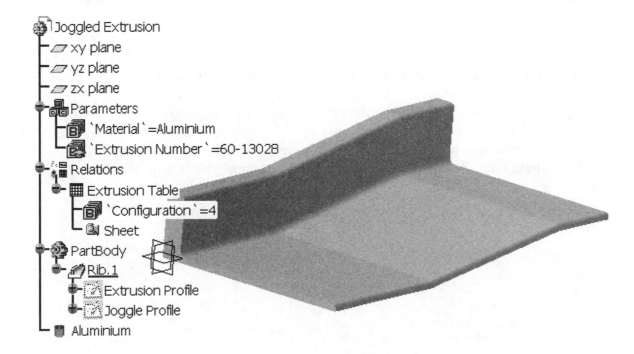

12. Editing the Extrusion Table

You now have the **Extrusion Table** linked to the **Joggled Extrusion CATPart**. As the previous step demonstrated, creating new extrusions are only a few clicks away. Editing the **Extrusion Table** (design table) is just as easy. Modifying the **Extrusion Table** can be done in CATIA V5 or outside of CATIA V5. To modify the **Extrusion Table** inside of CATIA V5, complete the following steps.

12.1   Double click on the **Extrusion Table** in the **Specification Tree**.

12.2   This brings up the **Extrusion Table Active** window. Click on the **Edit Table** button at the bottom left of the window.

12.3   This brings up the original spreadsheet that the **Extrusion Table** was created in. Modify the number **2** in row 2 (Extrusion Number 60-10677) and column C (header B (in)) to a **4**.

12.4   Save and exit the revised spread sheet program. CATIA V5 will notify you that the **Extrusion Table** has been revised. Select **Close** to update the link.

12.5   The part will turn red because it is the active row. Select **OK** to update the **Joggled Extrusion CATPart**.

Your part is now updated to the information edited into the spreadsheet without leaving CATIA V5. You can use this method to add rows of new information, in this case additional extrusion types. You can also delete rows of information. The second method of revising the spreadsheet is editing the spreadsheet outside of CATIA V5. CATIA V5 will still give you a warning and a chance to accept or reject the revised spreadsheet.

NOTE: 2″ is correct for the 60-10677 Extrusion Number, so be sure to change it back.

13. Displaying the Extrusion Type in the Specification Tree

Figure 1.18 shows the **Specification Tree** without the value displayed, and Figure 1.19 shows the **Specification Tree** after the following process to display the value. Select **Tools**, **Options**, **Parameters and Measure** under the **General** branch, **Knowledge** tab, **Parameters Tree View** section; check the **With Value** box.

Figure 1.18

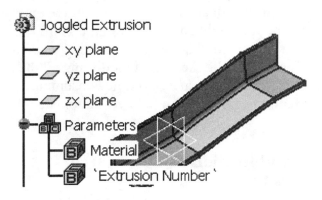

Figure 1.19

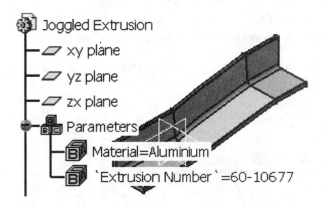

14. Modifying the Existing Joggle Profile Sketch

The previous steps showed you how to create, select and automate the creation of different types of extrusions. This was accomplished using a spreadsheet and the **Extrusion Profile** sketch. The following step will show you how to apply joggle information to the selected extrusion. This step uses/modifies the **Joggle Profile** sketch. If joggle information was standardized, you could create a spreadsheet with the required information and apply it to the **Joggle Profile** sketch as you did to the **Extrusion Profile** sketch. Joggle information is not standard; it is as varied as the parts and assemblies they are applied to. With the help of **Knowledgeware** tools this process can still be automated by getting information directly from the user in the place of the spreadsheet.

For this step, revise all the constraints in the **Joggle Profile** sketch to match the constraints shown in Figure 1.16.

The following steps will show you how this is accomplished. This step will start out real basic so you can better appreciate the power of CATIA V5's **Knowledgeware** tools. The **Joggle Profile** sketch controls the joggle of the extrusion. If you want to change the joggle depth, you could go into the **Joggle Profile** sketch and revise the constraint that controls the depth. Figure 1.7 shows that value of **Depth** is currently **.75″**. Entering the **Joggle Profile** sketch and modifying all the constraints for every individual part becomes very repetitious and time consuming. The following steps will show you how **Knowledgeware** can help you automate this process.

15. Automating the Modification Using a Marco

This step is similar to what was explained in Step 12. You go through the same steps except that you turn on the **Macro Recorder** to record everything you do. To accomplish this, complete the following steps.

   15.1   Enter the **Joggle Profile** sketch, as shown in Figure 1.7. The first thing you need to remember is to record only what is necessary, other wise you get a lot of information that only complicates the process.

   15.2   Select **Tools**, **Macro**, **Start Recording**. This will bring up the **Record Macro** window as shown in Figure 1.20.

   Figure 1.20

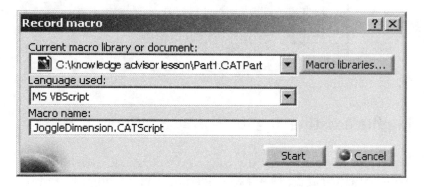

   15.3   The **Current Macro Library Or Document:** should default to your CATPart at its designated saved location. Select **CATScript** for the **Language Used:** box.

   15.4   Name the macro "**JoggleDimensions.CATScript**." CATIA V5 will default the name to **Macro1.catvbs** unless you specify a name. You must also add the **.CATScript** extension. Adding the extension allows CATIA V5 to save the macro externally not only as a macro but also a CATScript.

Figure 1.21

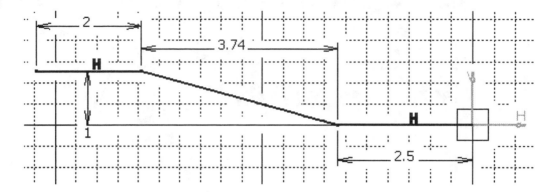

15.5   Before you start recording, make sure you know from start to finish what you are going to record. In this step you are going to modify all of the constraints in the **Joggle Profile** sketch to match the constraints shown in Figure 1.21.   Select the **Start** button to start recording. Notice when you start recording, CATIA V5 creates a **Stop Recording** toolbar with a **Stop Macro Recording** tool on it.

15.6   Revise the constraints to match the constraints shown in Figure 1.21 in the following order: **.75** to **1.0** (Depth), **5** to **3.74** (Transition), and **4** to **2.5** (Dist. To Endp.).

15.7   Stop the recording. You can stop the recording by selecting the **Stop Macro Recording** tool in the **Stop Recording** window explained in Step 15.4. Another method is to select **Tools**, **Macro**, **Stop Recording**.

15.8   Now go back to the **Joggle Profile** sketch and change the constraints to the previous values; the values shown in Figure 1.7.

15.9   Exit the **Sketcher** workbench.

15.10 Select **Tools**, **Macro**, **Macros**. This will bring up the **Macros** window as shown in Figure 1.22. Select the **JoggleDimensions.CATScript** macro.

Figure 1.22

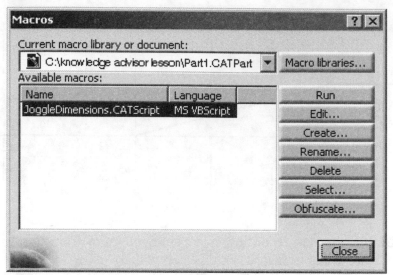

15.11   Select the **Run** button. This will run the **JoggleDimensions.CATScript** macro. Notice your **Joggled Extrusion.CATPart** will turn red and then update to the joggled dimensions you created in the macro.

15.12   The previous step demonstrates the result of the macro/script you just created. As you recorded the macro, CATIA V5 translated the action into the **VBScript Language**. CATIA V5 allows you to view and edit the scripted language. To view the **VBScript Language** you just created, select **Tools**, **Macro, Macros**, and then select the **JoggleDimensions.CATScript** file in the **Macros** window.

15.13   Select the **Edit** button. This will bring up the **Macros Editor** window shown in Figure 1.23.

The macro function is a powerful tool when it comes to accomplishing a process that is repeated over and over. The real power of the macro or CATScript you just created will be shown to you in the next step. Note: The values shown in the Macro Editor are shown in metric units.

Figure 1.23

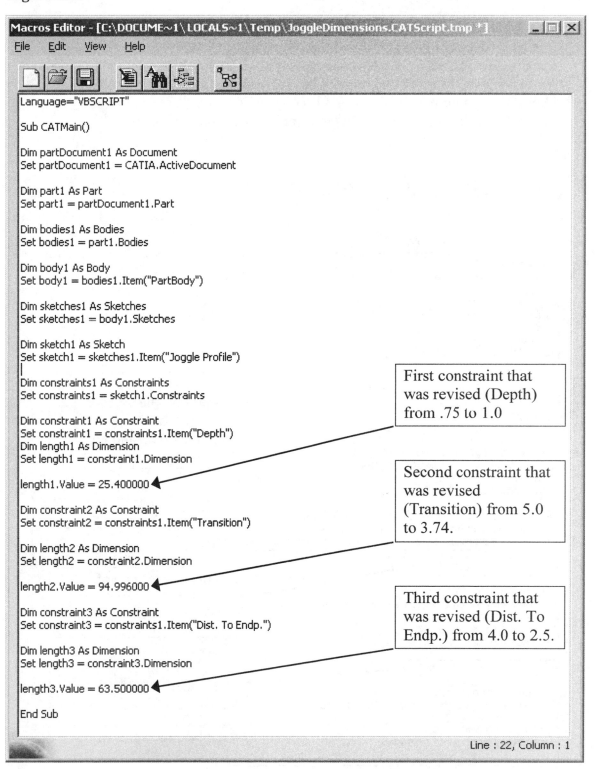

```
Macros Editor - [C:\DOCUME~1\LOCALS~1\Temp\JoggleDimensions.CATScript.tmp *]
File   Edit   View   Help

Language="VBSCRIPT"

Sub CATMain()

Dim partDocument1 As Document
Set partDocument1 = CATIA.ActiveDocument

Dim part1 As Part
Set part1 = partDocument1.Part

Dim bodies1 As Bodies
Set bodies1 = part1.Bodies

Dim body1 As Body
Set body1 = bodies1.Item("PartBody")

Dim sketches1 As Sketches
Set sketches1 = body1.Sketches

Dim sketch1 As Sketch
Set sketch1 = sketches1.Item("Joggle Profile")

Dim constraints1 As Constraints
Set constraints1 = sketch1.Constraints

Dim constraint1 As Constraint
Set constraint1 = constraints1.Item("Depth")
Dim length1 As Dimension
Set length1 = constraint1.Dimension

length1.Value = 25.400000

Dim constraint2 As Constraint
Set constraint2 = constraints1.Item("Transition")

Dim length2 As Dimension
Set length2 = constraint2.Dimension

length2.Value = 94.996000

Dim constraint3 As Constraint
Set constraint3 = constraints1.Item("Dist. To Endp.")

Dim length3 As Dimension
Set length3 = constraint3.Dimension

length3.Value = 63.500000

End Sub
                                                    Line : 22, Column : 1
```

First constraint that was revised (Depth) from .75 to 1.0

Second constraint that was revised (Transition) from 5.0 to 3.74.

Third constraint that was revised (Dist. To Endp.) from 4.0 to 2.5.

16. Customizing the Macro Using VBScript

CATIA V5 **Knowledgeware** allows you to customize the CATScript using
VBScript Language. This customization makes the **Macro** and **Scripting**
capabilities of CATIA V5 **Knowledgeware** almost limitless. You don't have to be a
VBScript guru to take advantage of this tool, but obviously the more you know
about it the more powerful a tool it becomes. To add the constraint variables you
created in the **Joggle Profile** sketch complete the following steps.

Figure 1.24

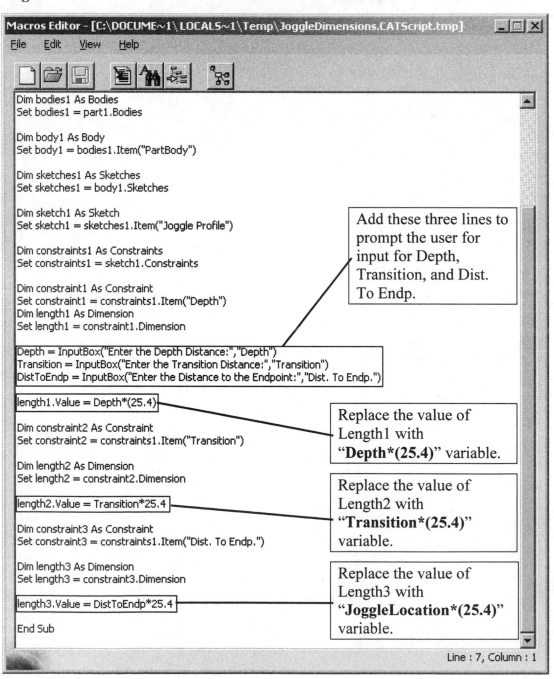

16.1   The macro you created in Step 15 assigned the constant value of **25.400000** to the first constraint you modified when recording the macro. The macro recorded the value as **length1.Value**. You will need to find the line where **length1.Value** is assigned the length. Figure 1.24 points out the approximate location of this line.

16.2   Insert the three lines indicated in Figure 1.24 above the line with the value as **length1.Value**. The purpose of doing this is to create prompt windows for the variables you are about to assign in place of the constant values that are assigned manually. Just adding variables would do you no good; you need some method of entering a value for the variables that you will create. The prompt window will allow the user to enter a value for the variable. (Make sure you type in the syntax exactly as it is shown.)

NOTE: It is obvious that each line represents a specific constraint variable. **Depth** is the variable. **InputBox** is VBScript syntax that creates a prompt window. **Enter the Depth Distance** is the text that will show up in the prompt window header. **Depth** at the end of the syntax creates a value input box.

16.3   Now back to the line that has the value as **length1.Value**. The macro converted the constant value to metric (mm). You will want to keep the units in inches so multiply the **Depth** value by **25.4**. The variable name used for the first constraint is **Depth*(25.4)**. This will convert the value back to inches. Reference Figure 1.24. Your modified line should look like similar to the line that is referenced.

16.4   Find the line that assigns **length2.Value**, the value you changed the constraint to in Step 15. Change the value to the variable constraint named **"Transition*(25.4)."** This variable needs to be converted back to inches as the one in Step 16.3 did. Reference Figure 1.24 to find the approximate location of the linen and for the way the revised line should look.

16.5   Find the line that assigns **length3.Value**, the value you changed the constraint to in Step 15. Change the value to the variable constraint named **"DistToEndp*(25.4)."** Note: There are no spaces between the words. This variable also needs to be converted back to inches in the same method used in Steps 16.3 and 16.4. Reference Figure 1.24 to find the approximate location of the line and for the way the revised line should look.

16.6   Save the changes and then close the **Macros Editor** window. The **Macros** window will still be available – don't close it.

It is important that you understand the relationship between the constraint that you renamed in Step 5 and the variable name that you are editing into the VBScript file. If you get them mixed up you could be changing things in ways you didn't expect. You must be sure and follow the VBScript syntax or it will not work. When editing the lines, make sure they match the lines pointed out in Figure 1.24 exactly. Reference the CATIA V5 online help and/or a VBScript manual for more in-depth information on VBScript syntax.

17. Testing the Customized Macro

This step will take you through the process of updating your **Joggled Extrusion** by running the macro. This will be a good test to see if you have entered all the syntax as required.

17.1   The **Macros** window should still be on the screen. Select the **Run** button.

17.2   This should bring up the first of the three prompt windows that were created previously (**Depth**). Reference Figure 1.25. Type in the original value assigned in Step 5 (**.75**), then select **OK**.

17.3   This will take you to the next prompt window (**Transition**). Again type in the original value (**5**) and then select **OK**.

17.4   The last prompt window created (**Dist. To Endp.**) will appear. Type in the original value (**4**) and select **OK**.

17.5   If the syntax was set up correctly, your extrusion should update automatically or turn red to indicate updating is needed. Your extrusion should be back to its original configuration.

NOTE: If the link is broken between the CATPart and the CATScript document, the macro will not be displayed in the Macro window. You can link the documents together by browsing to the directory where the CATScript is located. Run the JoggleDimension.CATscript macro by double clicking on the JoggleDimension.CATscript document. Once the macro is run it will show up in the Macro window.

Figure 1.25

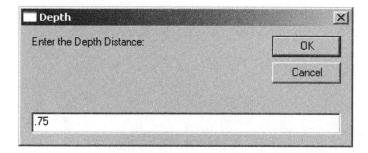

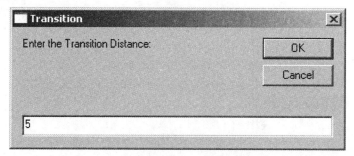

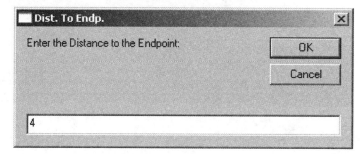

18. Creating a Tool Icon for the Macro

The macro (**JoggleDimensions.CATScript**) created and modified in the previous steps is a very powerful tool. CATIA V5 has developed another powerful tool that will save you additional time. This tool allows you to customize your CATIA V5 work environment by creating your own tool icons. Every time you wanted to run the **JoggleDimensions.CATScript** macro you could go through the same process of selecting **Tools**, **Macro**, **Macros,** select the macro, select **Run**, and finally be ready to run the macro; or, you could assign the macro a tool icon and just select the tool icon. Creating a tool icon for the macro would save five steps every time. The following steps show you how to assign a tool icon to the macro.

18.1   Select **Tools** and then select the **Customize** option

18.2   This will bring up the **Customize** window as shown in Figure 1.26.

Figure 1.26

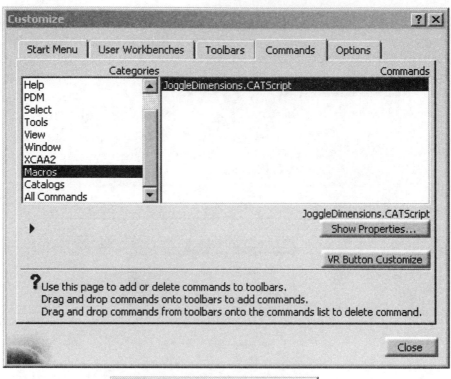

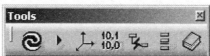

18.3   Select the **Commands** tab in the **Customize** window.

18.4   Select **Macros** from the **Categories** box. This will bring up all the macros that were created and saved with the ***.CATScript** extension.

18.5   Select the **JoggleDimensions.CATScript** located in the **Commands** box.

18.6   With the **JoggleDimensions.CATScript** file highlighted, drag it to the **Tools** toolbar. Drop the **JoggleDimensions.CATScript** on the toolbar as shown in Figure 1.26.

18.7   Close the **Customize** window and click on the newly created tool icon. This will start the **JoggleDimensions.CATScript** macro.

As you can see on the **Customization** window, CATIA V5 allows you many different ways to customize your CATIA V5 work environment. This step has shown you only one. Finding and using the tool from the toolbar is easier than going into the **Macro** option and searching for the macro.

19. Applying Correct Processes and Standards Using the Check Tool

Currently the **JoggleDimensions.CATScript** macro will accept the value of **1″** for the **Transition** dimension and **5″** for the **Depth** dimension. Any experienced joggle operator would tell you that is not a reasonable ratio for an aluminum extrusion. A safe standard for aluminum extrusions is about **4** (run or **Transition**) to **1** (rise or **Depth**). This is a basic standard, but not every one is aware of it. It is very possible that the engineer/planner creating the drawing is not aware of the standard, thus could violate the standard. The engineer/planner could spend time planning and drawing the **Joggled Extrusion**. The part could use up time and resources being prepped for the joggle operation. Only after the extrusion gets to the joggle process would it be discovered that the joggle dimensions are not within company and/or industry standards. All of the time, material and resources have gone to waste. All of this could have been avoided if the engineer/planner was aware of the standard. One way to safeguard yourself and/or company from such mistakes is by incorporating the standard into the intelligence of the part. CATIA V5 offers you the tools to capture the knowledge and/or standard and apply it to your CATParts. The following step explains how to incorporate the **JoggleRatio** standard to your **Joggled Extrusion.CATPart**.

19.1 Double click on the **Relations** branch of the **Specification Tree**. This will bring up the **Knowledge Advisor** workbench.

19.2 Select the **Check** tool. This will bring up the **Check Editor** window as shown in Figure 1.27.

Figure 1.27

Check Editor	
Name of Check :	
JoggleRatio	
Description :	
Check created 8/28/2004	
Destination :	
Joggled Extrusion\Relations	
OK	Cancel	Help

19.3 Label the check **"JoggleRatio."**

19.4 Select **OK**. This will bring up the **Check Editor: JoggleRatio Active** window as shown in Figure 1.28.

Figure 1.28

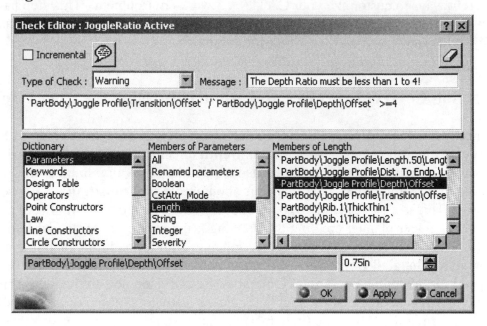

19.5   Select **Warning** as the **Type of Check**.

19.6   In the **Message** box, type "**The Depth Ratio must be less than 1 to 4!**"

19.7   Under **Dictionary**, select **Parameters**.

19.8   In the **Members of Parameters** box, select **Length**.

19.9   In the **Members of Length** box, double click on the "**PartBody Joggle Profile\Transition\Offset**" parameter. This will copy it to the input box above it.

NOTE: Depending on how the constraint was created, the type maybe "Length" or "Offset". The type should not matter as long as it constrains the correct features.

19.10 Type in the symbol for divide (/) after the inserted line. Reference Figure 1.28.

Figure 1.29

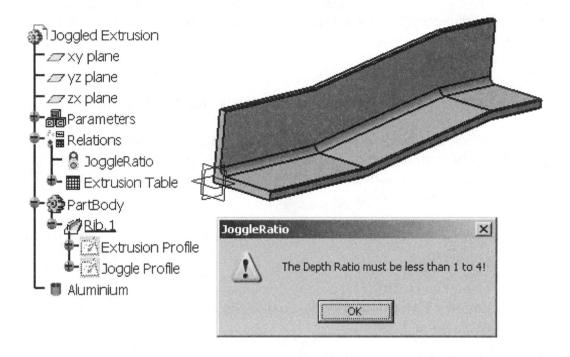

19.11   In the **Members of Length** box, double click the "**PartBody\Joggle Profile\Depth\Offset**" parameter. This will copy it to the end of the line you have been creating in the input box above it.

19.12   Type in **>=4** following the "**…\Depth\Offset**" parameter. Steps 19.9 through this step created a formula that tests the values the user enters when running the **JoggleDimensions.CATScript** macro. The formula needs to be the exact format as seen in Figure 1.28. If the **Transition** value divided by the **Depth** value is **>= 4**, everything is ok. If the value is not **>=4**, then a **Warning** window will appear on screen stating the message you created in Step 19.6, "**The Depth Ratio must be less then 1 to 4!**"

19.13   Select the **OK** button. Notice that CATIA V5 adds a **Check** branch labeled **JoggleRatio** on the **Specification Tree** under the **Relations** branch. When the conditions of the check are met, the **JoggleRatio** branch will show a **Green** light. When the conditions are not met, the **JoggleRatio** branch will show a **Red** light.

19.14   If the values you enter for the **JoggleDimensions.CATScript** macro are not **>=4**, the **JoggleRatio** warning window will appear as shown in Figure 1.29. In this particular **Check** the **Joggled Extrusion** will still be updated even though it did not pass the check. The **Type of Check** was a **Warning**. CATIA V5 let you know that it did not pass the check.

Even though this is a simplified application of the CATIA V5 **Check** tool, it is very useful. It also gives you a glimpse of how powerful this tool can be. This step should give you enough information to start building on more complex checks.

20. Practical Application...
Creating an Up-to-Date Production Drawing Automatically

So far this lesson has shown you some powerful **Knowledgeware** tools. This is the step that brings it all together. The objective from the beginning was to develop an automated process of creating **Detailed Production Drawings**. To accomplish this, complete the following steps.

NOTE: This lesson assumes that you know how to use the CATIA V5 **Drafting** workbench.

20.1   Using the **Drafting** workbench, create a basic **Production Drawing** of the **Joggled Extrusion**. Use the **Orthographic** views and one **Isometric** view as shown in Figure 1.30.

20.2   Dimension the characteristics of the **Joggled Extrusion**. The characteristics of the joggle are:

20.2.1   End of part to start of joggle.

20.2.2   Joggle transition.

20.2.3   Joggle depth.

There is no need to dimension the characteristics of the extrusion because the Tierany Metals Catalog contains all of the extrusion dimensions. The Joggle Operator determines the joggle characteristics, not the extrusion characteristics. The production drawing only need contain the information that is pertinent to the process it is designed for. The dimensions required are shown in Figure 1.30.

20.3   Add a title block and production notes as required, similar to what is shown in Figure 1.30.

20.4   Save the **Production Drawing** as "**Joggled Extrusion.CATDrawing**."

20.5   Print and/or plot as required.

20.6   Run the **JoggleDimensions.CATScript**. Change the joggle dimensions as shown:

    20.6.1   Depth = **.40″**

    20.6.2   Transition = **3″**

    20.6.3   Dist. To Endp. = **2″**

20.7   Bring up the **Joggled Extrusion.CATDrawing**. Update the drawing using the **Update** tool. Notice the view and dimensions automatically update to the newly selected extrusion and joggle dimensions.

This is where CATIA V5 Knowledgeware really saves time. The user can continue to automatically create production drawings for unique **Joggled Extrusion Parts**.

Figure 1.30

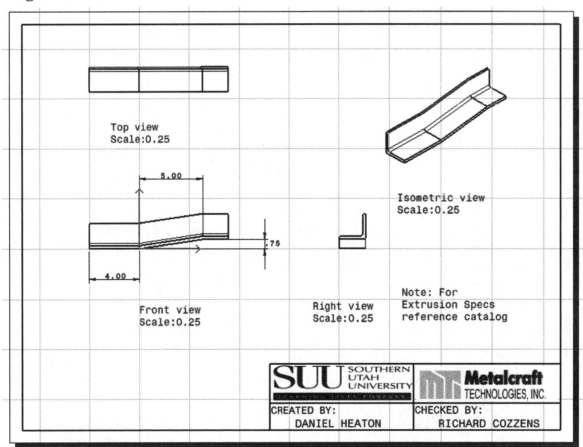

Summary

The **Knowledgeware** product is made up of the following workbenches: **Knowledge Advisor, Knowledge Expert, Product Engineering Optimizer, Product Knowledge Template, Product Function Optimization and Product Functional Definition**. This lesson used a small portion of the tools contained in each individual workbench. Even though only a few tools were used, a great deal of time was saved. The remaining tools offer similar opportunities for significant time saving. This lesson has supplied you with enough information to get you started. Your challenge is to find ways to implement them into your business and processes.

Review Questions

After completing this lesson, you should be able to answer the questions and explain the concepts listed below.

1. The name of a constraint can be changed by double clicking on:

    A. The constraint symbol in the **Specification Tree**.
    B. The entity/entities being constrained.
    C. The actual constraint in the sketch.
    D. Both A and C.

2. Where do you turn on the **Parameters** and **Relations** so that they appear in the **Specification Tree**?

    A. Tools, Options, General, Parameters and Measures.
    B. Start, Infrastructure, Product Structure.
    C. Tools, Customize, Knowledge Advisor.
    D. Tools, Options, Display, Tree Appearance.
    E. None of the above.

3. How can associations be created between the column headings in an Excel table, and CATIA parameters?

    A. By giving the column headings the same name as CATIA gives to the desired parameter and allowing CATIA to automatically associate the two.
    B. By going into the **Associations** tab of the **Extrusion Table** and clicking on the **Create Parameters** button.
    C. Manually select the column heading under the **Associations** tab then also highlighting the desired parameter in the **Parameters** box and click the **Associate** button.
    D. Both A and B.
    E. All of the above.

4. It is necessary to rename the constraints in order to associate the constraint with a column heading in a spreadsheet.

    A. True
    B. False

5. The "Offset" and "Length" type parameters/constraint (in reference to this lesson) are interchangeable.

    A. True
    B. False

6. How do you access an **Extrusion Table** created in CATIA so you can change the configuration row?

   A. Click on the **Extrusion Table** icon in the bottom toolbar of any workbench.
   B. Go into **Knowledge Advisor** and click on the **Extrusion Table** icon in the bottom toolbar.
   C. Double click on the **Extrusion Table** symbol in the **Specification Tree** which will take you directly into the table regardless of which workbench you are currently in.
   D. Double click on the **Extrusion Table** symbol in the **Specification Tree** which will first take you into the **Knowledge Advisor** workbench, if you are not already there, then you must double click again on the symbol (the actual design table) to open the table.
   E. Press **Ctrl + T**.

7. The CATscript document is embedded (part of) the CATpart document.

   A. True
   B. False

8. How do you edit an existing **Extrusion Table** to give it different values or add new configuration rows?

   A. Open the spreadsheet outside of CATIA and make the changes, then save them and close the file. When you open the table in CATIA, it will be automatically updated for you.
   B. Make the changes directly to the **Extrusion Table** by highlighting the rows to be changed and clicking the **Edit** button.
   C. Open the design table and click the **Edit table** button and then make the changes to the spreadsheet that comes up then save the changes and close the spreadsheet.
   D. Both A and C.
   E. Both B and C.

9. What must be added to a macro name in order to access it externally or link it to an icon?

   A. .CATPart
   B. .CATDrawing
   C. .CATKnowledge
   D. .CATScript
   E. .VBScript
   F. .com

10. You can customize your own tool to represent your macro. Therefore the macro could be run from the toolbar rather than going through all the macro options to locate and run your macro.

    A. True
    B. False

11. Which workbench contains a tool that allows you to create a **Check** that will monitor the parameter relations in the CATPart?

    A. Product Engineering Optimizer
    B. Generative Shape Design
    C. Generative Knowledge
    D. Assembly Design
    E. Knowledge Advisor

12. The Knowledgeware tools allows the user to capture, apply and enforce self defined standards.

    A. True
    B. False

13. Once a check has been created, CATIA indicates whether the part passes the check by:

    A. Turning the part red.
    B. A pop up window with your customized warning (text) in it.
    C. Making the part disappear.
    D. Highlighting a red or green light next to the check in the specification tree.
    E. Both B and D.

14. Each time you use the Knowledgeware functions to make changes to a CATPart, you must create a new CATDrawing if you want to show the dimension changes in a new production drawing.

    A. True
    B. False

15. The Rib tool requires two separate sketches to define a solid.

    A. True
    B. False

16. What is CATIA V5 indicating when your part turns red after running a macro.

    A. The macro did not work.
    B. A warning that the values entered are outside the acceptable check values.
    C. You need to manually force the solid model to update by selecting the Update tool.
    D. Your spreadsheet needs to be saved before proceeding.
    E. None of the above.

17. CATIA V5 allows you to convert a recorded macro to VBscript and/or CATscript language.

    A. True
    B. False

18. CATIA V5 allows several different types of checks. In this lesson you used the "Warning" check. What other option/options did CATIA V5 allow?

    A. Silent
    B. Crash
    C. Delete
    D. Information
    E. Both A and D.

19. Knowledgeware tools are located in only one specific workbench.

    A. True
    B. False

20. Macros are most useful when a particular process needs to be completed multiple times.

    A. True
    B. False

Practice Exercises

Complete the following practice exercises using the information and experienced gained by completing this lesson.

1. Create a new spreadsheet using the same format used in this lesson. Link the spread sheet with the CATPart document. Update the drawing documents with each new extrusion defined in the new spreadsheet. Save the CATDrawing documents as **"Lesson1 Ex1 Part1.CATDrawing,"** **"...Part 2.CATDrawing"** and so on.

2. Modify the **JoggleRatio Check** to **1** to **3**. Save the documents as **"Lesson1 Ex2 .CATPart"** and **"Lesson1 Ex2.CATDrawing."**

3. Modify the **Joggle Depth** window prompt so it displays a warning about entering a number that violates the depth ratio 1/3 used in Exercise 2. Save the document as **"Lesson1 Ex3.CATpart."**

4. Modify the Check to a type "Silent" and save it as **"Lesson1 Ex4.CATpart"**.

5. Modify the existing **"L Extrusion"** to a **"T Extrusion."** Modify the sketches, spreadsheet and other parameters as required. Save all related (required) documents.

Notes:

DMU Kinematics

Introduction

This lesson uses a **U-Joint Assembly.CATProduct**. You will need to have
the assembly already created in order to complete this lesson. If you have
not previously created a **U-Joint Assembly**, perhaps using the CATIA V5
Workbook, it can be downloaded from the internet at www.schroff1.com/
catia (select the **Advanced CATIA V5 Workbook** and then **Download
U-JointAssemblyTrace.zip**).

DMU Kinematics

This lesson will take you through a step by step example of how to use the **DMU
Kinematics** workbench to simulate the motion of a mechanical assembly.

Figure 2.1

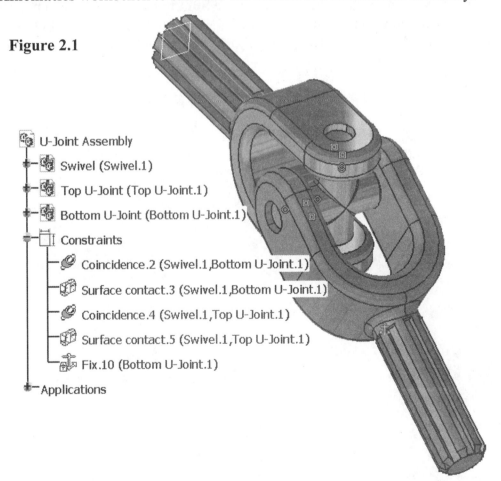

The first part of this lesson will introduce the features of the **DMU Kinematics**
workbench. It will then take you through a demonstration of how to use some of these
features to simulate the motion of the **U-Joint Assembly**.

Objectives

This lesson will take you through the process of creating and simulating **Kinematic Joints** on the **U-Joint Assembly**. This lesson will present the following processes:

1. Learn how to use some of the basic tools of the **DMU Kinematics** workbench.

2. Learn how to bring an existing assembly into the **DMU Kinematics** workbench.

3. Learn how to create **Joints** from existing constraints as well as from scratch.

4. Learn how to create a **Mechanism** and give it commands that allow it to be simulated.

5. Learn how to compile a **Simulation** and create a **Replay**.

6. Learn how to use the **Replay** to analyze the motion of an assembly.

Following the instruction section of the lesson, there is a **Summary** and **Review** to help re-enforce your understanding of the **DMU Kinematics** workbench. The last section of this lesson is the **Practice Exercises** where you will be given the opportunity to test your new knowledge.

Workbench Tools and Toolbars

The following section lists the toolbars and their tools along with a brief explanation for each. This lesson does not use all of the tools listed in the workbench. There are four standard toolbars that have **Kinematics** tools.

The <u>DMU Kinematics</u> Toolbar

DMU Kinematics ☒

TOOL ICON	TOOL NAME	TOOL DEFINITION
Simulation Toolbar		
	Simulation with Commands	Indicates if joints have enough commands to be simulated and what is lacking if there is not.
	Simulation with Laws	Indicates if joints have enough laws to be simulated and what is lacking if there is not.
	Mechanism Dressup	Adds or subtracts products from an already existing mechanism.
Kinematic Joints Toolbar		
	Revolute Joint	Revolving joint consisting of a coincidence constraint and a surface contact constraint.
	Prismatic Joint	Sliding joint consisting of two coincidence constraints.
	Cylindrical Joint	Axial joint consisting of a coincidence constraint.
	Screw Joint	Axial joint consisting of a coincidence constraint and a pitch value.
	Spherical Joint	Ball and socket joint that consists of a coincidence constraint between two points.
	Planar Joint	Sliding joint that consists of a coincidence constraint between two planar faces.
	Rigid Joint	A joint that holds two parts of an assembly together so they can not move in relation to each other.
	Point Curve Joint	A joint that keeps a point on one object tangent to a curve on another object.

		Slide Curve Joint	A joint that keeps a curve on one object tangent to a curve on another object allowing one to slide along the other.
		Roll Curve Joint	A joint that keeps curves on separate objects tangent and allows them to move in relation to each other using a specified joint limit.
		Point Surface Joint	A joint consisting of a point on one object that is forced to remain tangent to a surface of another object.
		Universal Joint	A joint consisting of two axes that spin as though they are two shafts connected by a U-Joint.
		CV Joint	A joint consisting of two universal joints that share one common spin axis.
		Gear Joint	A joint consisting of two revolute joints and a ratio relating the rotation between them.
		Rack Joint	A joint consisting of a revolute joint and a prismatic joint and a ratio between the rotation and linear movement of each.
		Cable Joint	Relation joint consisting of two prismatic joints and a ratio between them. Represents two sliding objects acting as though they are connected by a cable.
		Axis-based Joint	Creates a Spherical, Cylindrical, Revolute, Prismatic, or U-Joint between two axis systems.
		Fixed Part	Fixed constraint that designates which part of the assembly will remain stationary and act as the point of reference for the assembly motion.
		Assembly Constraints Conversion	Automatically converts already existing assembly constraints into the comparable Kinematic joints.
		Speed and Acceleration	Applies the factors of velocity and acceleration to the motion of an assembly.
		Mechanism Analysis	Details all of the parts of a mechanism that have been created and indicates what else needs to be created before the mechanism can be simulated.

The <u>DMU</u> Generic Animation Toolbar

TOOL ICON	TOOL NAME	TOOL DEFINITION
DMU Generic Simulation Commands Toolbar		
	Simulation	Sets commands and laws that will define the motion of the mechanism that is to be simulated.
	Compile Simulation	Takes the commands and laws designated in the Simulation feature and applies them to the assembly creating a recorded replay of the motion.
	Replay	Replays the recorded simulated motion of the assembly so it can be analyzed.
DMU Player Commands Toolbar		
	Simulation Player	Plays a simulation that has been created allowing an opportunity to see how it will look.
	Edit Sequence	Provides the opportunity to order and re-order simulations and sequences prior to compiling.
Automatic Clash Detection Toolbar		
	Clash Detection (Off)	Turns the Clash Detection feature Off.
	Clash Detection (On)	Turns the Clash Detection feature On.
	Clash Detection (Stop)	Turns on the feature that stops the motion of the assembly when a clash is detected.
	Swept Volume	Creates a volume that represents the entire area taken up by the simulated motion of the assembly.
	Trace	Traces the motion of a single point on the assembly as it moves through a simulated motion.

The <u>DMU Space Analysis</u> Toolbar

TOOL ICON	TOOL NAME	TOOL DEFINITION
	**Clash**	Designates which parts of the assembly to perform a clash analysis between.
	Distance and Band Analysis	Measure minimum distances and distances along X, Y and Z.

The <u>Kinematics Update</u> Toolbar

TOOL ICON	TOOL NAME	TOOL DEFINITION
	Update Positions	Updates all changes made to the positions and joints of the assembly.
	Import Sub-Mechanisms	Imports additional mechanisms into the workbench so they can be interrelated.
	Reset Positions	Resets the entities back to their original positions.

Steps to Simulating an Assembly Using the DMU Kinematics Workbench

An assembly can be analyzed for such things as clashing components in the **Assembly Design** workbench. You can also measure the distance between components as well as the physical properties of the entire assembly. These analyses and measurements are taken from a static frame of reference. You will now learn how to use the **DMU Kinematics** workbench to analyze and measure the **U-Joint Assembly** from a kinematics frame of reference, which will allow you to analyze and measure these same properties as the assembly moves.

1. Preparing the Assembly

The most important thing to remember when using the **DMU Kinematics** workbench, is that in order to simulate an assembly, it must be **fully constrained** just as it would be if you were testing an actual assembly that you have physically built. The **U-Joint Assembly** is currently just floating in space and therefore cannot be simulated without first mounting it to a **fixed frame of reference**. A practical example of this would be the carrier bearings and brackets that hold the driveline attached to the **U-Joint** on an automobile drive train.

2. Creating the Mounting

In order to simulate the **U-Joint Assembly** in CATIA V5, you will have to first create a **Mounting** and add it to the assembly. The specific design of the mounting is not important, just as long as it holds the **U-Joint Assembly** in a way that allows it to rotate correctly. For this exercise, a simple mounting design is used that is constrained in a way that will allow you to change the angle between the shafts of the **Top** and **Bottom U-Joints.** This will allow the assembly to be tested more completely using the **DMU Kinematics** workbench. To create this **Mounting**, complete the following:

2.1 Open the **U-Joint Assembly.CATProduct** and take it into the **Product Structure** workbench.

2.2 Add a new part to the assembly by **Inserting** the **New Part**.

2.3 Change the name of the new part to **Mounting**.

2.4 Open the **Part Design** workbench (**Mounting.CATpart**).

2.5   Use the **YZ plane** as the first sketch plane and create the sketch shown in
      Figure 2.2. It is easiest if you create the first arc using the **arc** command
      and constrain the arcs center to the origin of the sketch. Then, create the
      second arc using the **offset** command and attach the ends of the arcs with
      lines.

NOTE: Be sure that the sketch is exactly like the one shown in Figure 2.2. If any
          horizontal or vertical constraints are automatically attached to the lines, it will
          cause problems later on when you try to change the angle of the arcs.

Figure 2.2

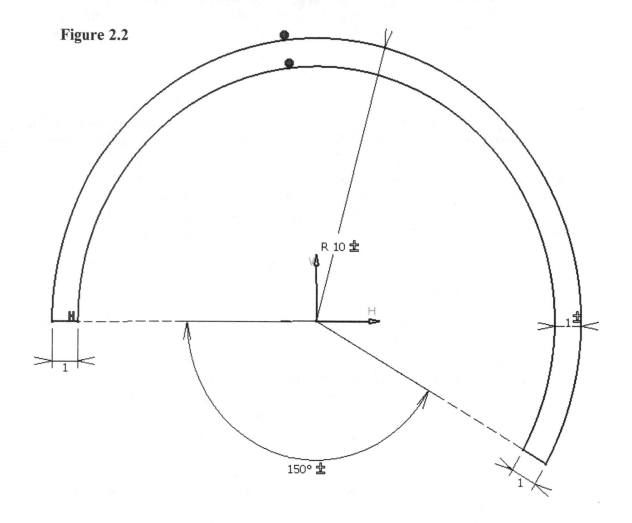

2.6   Once this sketch is complete, extrude it **2″** using the **Pad** tool.

2.7   Use both rectangular ends of the part just created as sketch planes for two
      more pads. These pads are rectangles that are constrained to the shape of
      the ends of the extruded arc just created as shown in Figure 2.3.

2.8   Extrude each of these pads **1″**, creating a rectangular box at each end of the
      arc pad.

2.9   Complete the mounting by rounding off the ends using **Tri-tangent** fillets.

2.10   Put **1.5″** diameter holes through the center of the flat surface of each rounded end so that the final part looks like the part shown in Figure 2.3.

NOTE: This design will provide (2) axial holes to constrain the **U-Joint** shafts to as well as the ability to change the angle between those two axes.

Figure 2.3

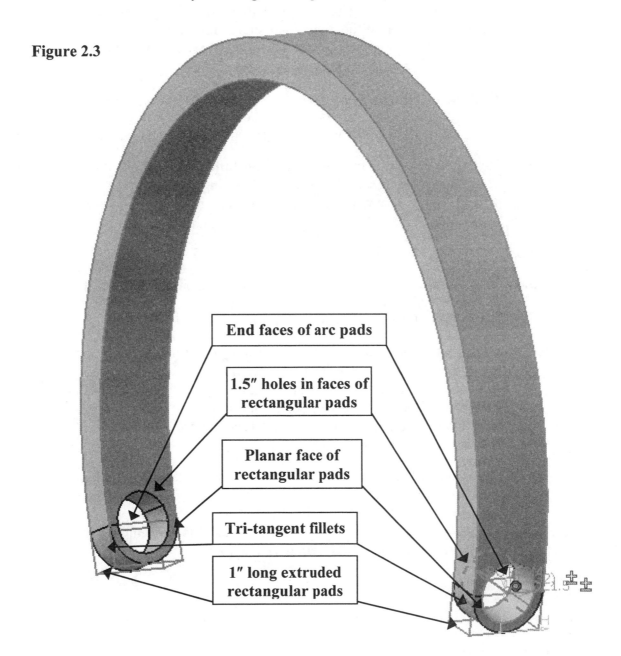

End faces of arc pads

1.5″ holes in faces of rectangular pads

Planar face of rectangular pads

Tri-tangent fillets

1″ long extruded rectangular pads

3. Assembling the U-Joint into the Mounting

Once you have completed the **Mounting**, you can use the **Assembly Design** workbench to assemble the **U-Joint Assembly** into the **Mounting**. This is accomplished by adding 4 new constraints and deleting one old constraint as described below:

3.1   Constrain each of the shafts of the **Top** and **Bottom U-Joints** axially to the holes in each end of the mounting using **Coincidence** constraints. Doing this should automatically move the **U-Joint Assembly** to the center of the mounting when the assembly is updated.

NOTE: Be sure the mounting is oriented so that the holes are at least close to the shafts you desire to constrain them to or else CATIA may determine to move the part so that it is aligned opposite from where you intended it to be.

3.2   Lengthen the shafts on the **Top** and **Bottom U-Joints** so that they pass completely through the holes in the mounting (if they aren't already). This will make the assembly easier to work with and visualize. For this lesson, extrude the second limit of the shaft pads an additional **6″**.

3.3   Delete the **Fix** constraint from the **Bottom U-Joint**.

3.4   Fix the mounting so that it cannot move. This can be accomplished using the **Fix Component** constraint represented by an anchor just like the one just deleted from the **Bottom U-Joint**.

3.5   Create an **Offset Constraint** between the end of one of the shafts and the face of the mounting hole that it passes through. It may not be obvious, but with both shafts only fixed axially, they would be able to slide along their axes and this would cause the assembly to bind up as it attempts to rotate. This **Offset Constraint** fixes that problem by preventing one shaft from moving along its axis.

NOTE: If you leave off this constraint, the **Mechanism Analysis** function of the **DMU Kinematics** workbench may have indicated that the assembly could not be simulated without adding the constraint. The completed assembly should look like the one shown in Figure 2.4. The assembly is now ready to be taken into the **DMU Kinematics** workbench.

Figure 2.4

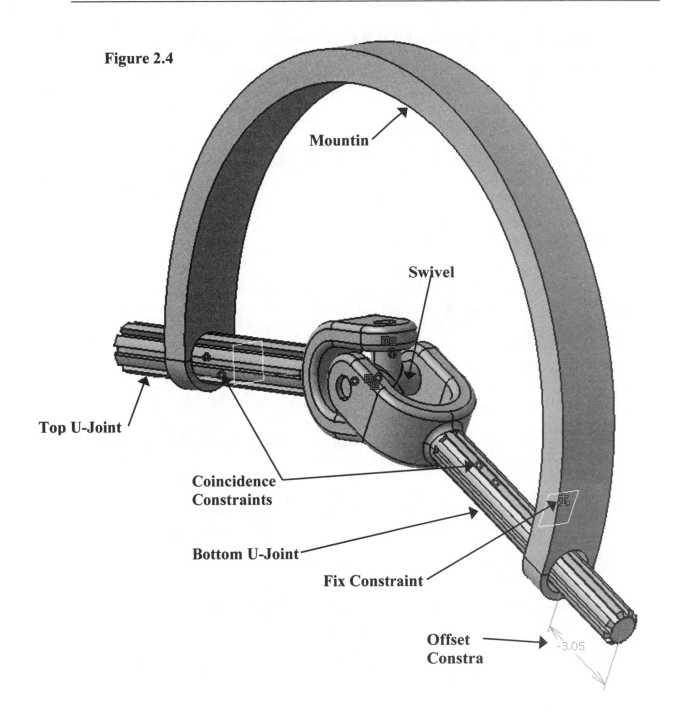

Mountin

Swivel

Top U-Joint

Coincidence
Constraints

Bottom U-Joint

Fix Constraint

Offset
Constra

3.05

4. Moving an Assembly into the DMU Kinematics Workbench

Now that the assembly has been completed and fully constrained, it can be taken into the **DMU Kinematics** workbench. This workbench is located under **Start, Digital Mockup, DMU Kinematics**. As usual, make sure the assembly is highlighted in the **Specification Tree** before selecting the workbench so that the entire assembly is moved into the new workbench. Now that the assembly is in the **DMU Kinematics** workbench, you can begin the process of simulating and testing the assembly in kinematical motion.

5. Automatic Joint Creation

In order to simulate an assembly in the **DMU Kinematics** workbench, it must first have joints created that constrain its range and type of motion. A joint is a combination of several constraints that work together to simulate a specific type of kinematical motion. These joints can be created in two ways, automatically from existing constraints, or manually using the pre-created joint options found under the **Kinematics Joints** toolbar 🔧 of this workbench. Because the assembly was already fully constrained in the **Assembly Design** workbench, CATIA can use those constraints to automatically create all of the equivalent joints.

5.1   First click on the **Assembly Constraints Conversion** icon 🔧. This will bring up the **Assembly Constraints Conversion** window as shown in Figure 2.5.

5.2   Click on **New Mechanism** to bring up the **Mechanism Creation** window. The default name of the mechanism should be **Mechanism.1**.

5.3   At this point you can re-name the mechanism, for this lesson we will call the mechanism "**U-Joint**."

5.4   Select **OK** to close the **Mechanism Creation** window after you have finished naming the mechanism.

5.5   Select the **Auto Create** button. This will automatically convert the existing assembly constraints into kinematical joints that the workbench can use to simulate the assembly.

Figure 2.5

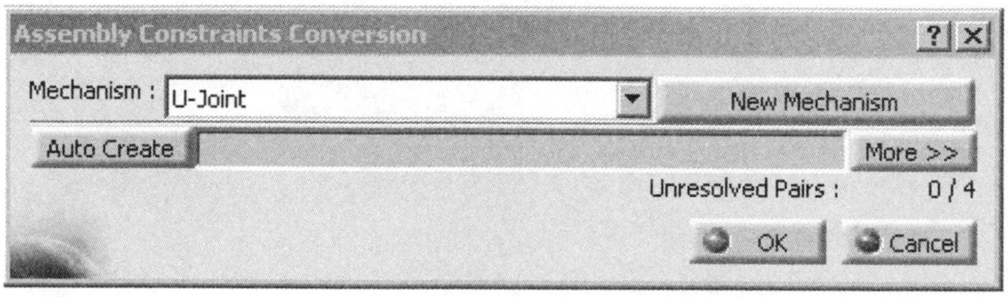

NOTE: At this point it may not be obvious what you have done, other than the **Applications** section of the **Specification Tree** is now expandable. Select the **OK** button to close the **Assembly Constraints Conversion** window. To see what you have done, expand the **Applications** branch of the **Specification Tree**. Notice that the new joints appear in the **Specification Tree** under **Applications, Mechanisms, U-Joints, Joints** as shown in Figure 2.6. In this case the assembly constraints were used to create three revolute joints and one cylindrical joint. Notice also, that the **Mounting** was added to the **Specification Tree** under **U-Joint, Fix Part**. This means that the work bench recognizes the **Fix Component** assembly constraint and has made the **Mounting** the part of the assembly that will not move thus becoming the point of reference for all kinematical motion of the assembly.

Figure 2.6

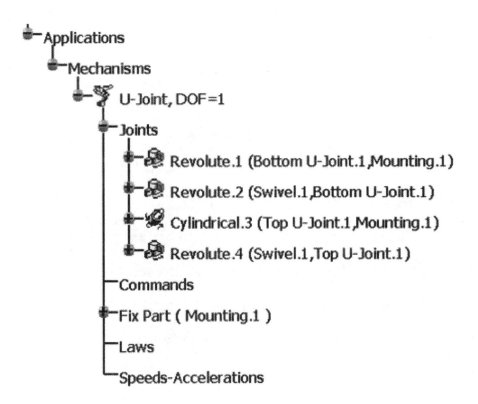

6. Manual Joint Creation

The **Assembly Constraints Conversion** tool is the quickest and easiest way to create **Kinematical Joints** in the **DMU Kinematics** workbench. However, in many instances you will need a joint that is not equivalent to any of the already existing assembly constraints. Therefore, as part of this lesson, you will delete one of the joints that were just automatically created and re-create it manually. In this lesson, you will only have to create this one joint manually, but the basic steps and processes can be applied to later problems that require more complex manual joint creation. To create a joint manually, complete the following steps:

6.1 Delete the old joint that was created automatically. Delete the **Revolute Joint**, the one between the **Mounting** and the **Bottom U-Joint**, from the **Specification Tree** as shown in Figure 2.7. This can be accomplished by simply highlighting the **Revolute Joint** in the **Specification Tree** and pressing the **Delete** key.

Figure 2.7

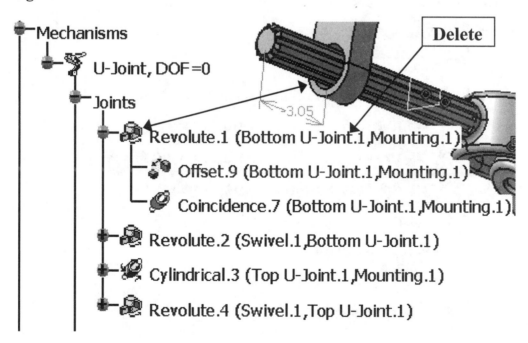

6.2 Select the **Revolute Joint** [icon] tool. This will bring up the **Joint Creation: Revolute** window as shown in Figure 2.8.

6.3 Select the **Mechanism** to create the joint on. This should be the **U-Joint** mechanism you created in the previous steps.

6.4 Select the two lines to be constrained axially. The axis of the **Bottom U-Joint** shaft should be selected as **Line 1** and the axis of the hole in the end of the **Mounting** as **Line 2**. (You may have to hover the mouse over the area of the base of the shaft in order to make the axis line appear.)

6.5 Select the two planar faces to be constrained parallel. The face at the end of the **Bottom U-Joint** shaft should be selected as **Plane 1** and the planar face at the end of the **Mounting** that the hole is through as **Plane 2**.

6.6 Select the **Offset** setting to be used for the planar constraint. **Null Offset** means that the planar faces are in contact and **Offset** means that there is a set distance between them. Selecting **Offset** should cause the distance value of **3.05in** to appear since that is the current distance between the faces.

6.7 Once all of the settings are selected as described above, create the joint by clicking the **OK** button.

NOTE: The **Revolute Joint** that you just created will appear in the **Specification Tree** in place of the joint that was deleted. You can follow these same basic steps for creating any of the **Kinematic Joints** that are used in the **DMU Kinematics** workbench. Just click on the tool of the desired joint and select the features of the assembly that are asked for in the **Joint Creation: Revolute** window.

Figure 2.8

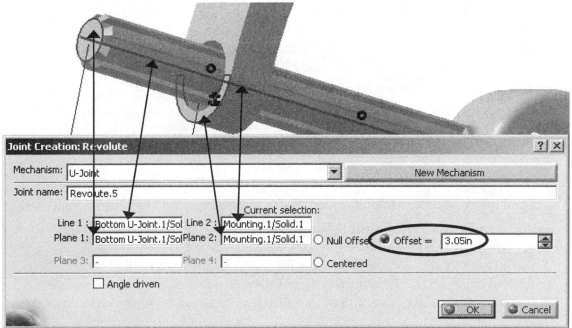

7. Mechanism Analysis

In order to be simulated, every mechanism must have at least one command and one fixed component. The **Mechanism Analysis** tool can now be used to find out if the assembly can be simulated, click on the **Mechanism Analysis** 🔍 tool. This will bring up the **Mechanism Analysis** window as shown in Figure 2.9. This feature lets you know what parts of the mechanism you have successfully created and what still needs to be done before the mechanism can be simulated. At this point the assembly cannot yet be simulated as indicated by the word **No** in the box next to the **Mechanism can be simulated** line. The other lines in the window will indicate what else is required before the mechanism can be simulated. Notice that the **Number of commands** at this point is **zero**. The mechanism still needs a command to tell it how to move. Now that you know what else the mechanism needs, close the **Mechanism Analysis** window.

Figure 2.9

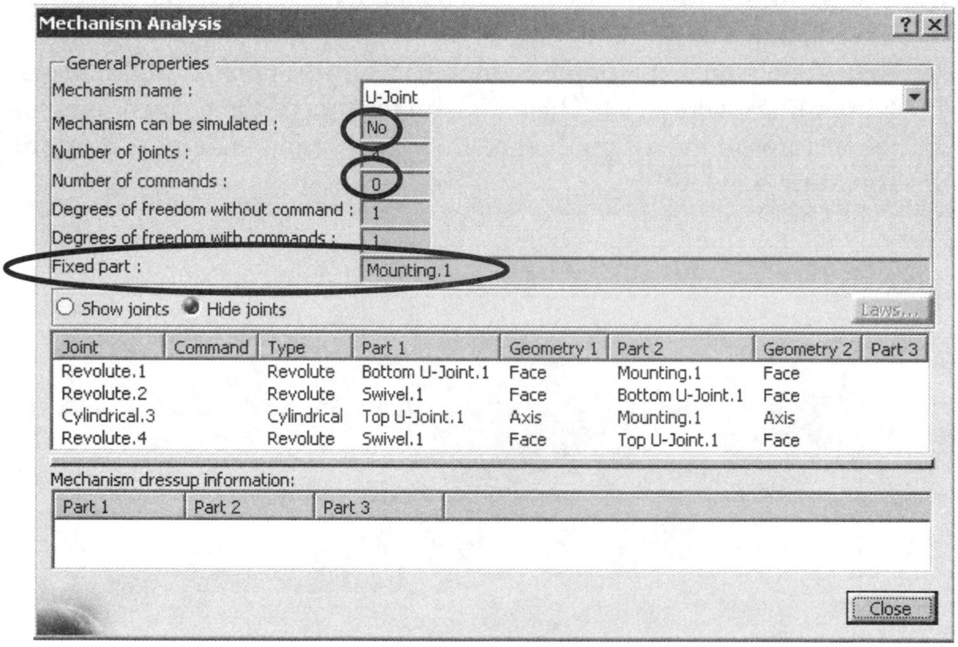

Another way to determine what else the mechanism needs is to click on **Simulation with Commands** 🔧 or **Simulation with Laws** 📋. This will tell you if the mechanism cannot be simulated and the reasons why. In this case, click on **Simulation with Laws** found by expanding the **Simulation with Commands** tool. This will bring up the **Kinematics Simulation** window as shown in Figure 2.10. In this case you should get the following message: "**Add at least one command on a joint**." This feature gives a specific reason why the mechanism cannot yet be simulated.

Figure 2.10

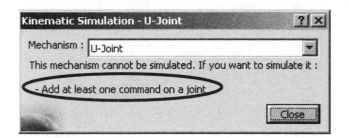

Figure 2.11

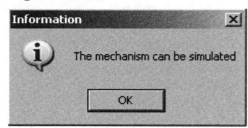

8. Adding a Command

CATIA has indicated that a command needs to be added to the mechanism before it can be simulated. This means that you need to add a **numerical value** to the motion of one of the joints so that CATIA knows how far to move it and in what direction. To do this, you must first select which joint you want to use to drive the motion of the assembly. You can then give that joint a command to constrain its motion. For this step you will have the cylindrical joint on one of the shafts rotate.

8.1 Locate in the **Specification Tree** the cylindrical joint that connects the **Top U-Joint** to the **Mounting**.

8.2 Double click on the cylindrical joint in the **Specification Tree**. This should bring up the **Joint Edition** window shown in Figure 2.12. This joint has the options of being **Angle driven** or **Length driven**.

8.3 Select the **Angle driven** option.

8.4 Enter the upper and lower limits of rotation. For this step use **-360** to **360** as the rotational limits. Reference Figure 2.12.

8.5 Select **OK** to close the window.

NOTE: An **Information** box like the one shown in Figure 2.11 should appear telling you that the mechanism can now be simulated. If the information box does not appear, then you should again check the **Mechanism Analysis** window or the **Simulation with Laws** window to determine what else the mechanism needs in order to be simulated. Once CATIA has indicated that the mechanism can be simulated, you can move on to the next step.

Figure 2.12

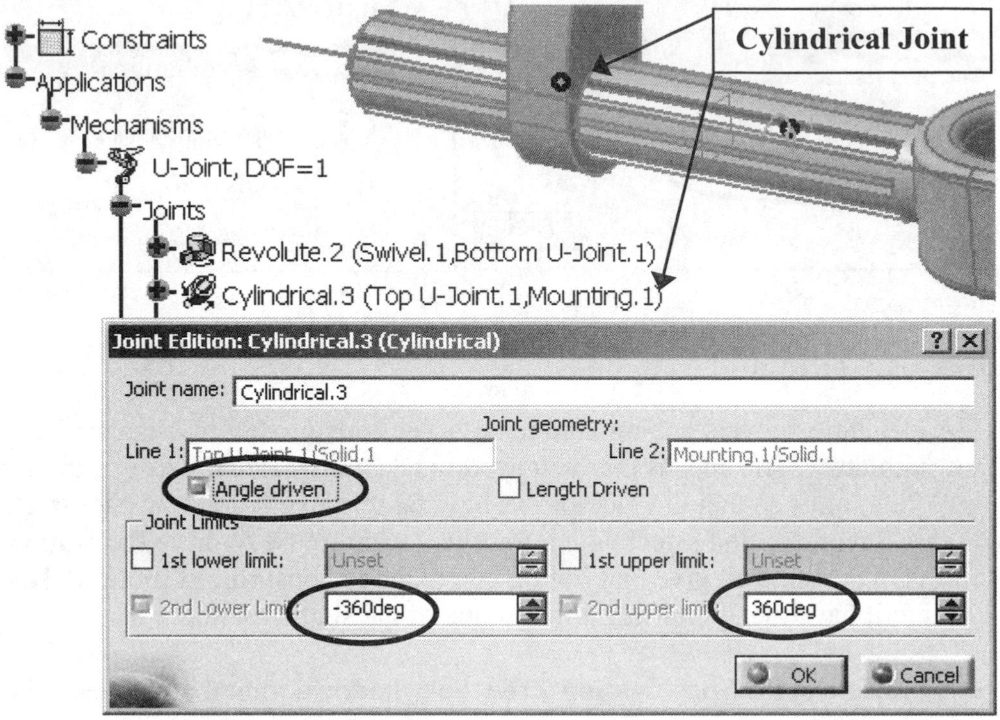

9. Editing a Simulation

The first step in creating a simulation is to configure the parameters of the simulated motion. This is accomplished using the **Edit Simulation** window of the workbench.

To access this window, click on the **Simulation** [icon] tool. If you have created more than one mechanism, this will bring up a **Select** window where you can chose which mechanism to simulate. If this window appears, select the **U-Joint** mechanism that you have created and click the **OK** button. This will bring up the **Edit Simulation** and **Kinematic Simulation** windows shown in Figure 2.13. You will note that the limits you set as a command for the cylindrical joint are shown in the **Kinematic Simulation** window. The first thing to note is the initial value that it is set to. This value is shown in the display box and represented by the position of a slider tool in the Kinematics Simulation – U-Joint window. This is the initial position of the simulated motion (should be **-360** or **0** degrees, depending on how you set your command parameters). The features of these windows can be used to configure the parameters of the simulation as follows:

9.1 Make sure the initial value is what you want. In this case, it would be the lower limit value of **-360**.

9.2 If the initial value is not what you desire, then you can change it by first typing the desired value into the display box or moving the sliding switch to the desired value.

Figure 2.13

9.3 Click the **Modify** button in the **Edit Simulation** window. This modifies the initial position of the motion.

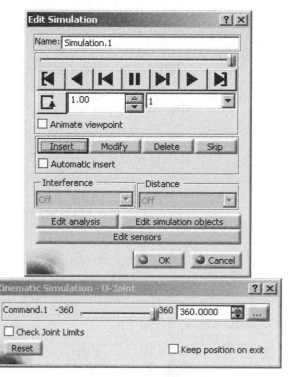

9.4 To define your simulation, change the value to the end position of the intended motion. Again, this is accomplished by either typing the value into the display box, or moving the sliding switch to the desired value. In this case we want the assembly to rotate to the upper limit of **360** degrees. Notice that you can see the assembly move as the sliding switch is moved.

9.5 Record this value change by clicking on the **Insert** button of the **Edit Simulation** window. You will notice that this moves the sliding switch of the **Edit Simulation** window across to the right side. This means that the movement from the initial to final positions has been recorded.

9.6 If you wish to erase what was just recorded and start over, this can be done using the **Delete** button.

9.7 Note that the name of this simulation is given in the **Name** display box at the top of the **Edit Simulation** window. The default name should be **Simulation.1**. A different name can be typed into this box if desired. The other settings options in this window will not be used in this exercise.

9.8 Once you have finished configuring the simulation, close the **Edit Simulation** window by selecting on the **OK** button.

10. Playing a Simulation

At this point you can not tell if the simulation that you have just configured is actually what you meant it to be. In previous releases of CATIA V5, you had to use the **Compile Simulation** tool to compile the simulation into a replay in order to see if the motion is truly what you intended it to be. By that time, however, you had already gone to all of the trouble of creating a replay of the motion. A new feature added to this workbench in **Release 9** is the **DMU Player Commands** toolbar. To use this feature, complete the following steps:

10.1 Click on the **Simulation Player** ▦ icon. This should cause the **Player** toolbar to appear as shown in Figure 2.14. This tool allows you to play the simulation that was just recorded as follows:

    10.1.1 Select the simulation to play from the **Specification Tree**. If you have recorded only one simulation, then by default it will be the one played.

    10.1.2 Click on the **Parameters** icon ▦ on the **Player** toolbar to bring up the **Player Parameters** window.

    10.1.3 Change the **Sampling Step** value to **0.01 s**. This value is the fraction of a second that the motion will be divided up into. If you accepted the default value of **1 s**, the entire motion will occur in one step and you will not be able to see the assembly move.

    10.1.4 Click on the **Play Forward** button ▶ of the **Player** toolbar. This should cause the assembly to move through the motion of the simulation that was just compiled.

NOTE: If the assembly does not move, first check to see if the **Sampling Step** value of the **Player Parameters** window is set to **0.01 s** as indicated above. If this value is set correctly and the assembly still does not move, go back to the **Editing a Simulation** section and re-create the simulation according to the steps listed making sure that the steps are followed exactly. Once you have successfully played the motion of the simulation, you can move on to the next step of **Compiling the Simulation**.

Figure 2.14

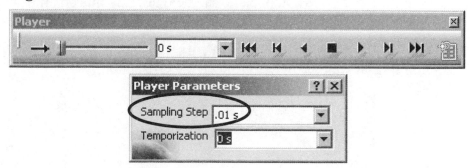

11. Compiling the Simulation

Having configured the simulation using the **Edit Simulation** tool and playing its simulated motion using the **Simulation Player** tool, the next step is to compile the simulation. To do this:

11.1 Click on the **Compile Simulation** icon under the expanded **DMU Generic Simulation Commands** toolbar. This will open the **Compile Simulation** window shown in Figure 2.15.

Figure 2.15

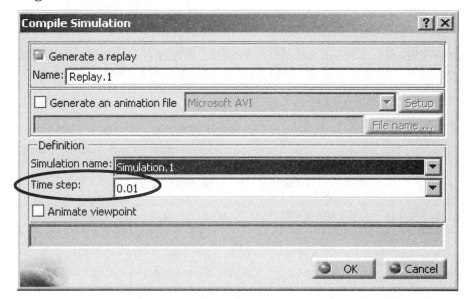

11.2 Select whether you want to generate a **replay** or an **animation file**. A replay can be used to analyze the motion of the assembly in CATIA V5. An animation file is a **Microsoft AVI** file that can be used to show the motion of the assembly on a media player. In this case, we want to analyze the motion of the assembly, so make sure that the **Generate a replay** option is selected.

11.3 Note the name of the replay. The default name of the replay should be **Replay.1,** but can be changed if desired.

11.4 Select which simulation to compile. In this case, **Simulation.1** should be the default simulation in the **Simulation name:** box. If you had created more than one simulation, then the desired simulation could be selected from the drop down menu of this box.

11.5 Set the **Time step**. By default, the **Time step:** value should be set to **1**. In this case, you should change this value to **.01** by selecting it from the drop down menu. This causes the replay of the motion to be shown in finer time step increments just like the **Simulation Player** tool.

11.6   Once you have selected the desired settings, click the **OK** button. This
        will cause CATIA V5 to begin to compile the simulation into a **Replay**.
        You should be able to see the assembly move through its configured
        motion as the simulation is being compiled. If you do not see the assembly
        move, then you will have to go back through the process of editing the
        simulation and checking to make sure it was done correctly by again using
        the **Simulation Player** tool. Once the simulation is compiled, you can
        move on to replay and analyze the simulated motion of the assembly.

12. Replaying the Simulation

12.1   To view the replay that was just created, click on the **Replay** icon
        under the expanded **DMU Generic Simulation Commands** toolbar.
        This will open the **Replay** window shown in Figure 2.16. You can also
        double click on **Replay.1** in the **Specification Tree**.

12.2   Select the replay to be
        replayed from the **Name** box   **Figure 2.16**
        at the top of this window.
        Replay.1 should be shown by
        default, but if more than one
        replay has been created, then it
        can be selected from the drop
        down menu of the **Name** box.

12.3   Select the desired play speed
        of the replay from the play
        speed drop down menu. By
        default it should be set to **x 1**,
        and it can be set for up to **x 10**,
        meaning 10 times faster than
        the standard replay speed.

12.4   You can now use this window to view the simulated motion of the
        assembly by clicking on the **Play Forward ▶** button. This should cause
        your assembly to move through the simulated motion you just compiled.
        (There are also other standard viewing buttons such as **Pause ❙❙**, **Play
        Backward ◀**, **Step Forward ▶❙**, **Step Backward ❙◀**, **Jump to Start ❙◀**,
        and **Jump to End ▶❙**.)

12.5   You can also change the play back loop to play only **one time through**,
        continuous, or **back and forth**. Take some time to figure out these
        different features for replaying the simulation.

NOTE: At this point, you should note that the **Simulation.1** and **Replay.1** that you have just created have been added to the **Specification Tree** under the **Applications** branch. If you wish to access either of these to view what you have done or make changes, they can either be selected from the **Specification Tree** or by opening the windows and using the tools that were utilized in creating them.

13. Distance and Band Analysis

Now that a simulation has been compiled and stored in the form of a **Replay**, you can use the **DMU Kinematics** workbench to analyze the motion of the assembly. The first thing we will use to analyze the motion of the assembly is the **Distance and Band Analysis** tool. This will show how close the different components of the assembly are to each other as the assembly moves. To use this tool:

13.1 Click on the **Distance and Band Analysis** icon ![icon]. This will bring up the **Edit Distance and Band Analysis** window shown in Figure 2.17.

13.2 As usual, the first thing you have the option of doing is customizing the name of the analysis. We will accept the default name of **Distance.1**.

13.3 The next thing to set is the **Type** of distance analysis that you would like to perform. In this case the default should be **Minimum**, which is the type of analysis we want in this case.

Figure 2.17

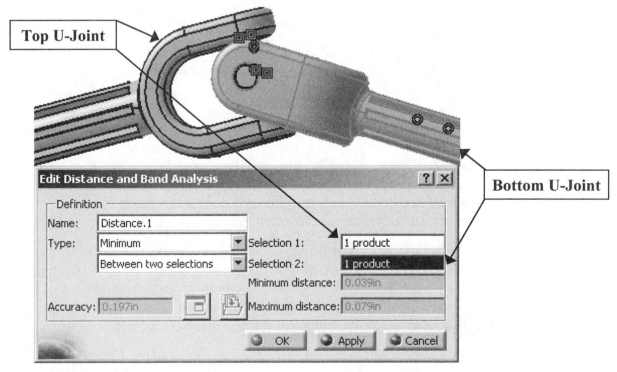

13.4   The next part of setting the type of distance analysis is determining what objects you would like to analyze the distance between. In this case we will change the type from **Inside one selection** to **Between two selections**. This will allow us to analyze the minimum distance between the **Top** and **Bottom U-Joints** as the assembly rotates.

13.5   Select which parts of the assembly to analyze the distance between. To do this, make sure that the **Selection 1** box is highlighted, and then select the **Top U-Joint**. This should cause **1 product** to appear in the **Selection 1** box.

13.6   Next, highlight the **Selection 2** box and select the **Bottom U-Joint**. Again, **1 product** should appear in the **Selection 2** box. This indicates that **Selection 2** is composed of only one product or part.

Figure 2.18

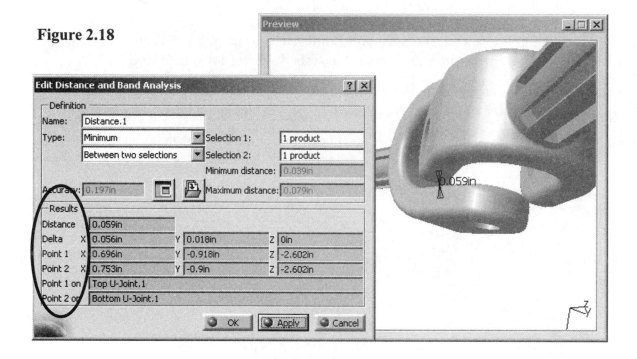

NOTE: If you desired, you could select multiple parts that would all be contained in **Selection 2**. For example, you could also select the **Mounting** or **Swivel** to be part of **Selection 2** and the minimum distance would be between whichever of those parts was closest to the parts of **Selection 1**.

13.7   To apply the **Distance and Band Analysis** to the current orientation of the assembly, select the **Apply** button at the bottom of the window. This will create a **Preview** window that shows the current distance relationship of the two selections and where the **minimum distance** occurs. You may need to **zoom in** a little to see the minimum distance location in the preview.

13.8   Click the close button in the upper right hand corner of the **Preview** window.

13.9 After closing the **Preview** window, take note of the analysis **Results** that the **Edit Distance and Band Analysis** window is displaying as shown in Figure 2.18. The results will show the **minimum distance**, the **X, Y**, and **Z location of the points** on each of the selections where the minimum distance occurred, and the **parts** on which those points are located. This information is saved under the **Distance** branch of the **Specification Tree** as the default name that it was given of **Distance.1**.

13.10 Close the **Edit Distance and Band Analysis** window by clicking the **OK** button at the bottom of the window.

14. Clash Analysis

In this lesson, we will also use the **Clash** analysis tool. This will tell you if there is interference between any of the parts of the assembly. To use this tool:

14.1 Click the **Clash** icon . This should bring up the **Check Clash** window shown in Figure 2.19.

14.2 Again, we can first give this analysis a name or in this case, accept the default name of **Interference.1**.

14.3 Select the **Type** settings of **Contact + Clash**, and **Between two selections**.

14.4 Select the **Top U-Joint** to be **Selection 1** and the **Bottom U-Joint** as **Selection 2** just like with the **Distance and Band Analysis** tool.

14.5 Once you have done this, click the **Apply** button at the bottom of the window. The results of the analysis should now be displayed. Notice that if there are no results listed that there is a **green light** shown under the word **Results**. Next to that it should indicate the **Number of interferences**, which in this case should be **zero**. This indicates that there is no interference between these two selections at this time.

Figure 2.19

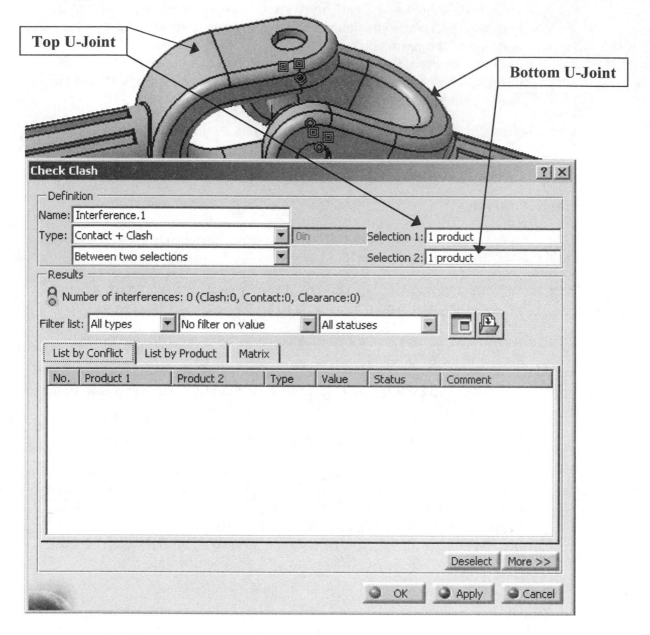

14.6   When you have obtained all the information that you want from this
       window, you can close it by clicking the **OK** button at the bottom of the
       window.

14.7   Notice that the interference analysis you just created now appears in the
       Specification Tree under **Applications**, **Interference** as **Interference.1**.

15. Edit Analysis

The real power of the analyses that you have just performed is applying them to the simulated motion of the assembly that you have created and stored as a **Replay**. To do this:

15.1 First, open the replay that you have created by double clicking on it in the **Specification Tree** or by clicking on the **Replay** icon 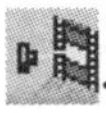.

15.2 Select the desired **Replay**. If you have created multiple replays, then you can select the desired one from the drop down menu of the **Name** box.

NOTE: Once you have selected the desired **Replay**, you can now adjust the **Edit analysis** settings at the bottom of the window. Notice that you can apply **Interference** or a **Distance** analysis to the **Replay**. Notice that the **Interference** and **Distance** boxes are not lit up at this time, indicating that they can not yet be used. In order to apply an analysis, you must first add it to the **Replay**.

15.3 Click on the **Edit analysis** button. This should bring up the **Edit Analysis in Replay** window shown in Figure 2.20. At this time the window should be empty, because you have not added an analysis yet.

Figure 2.20

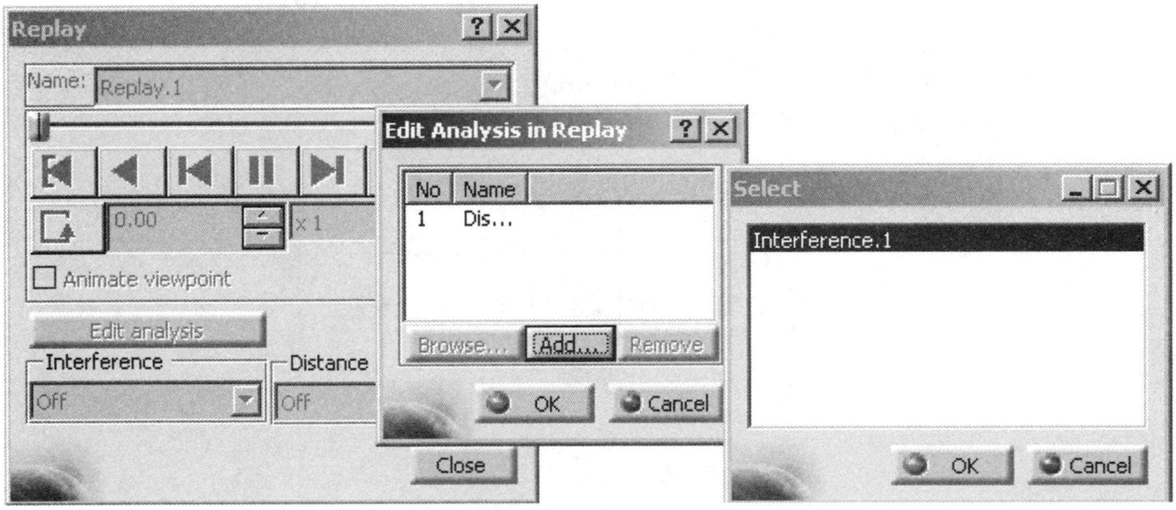

15.4 Click on the **Add...** button in this window to bring up the list of analyses that have been created for this mechanism. The names of the two analyses that you created should appear on this list. You can only add one analysis at a time.

15.5 Click on **Distance.1** to highlight it.

15.6   Click the **OK** button. Notice that it is now added to the **Edit Analysis in Replay** window.

15.7   Click the **Add...** button again and repeat the process to add your **Interference.1** analysis to the window as well.

15.8   Once you have both analyses added to the **Edit Analysis in Replay** window, click the **OK** button at the bottom of the window.

NOTE: Now the **Interference** and **Distance** boxes should both be lit up, meaning that you can use them. They should also both be turned **Off** by default at this time. From the **Interference** drop down menu you can also select whether you want the interference analysis set to **On** or **Stop**. When it is set to **On**, the parts will turn **red** when they are colliding, but they will continue to move. When it is set to the **Stop** option, the replay will stop as the parts begin to clash as though they were real. The distance analysis can be set only to **On** or **Off**.

Figure 2.21

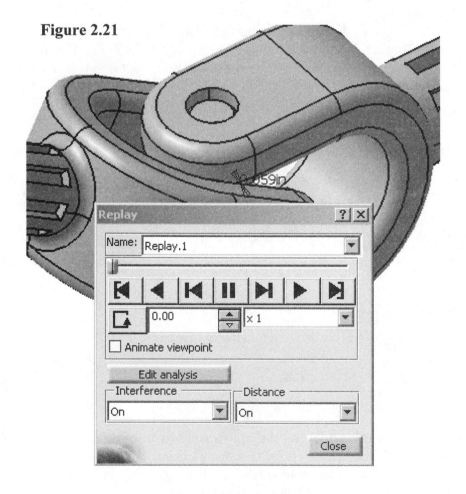

15.9   Turn both the **Interference** and **Distance** analyses **On** at this time as shown in Figure 2.21.

15.10 Now, run the replay by playing it forward. You will notice that the **Distance** analysis is continually running and displaying the distance as it changes through the motion. This distance is displayed on the assembly as (zero) **0in** if the parts interfere. You may need to **zoom in** on the part to see the actual distance value displayed clearly. If none of the parts are turning red, then you know for certain that there is no interference in this simulated motion.

16. Swept Volume

Another useful feature of the **DMU Kinematics** workbench is the **Swept Volume** analysis feature. This allows you to see exactly how much space is taken up by the motion of an assembly. To use this tool:

16.1 Click on the **Swept Volume** icon . This should bring up the **Swept Volume** window shown in Figure 2.22.

16.2 Select which **Replay** you would like to create the **Swept Volume** from, by default it should be **Replay.1**.

Figure 2.22

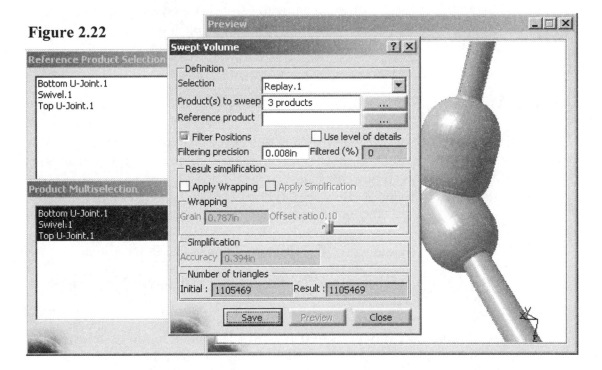

16.3 Adjust the **Product(s) to sweep** box. By default it should have **3 products** written in it. The products can be viewed by clicking the button at the right side of the box. In this case, the **Top U-Joint**, **Bottom U-Joint** and **Swivel** should all be listed and highlighted. These are automatically selected, because they are the only parts of the assembly that move.

16.4　If you want to change the products to create a **Swept Volume** from, do so at this time by only highlighting the desired products.

16.5　Click the **OK** button to close the **Product Multiselection** window.

16.6　Select your **Filtering precision** and **Reference product**. For this lesson, we will leave the default values for these options.

16.7　Click on the **Preview** button to see what the swept volume of the selected products will look like as they move through the **Replay.1** recorded motion. The computer will need some time to compute the swept volume, so you may have to wait 30 seconds to a minute before the results are displayed. After the swept volume is computed, a **Preview** window showing the **Swept Volume** of the **U-Joint Assembly** should appear.

16.8　After you have previewed the swept volume, close the **Preview** window. You now have the option of saving the **Swept Volume**.

16.9　Click on the **Save** button at the bottom of the **Swept Volume** window. A **Save As** window should appear that allows you to save the swept volume as a **cgr**, **wrl**, **model**, or a **stl** file.

16.10　Give the **Swept Volume** the name of "**U-Joint Assembly Motion**" and save is as a **cgr** file. Now you will be able to open or insert the **Swept Volume** file into other files as it is needed in the future.

17. Trace Analysis

Another useful feature of this workbench is the **Trace** analysis function. This allows you to compute the motion of a given point on the assembly as it moves through one of the recorded **Replays**. Thus, you can see exactly how far and in what path a particular point on the assembly travels as the assembly moves. To access this tool:

17.1　Click on the **Trace** icon ![icon]. This should open the **Trace** window.

17.2　First, select the **Object to trace out** that you wish to use. For this lesson, we will use **Replay.1**.

17.3　Next, select the **Elements to trace out**. This point has to be selected from the edge curve geometry of one of the parts of the assembly. For this exercise, we will select a vertex point of the **Top U-Joint** as shown in Figure 2.23. To select the vertex, hover the mouse pointer over the area of the tri-tangent fillet until the vertex point appears, then left click.

Figure 2.23

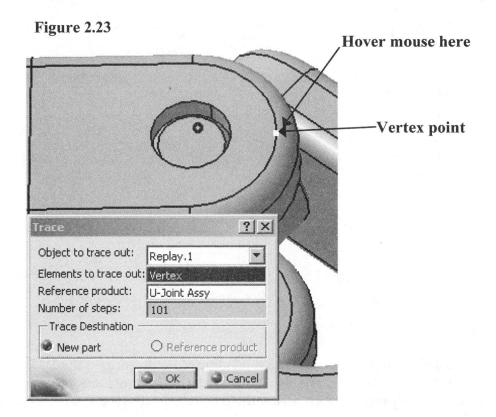

Hover mouse here

Vertex point

17.4   Once you have selected this point, click the **OK** button. It may take
        the computer a few seconds to compute the path of the selected point.

NOTE: After the path of the point has been computed, a new CATPart will be
          created titled **Trace1** as shown in Figure 2.24. This part file consists of
          many points showing the location of the selected point at increments along
          the path of its motion and a spline connecting these point locations. At this
          point you can decide if this point trace is what you wanted and you can
          either save it or close it without saving.

17.5   Save the point trace file as "**U-Joint Assembly Trace.CATPart**."

17.6   After saving the file, close or minimize the trace so that you can go back
        to the original **U-Joint Assembly** file that you have been working on.

NOTE: The **Swept Volume** and **Trace** files that you have saved can now be used
          in future designs and other assemblies that surround or mate up to the
          U-Joint Assembly. Thus helping you to minimize wasted space and avoid
          clash and interference that may occur as different assemblies move
          simultaneously. An example of a situation where this feature is useful is in
          designing a wheel well that will allow the front tire of an automobile to
          turn back and forth as it moves up and down on the suspension system or in
          other complex motions.

Figure 2.24

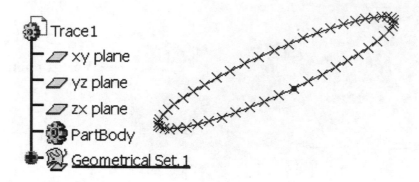

Summary

This lesson has demonstrated the application of some of the features of the **DMU Kinematics** workbench. Having completed this lesson, you should now be familiar with the basic steps of **preparing an assembly** to be simulated, **setting up a simulation**, **creating a simulation**, and **replaying and analyzing a simulation**. The basic steps and features demonstrated in this lesson can be applied to virtually any mechanical assembly. Some of the more advanced and unique features available in this workbench have not been discussed in this lesson such as the **speed and acceleration** feature and many of the available **joint types**. To become more proficient at this workbench, take some time to complete the **Review Questions** as well as the **Practice Exercises** provided at the end of this chapter.

Review Questions

After completing this lesson, you should be able to answer the questions and explain the concepts listed below.

1. Where is the **DMU Kinematics** workbench located?

2. How many standard toolbars are there in the **DMU Kinematics** workbench?

3. An assembly must be fully constrained and held by a fixed component just like a physical assembly in real life before it can be simulated.

   A. True
   B. False

4. What are the **two** ways of creating **Kinematic Joints**?

5. What **two** assembly constraints make up the **Revolute Joint** used in the **DMU Kinematics** workbench?

6. Name the **three** tools that can be used to **analyze** a mechanism to see if it can be **simulated**?

7. Mechanisms do not necessarily need a **command** in order to be **simulated**.

   A. True
   B. False

8. What are the **two** kinds of **commands** that can be added to a **joint**?

9. What are at least **two** ways that can find out if the **mechanism** can be **simulated**?

10. What button of the **Edit Simulation** window must be clicked after setting the value of the final position of the motion to finish **configuring** the **simulation**?

11. What tool can be used to check if the **simulation** was **configured** correctly **before** compiling it into a replay?

12. What feature if the **Player** and **Compile Simulation** tools must be set to a lesser value in order to see the mechanism move more **slowly** and **smoothly**?

13. What feature of the **Replay** window allows you to add analysis tools to the **replayed motion**?

14. What **two** analysis tools can be added to the replayed motion of an assembly?

15. A **Distance and Band Analysis** can not be added to a **Replay** unless it is first created using the **Edit Distance and Band Analysis** tool.

    A. True
    B. False

16. There are **Six** different items of information given in the **Results** section of the **Edit Distance and Band Analysis** window; name **three**.

17. What are the **two** things that every mechanism must have in order to be **simulated**?

18. What are the **three** settings that the **Interference** feature of the **Replay** window can be set to?

19. What are the **three** types of files that a **Swept Volume** can be saved as?

20. What type of new file is created by the **Trace** tool?

Practice Exercises

Now that you have simulated the motion of an assembly using the **DMU Kinematics** workbench, you can strengthen your newfound knowledge by completing the following practice exercises.

1. Modify **Sketch.1** of the **Mounting** of the **U-Joint Assembly** by changing the 150° angle constraint to 140°. This will change the angle between the axes of the holes that the shafts of the **Top** and **Bottom U-Joints** pass through as shown below. Then update the assembly in the **DMU Kinematics** workbench using the **Update Positions** tool 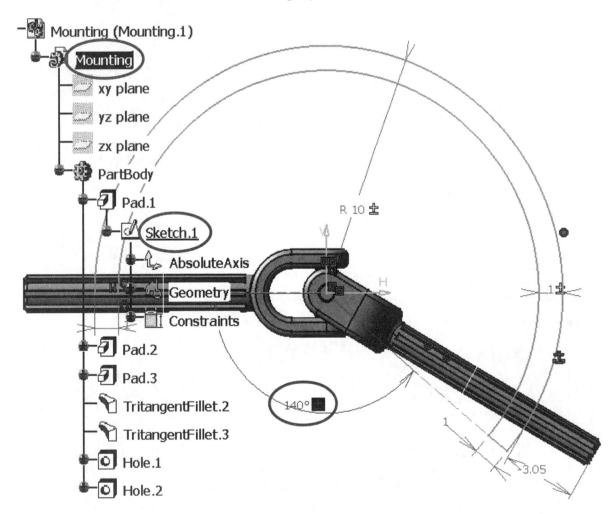 and create a new **Replay** with the **U-Joint** rotating at this new angle. Try to determine visually if the parts are now interfering, then apply the **Interference** analysis to this new replay to see if there really is any clash between the **Top** and **Bottom U-Joints** now. Take the opportunity to see the difference between the **On** and **Stop** settings of the **Interference** feature of the **Replay** tool.

2. Now replace the **Two Revolute Joints** that were automatically created using the **Assembly Constraints Conversion** tool with a single **Universal Joint**. Use the axes of the shafts of the **Top** and **Bottom U-Joints** as **Spin 1** and **Spin 2**. Accept the default setting for the **cross-pin axis** as being normal to one of the spins. If you have done this correctly, CATIA should bring up an information box telling you that the mechanism can be simulated. Notice that this eliminates the need for the **Swivel.CATPart** because the new joint is only between the **Top** and **Bottom U-Joints**. Therefore, when you create a new **Replay** of the assembly motion, the **Swivel** should no longer move.

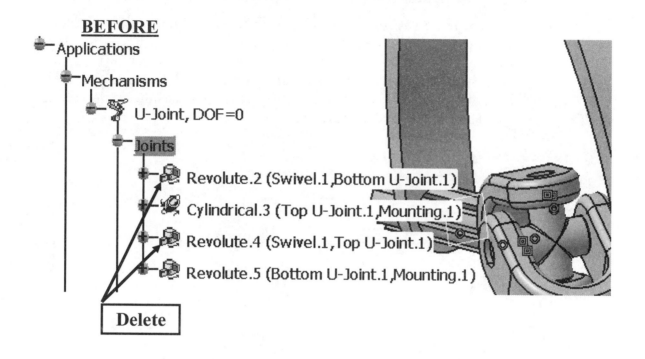

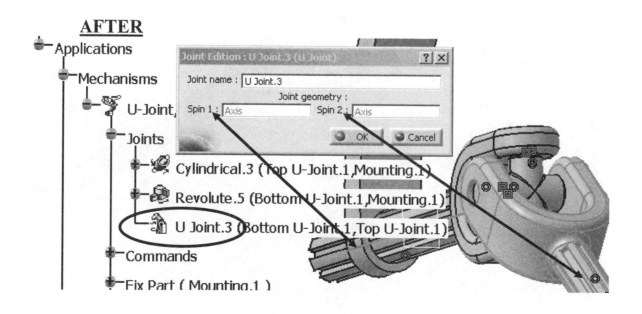

3. Go to www.schroff1.com/catia and download the **Arbor Press Assembly** file. Once you have the Arbor Press fully assembled, the challenge is to apply **Kinematical Joints** to it in order to make it move just like it would in real life. Apply a **Rack Joint** which consists of a **Revolute Joint** between the geared shaft and the frame, and a **Prismatic Joint** between the rectangular geared press bar and the frame. This one can be challenging, but it is a simple joint once you figure it out. The trick to simulating this assembly is that there are several separate parts attached to the geared shaft. If you would like to have these parts move with the rotation of the geared shaft, then you will have to attach them using **Rigid Joints**. (**Hint:** You can either apply a **Length Driven** command to the **Prismatic Joint** or an **Angle Driven** command to the **Revolute Joint**. The trick is figuring out a good gear ratio between the two joints that shows a correct simulation of the assembly. You will have to experiment and may even need to use a **negative** value to get it right. If you are having trouble, you may also download the **Arbor Press Assembly Kinematics** file from the same web sight. It should already have the **Kinematical Joints** and **Replay**.)

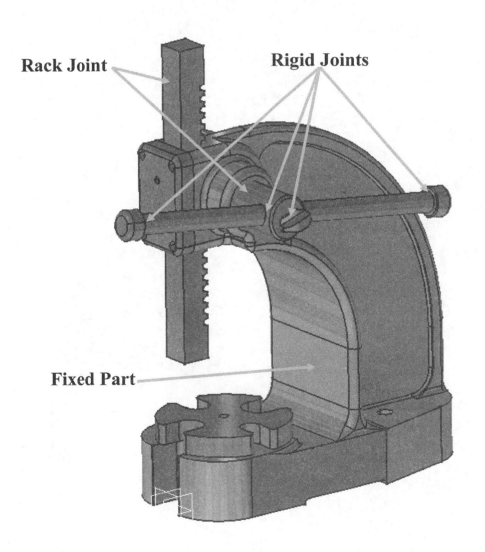

4. Go to www.schroff1.com/catia and download the **Slider Assembly** file. The
   Slider should already be assembled as shown below. Try to make it work by
   applying the **Kinematical Joints** and commands shown below. Then, create a
   Replay of the simulated motion of the assembly by setting the **First Angle
   Driven** command to move from **-360** to **360**. The motion of this assembly may
   surprise you. (**Hint:** If you can not get it to work, you may want to download the
   Slider Assembly Kinematics file from the same web sight to use as a guide.)

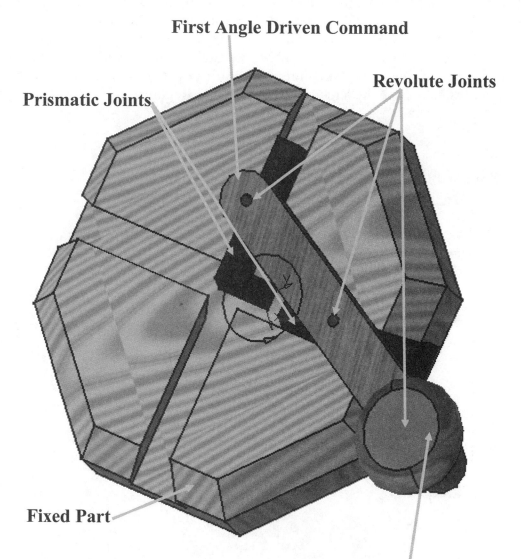

5. **Extra Credit:** Go to www.schroff1.com/catia and download the **Engine Assembly** file. The engine and drive train should already be assembled as shown below. Try to make it work by applying **Kinematic Joints** and commands shown below. Then, create a **Replay** of the simulated motion of the assembly by setting the **Angle Driven** command of the crank shaft to move from **-360** to **360**. This assembly will require a second **Angle Driven** command applied to one of the wheels as shown below. This second command is necessary to account for the extra degrees of freedom created by the differential gear box. The motion of this assembly may be simulated in **two** ways. The first is by creating a **Replay** using the first command. This should cause the assembly to move like a normal drive train being rotated by an engine. The second simulated motion can be seen by creating a second **Replay** that uses the second command. This second simulation should show how the engine driven wheels of a car act when the engine is stopped and the wheels are free to move. (**Hint:** You may have to experiment with the gear joints to get the ratios and directions right. If you can not get it to work, you may want to download the **Engine Assembly Kinematics** file from the same web sight. This file should already have all of the joints and replays created for you to look at.)

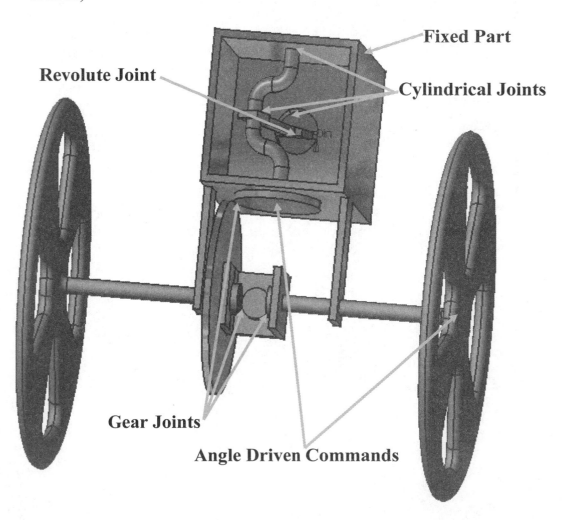

NOTES:

Lesson 3
Generative Structural Analysis

Introduction

The **Generative Structural Analysis** workbench is a powerful tool in CATIA V5. It allows the user to quickly model a part's mechanical behavior with very few steps. This lesson will demonstrate how to perform first order mechanical analysis for 3D parts. It will be beneficial to have an understanding of the principles of mechanics, the branch of science that deals with the state of a body when that body is subjected to forces. It is also assumed that you are familiar with **Sketcher**, **Part Design**, and **Assembly Design** workbenches.

Figure 3.1   **Example of a completed analysis**

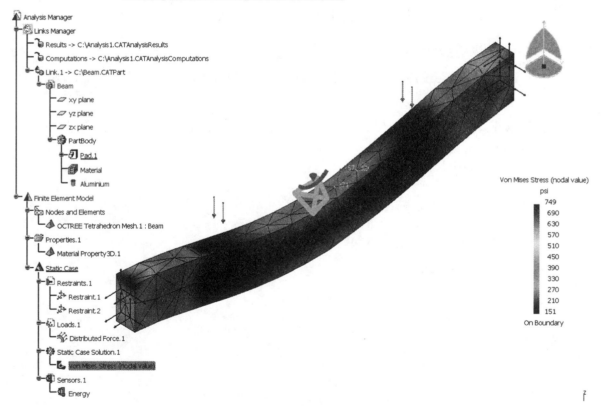

The toolbars associated with the **Generative Structural Analysis** workbench are shown to help you become familiar with the features and tools/icons related to the **Generative Structural Analysis** workbench. However, some tools will not be covered in this lesson and some tools are non-functional. The functionality depends on the type of analysis you are performing.

Objectives

This lesson covers an advanced workbench at a basic level. In this lesson you will create a **Beam.CATPart** in the **Part Design** workbench and conduct a **Static Case**, **Buckling Case**, and **Frequency Case** analysis on the **Beam.CATPart**. Even though you will be creating a simple part that could easily be analyzed using conventional methods, the power behind the **Generative Structural Analysis** workbench is analyzing complex surfaces, which would otherwise be almost impossible. However, with that complexity, how do you know your results are remotely accurate? You will use a simple beam part so you can follow and relate the workbench tools to the conventional methods. After completing this lesson you should be able to do and/or know the following:

1. Set up the analysis by assigning a material to the part, customize the view mode and set the units.

2. Five structural properties associated with the material.

3. Create restraints and loads.

4. Apply **Loads** at a specified location and direction.

5. Store the results.

6. View and evaluate the analysis using most of the **Image** and **Analysis Tools** toolbars.

7. Understand how **Mesh Size** and **Sag Values** determine the accuracy of the results.

8. Create **Virtual Parts**.

9. Adjust the **Color Pallet**.

10. Incorporate **Knowledge Advisor** into the analysis.

11. Generate a report.

Tools and Toolbars

The following section lists the toolbars and their tools along with a brief explanation for each. This lesson does not use all of the tools listed in the workbench. **Generative Structural Analysis** workbench has nine standard toolbars.

The Solver Tools Toolbar

TOOL ICON	TOOL NAME	TOOL DEFINITION
	Storage Location	Specify external storage in a particular case.

The Load Toolbar

TOOL ICON	TOOL NAME	TOOL DEFINITION
	Distributed Force	Force systems statically equivalent to a given pure force resultant at a given point.

The Compute Toolbar

TOOL ICON	TOOL NAME	TOOL DEFINITION
	Compute	Compute objects sets.

The <u>Restraint</u> Toolbar

TOOL ICON	TOOL NAME	TOOL DEFINITION
	Clamp	Restraints applied to surface or curve geometries.
Mechanical Restraint Toolbar		
	Surface Slider	Allows points of a surface to slide along a coinciding rigid surface.
	Slider	Prismatic join restraints applied to handle points of virtual parts.
	Sliding Pivot	Cylindrical join restraints applied to handle points of virtual parts.
	Ball Join	Spherical join restraints applied to handle points of virtual parts.
	Pivot	Hinge *(conical join)* restraints applied to handle points of virtual parts.
Advanced Restraint Toolbar		
	Advanced Restraint	Generic restraints allowing you to fix any combination of available nodal degrees of freedom on arbitrary geometries.
	Isostatic Restraint	Statically definite restraints allowing you to simply support a body.

The <u>Virtual Part</u> Toolbar

TOOL ICON	TOOL NAME	TOOL DEFINITION
	Smooth Virtual Part	A rigid body connecting a specified point to specified part geometries.
	Periodicity Condition	Simulate periodicity conditions by linking together the degrees of freedom of two faces that undergo transformation.

The <u>Image</u> Toolbar

TOOL ICON	TOOL NAME	TOOL DEFINITION
	Deformation	Used to visualize the finite element mesh in the deformed configuration of the system.
	Von Mises Stress	Used to visualize Von Mises Stress field patterns.
	Displacement	Used to visualize displacement field patterns.
	Principal Stress	Used to visualize principal stress field patterns.
	Precision	Used to visualize computation error maps.

The <u>Analysis Tools</u> Toolbar

TOOL ICON	TOOL NAME	TOOL DEFINITION
	Animate	A continuous display of a sequence of frames obtained from a given image.
	Cut Plane Analysis	Visualizes results in a plane section through the structure.
	Amplification Magnitude	Scales the maximum displacement amplitude for visualizing a deformed image.
	Image Extrema	Localize points where a results field is maximum or minimum.
	Information	Get information on one or more images and extrema you generated.
	Images Layout	Generated images corresponding to analysis results are superimposed into one image that cannot be properly visualized.
	Simplified Representation	Display a simplified representation while moving an image.

The <u>Analysis Results</u> Toolbar

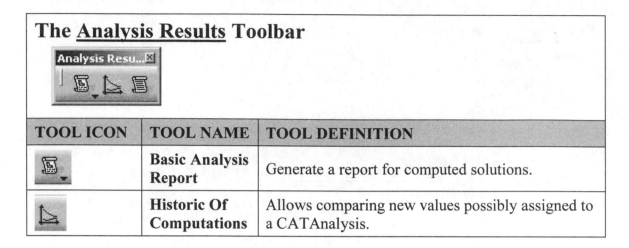

TOOL ICON	TOOL NAME	TOOL DEFINITION
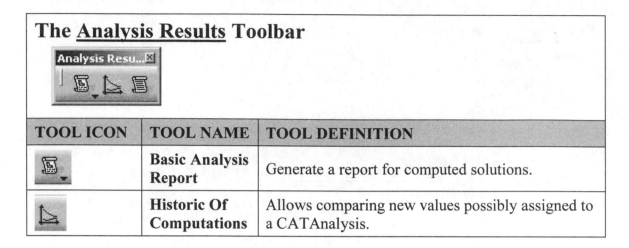	**Basic Analysis Report**	Generate a report for computed solutions.
	Historic Of Computations	Allows comparing new values possibly assigned to a CATAnalysis.

The <u>Mass</u> Toolbar

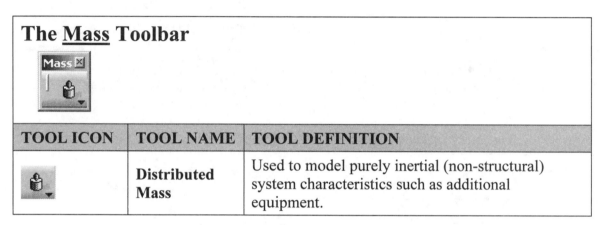

TOOL ICON	TOOL NAME	TOOL DEFINITION
	Distributed Mass	Used to model purely inertial (non-structural) system characteristics such as additional equipment.

Creating and Analyzing a Beam

1. Create the Beam.CATPart

Figure 3.5 shows the dimensions that will be used to create the **Beam.CATPart**. The steps to create it are listed below.

1.1 Start CATIA V5 and select **Start** and **Mechanical Design** and **Part Design** commands from the **Standard Windows** toolbar to create a new **CATPart** document (see Figure 3.2).

Figure 3.2

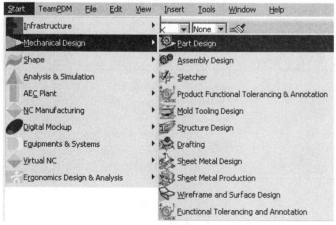

1.2   Select **Tools** and **Options...** from the **Standard Windows** toolbar (see Figure 3.3). This will bring up the **Options** window shown in Figure 3.4.

Figure 3.3

1.3   Select the **Parameters and Measures** branch on the option tree at the left. The tabbed options change accordingly.

1.4   Select the **Units** tab to change the units.

   1.4.1   To change the units from feet to inches, select/highlight the **Length** option at the top of the list.

Figure 3.4

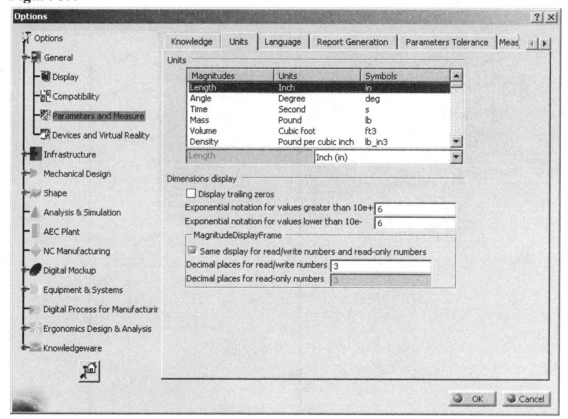

1.4.2   The **Length** option will appear at the bottom of the window list.

1.4.3   Selecting the **pull down arrow** will give you a list of all the types of length measurements. For this exercise, select **inches**.

1.4.4   Repeat the process of Steps 1.4.1 to 1.4.3 to change the other units to match the units as follows. The important units to verify are Mass (**lb**), Volume (**ft3**), Density (**lb_in3**), Area (**in2**), Energy (**ftlbf**), Force (**lbf**), Inertia (**in4**), Massic flow (**lb_min**), Moment (**lbfxin**), Pressure (**psi**), Angular stiffness (**lbfxin_rad**), Linear mass (**lb_in**),

Acceleration (**ft_s2**), Strain Energy (**lbfxin**), Volumic force (**lbf_in3**), Surfacic mass (**lb_in2**), Velocity (**mph**).

1.4.5   Then select the **OK** button.

1.5   In the **Specification Tree** rename **Part1** to "**Beam**."

1.6   Enter the **Sketcher** workbench using the **YZ** Plane.

1.7   Create the rectangular profile using the **Rectangle** tool. Use dimensions **3.5″** wide by **7.25″** tall, centered at the axis by creating constraints as shown in Figure 3.5.

Figure 3.5

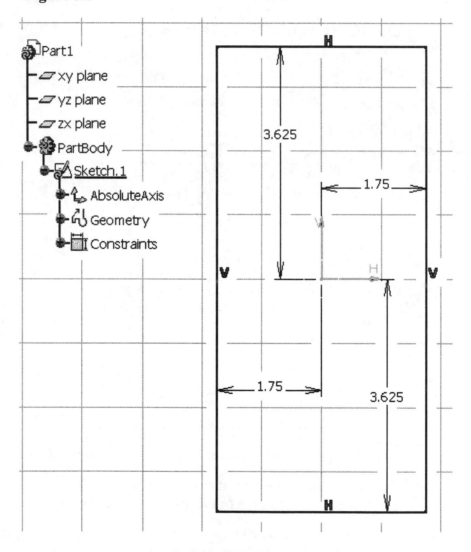

1.8   Select the **Exit** workbench tool.

1.9   In the **Part Design** workbench select the **Pad** tool.

1.10 The **Pad Definition** window will appear; type **"72in"** in the **Length** field.

1.11 Then select the **OK** button.

1.12 Select the **Fit All In** tool.

2. Apply Material and Apply View Properties

Figure 3.6

Before you enter the **Generative Structural Analysis** workbench or do any analysis on the **Beam.CATPart**, it must have a material assigned to it. Each material in CATIA V5 has mechanical properties for computing the analysis. These properties are Young's Modulus, Poisson Ratio, Density, Thermal Expansion, and Yield Strength. You will apply aluminum to the **Beam.CATPart**. You must also customize the view mode to the proper selections (see Figure 3.7) to view the results of the **Generative Structural Analysis** workbench correctly. Complete the following steps to apply aluminum to the **Beam.CATPart** and to modify the **Customized View**.

2.1 Select **Beam** in the **Specification Tree** so it is highlighted as shown in Figure 3.6.

Figure 3.7

2.2 Select the **Apply Material** 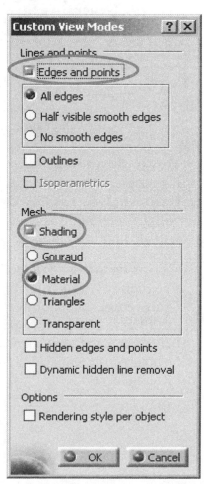 tool.

2.3 Select the **Metal** tab in the **Library (Read Only)** window.

2.4 Select **Aluminum** and then select the **OK** button.

2.5 Double click on **Aluminum** in the **Specification Tree** to modify the structural properties.

2.6 Select the **Analysis** tab and the five structural properties of **Aluminum** appear. You can change these values to reflect the different alloys of aluminum. For this lesson use the default values.

2.7 Select the **OK** button.

Complete the following steps to change the **Customized View**. Refer to Figure 3.7.

2.8　Set the view mode by selecting **View** and **Render Style** and **Customize View**.

2.9　The **Custom View Modes** window will appear. Select **Edges and points**, **Shading** and **Material**.

2.10　Select the **OK** button.

2.11　Save this document as **Beam.CATPart** in your working directory.

3.　Starting the Generative Structural Analysis Workbench

With the **Beam.CATPart** document open, you are now ready to enter the **Generative Structural Analysis** workbench. During this lesson you can stop at any time and save the document you are working on. The file extension will be ***.CATAnalysis**. Follow the same procedure for saving this document as you have for previous documents. Save the document as **BeamAnalysis.CATAnalysis** for the **File name** when you are ready to do so.

Figure 3.8

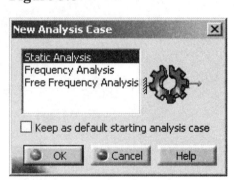

3.1　Select **Start** from the menu bar then **Analysis & Simulation** and finally **Generative Structural Analysis**.

3.2　A **New Analysis Case** window will appear in the document as shown in Figure 3.8. Select the **Static Analysis** text.

3.3　Select the **OK** button.

The **Static Analysis** selection allows you to evaluate the fixed boundary environment for the **BeamAnalysis.CATAnalysis** document. Notice the **BeamAnalysis.CATAnalysis** document will generate a default **Specification Tree** with two default branches called **Links Manger** and **Finite Element Model**. You will also notice that some tools will not be activated throughout the **Static Analysis**, such as the **Mass** toolbar. The **Mass** toolbar is activated when choosing **Frequency Analysis** or **Free Frequency Analysis** in Step 3.2. The **Advanced Connections** and **Connections** toolbars are not activated when analyzing a **CATPart**. These tools are activated when a **CATProduct** (with more than 1 part) is being analyzed; this is known as **Generative Assembly Structural Analysis** and can be entered the same as in Steps 3.1 through 3.3, with CATIA V5 recognizing the difference.

4. Links Manager

The **Links Manager**, which appears in the **Specification Tree**, contains the link to the **Results** and **Computations** files directory. It also contains the link to the **Beam.CATPart** document you created in the previous sections; the default name is **Link.1**. Notice that if you expand **Link.1** that it contains a copy (which is actually a link) of the **Specification Tree** found in **Beam.CATPart**. If you minimize the **BeamAnalysis.CATAnalysis** you just created in Section 3 you will observe that the **Beam.CATPart** created in Sections 1 and 2 is still open in CATIA V5, providing you did not close it.

The **Links Manager** allows you to save the **Results** and **Computations** files in whatever directory you specify. This is a nice feature if you are on a network and want to change the directory of the results. The steps to modify the files directory are given below. Skip Steps 4.1 through 4.4 if the file storage location is okay.

4.1   Select the **Storage Location** 🔓 tool.

4.2   This will bring up the **Current Storage Location** window with two **Modify** buttons that allow you to select the file path for storing the **BeamAnalysis.CATAnalysisResults** and for storing the path of the **BeamAnalysis.CATAnalysisComputations** files shown in Figure 3.9.

Figure 3.9

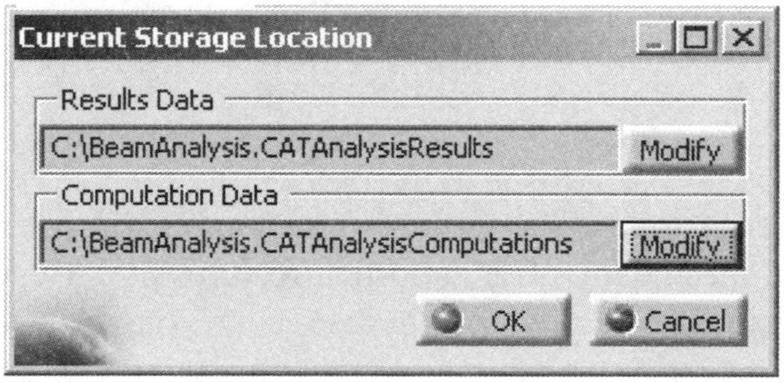

4.3   Select the **Results Data Modify** button. Navigate to the folder you want to store your **Results Data**, then select **Save**. Do the same thing for the **Computation Data**.

4.4   Select the **OK** button.

5. Finite Element Model

The second branch from the default **Specification Tree** is the **Finite Element Model**. It always contains **Nodes and Elements, Properties.1, Materials.1**, and either a **Free Frequency Case, Frequency Case** or in this instance, a **Static Case** as shown in Figure 3.10.

Figure 3.10

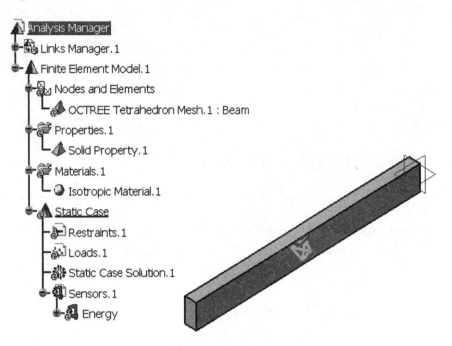

Nodes and Elements are used to turn the model into a discrete numerical problem through the use of mesh data. The important features of a **Mesh** are **Size, Sag** and **Order**. If you require more precision in the results you will need to decrease the mesh size and sag.

You will spend most of the time building the **Static Case** in the **Specification Tree**. This is where the object sets for **Restraints, Loads,** and **Solutions** are built.

Restrain and load the **BeamAnalysis.CATAnalysis** as a cantilevered beam. A cantilevered beam is a projecting structure, which is fixed at one end and carries a load at the other end or along its length. Figure 3.11 shows a cantilever beam with a uniform load *w* and its accompanying formula for maximum displacement. Figure 3.12 shows a cantilever beam with an end load *P* with its accompanying formula for maximum displacement. In the next sections you will apply a restraint and a load to the **BeamAnalysis.CATAnalysis** so that it behaves like the cantilever beams shown in Figures 3.11 and 3.12. You will then compare the conventional displacement formula result in Figure 3.11 with CATIA V5's displacement result.

Figure 3.11

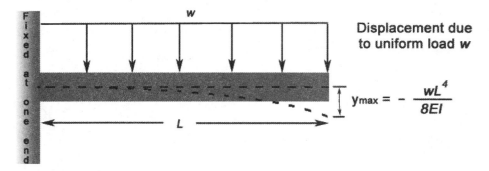

Displacement due
to uniform load **w**

$$y_{max} = - \frac{wL^4}{8EI}$$

Figure 3.12

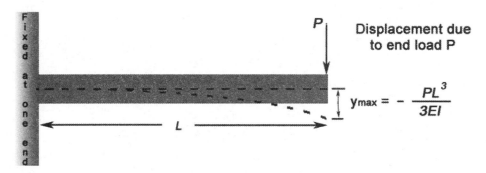

Displacement due
to end load P

$$y_{max} = - \frac{PL^3}{3EI}$$

6. Applying Advanced Restraints

A **User Defined Restraint** tool removes translation and rotational degrees of freedom and blocks these points from the analysis. The **User Defined Restraint** tool allows translation directions to be blocked from the analysis. The **Clamp** tool is also a restraint; however it restrains *all* translations and rotations. The following steps show how to apply an **User Defined Restraint** to fix one end of the **BeamAnalysis.CATAnalysis** to simulate a cantilevered beam.

6.1 Select the **User Defined Restraint**  tool. The **User Defined Restraint** window will appear as shown in Figure 3.13.

Figure 3.13

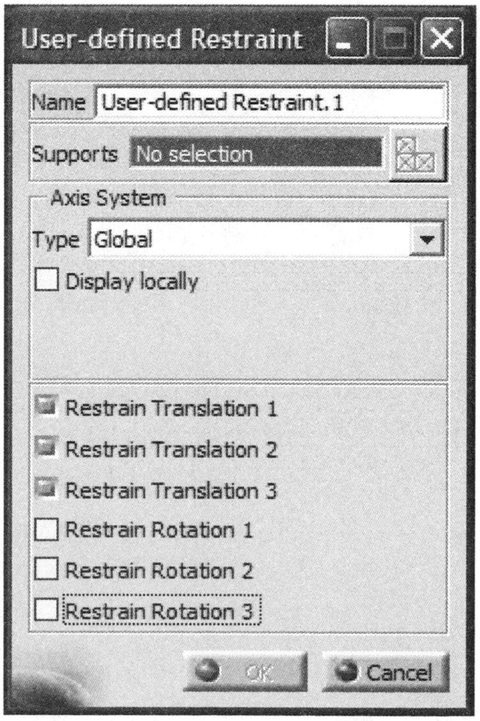

User-defined Restraint

Name User-defined Restraint.1

Supports No selection

Axis System

Type Global

☐ Display locally

☑ Restrain Translation 1
☑ Restrain Translation 2
☑ Restrain Translation 3
☐ Restrain Rotation 1
☐ Restrain Rotation 2
☐ Restrain Rotation 3

OK   Cancel

6.2   The **Supports** field should be highlighted
        in blue. The text will read **No selection**.

6.3   Only the **Restrain Translation 1, Restrain Translation 2,** and **Restrain
        Translation 3**
        options should be selected as shown in
        Figure 3.13.

Figure 3.14

6.4   Now select the front surface of the
        BeamAnalysis.CATAnalysis nearest
        the screen as shown in Figure 3.14.
        The **Supports** field text should now
        read **1 Face**.

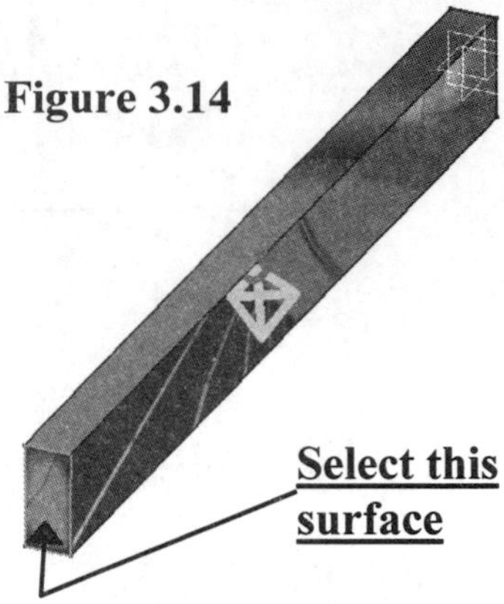

6.5   Finally select the **OK** button on the
        Advanced Restraint window.

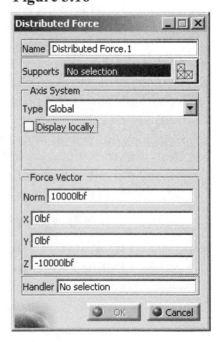

**Select this
surface**

Figure 3.15

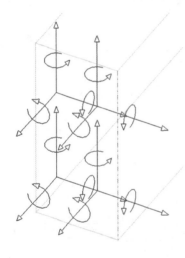

After completing Step 6.5 the restraint symbol will appear as
red arrows as shown in Figure 3.15. These arrows show that
this support is restrained in those directions and rotations.
The clamp tool could also have been used instead, since all
rotations and translations are restrained on this surface.

Figure 3.16

7. Applying a Force

To apply a force like the cantilever beam equation in
Figure 3.11, follow the steps below.

7.1   Select the **Force**    tool.
        The **Distributed Force** window
        will appear as seen in Figure 3.16.

7.2   The **Supports** field should be highlighted
        in blue. The text will
        read **No selection**.

7.3   Select the top surface of the
        BeamAnalysis.CATAnalysis in Figure

3.17. The **Supports** field text should now read **1 Face**. **Note:** It is important that you select the surface of the beam, not just an edge (line).

7.4   Type "**10000lbf**" in the **Force Vector** field **Norm**.

7.5   Type "**0lbf**" in the **Force Vector** field **X**.

Figure 3.17

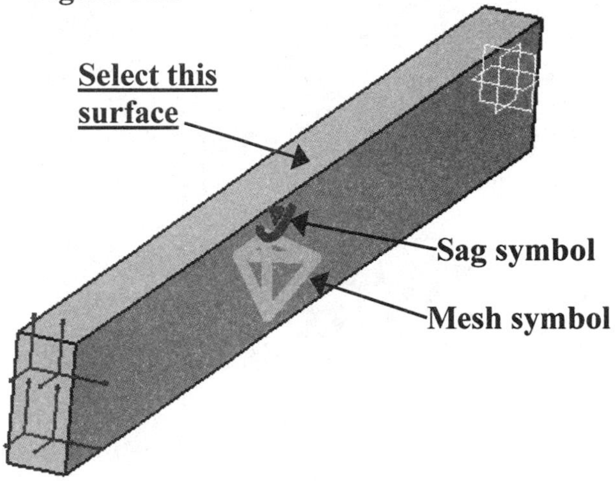

Select this
surface

Figure 3.18

Sag symbol

Mesh symbol

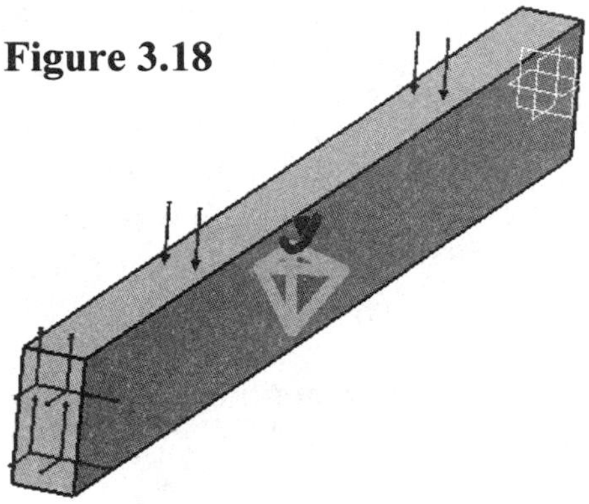

7.6   Type "**0lbf**"in the **Force Vector** field **Y**.

7.7   Type "**-10000lbf**" in the **Force Vector** field **Z**.

7.8   Select the **OK** button.

The force symbols appear as red arrows shown in Figure 3.18. The resultant force is applied to the centroid of the top surface. Choosing an edge would apply the resultant force at the middle point (centroid) of the edge. The **Structural Analysis** workbench now has enough information to compute the analysis.

8. Compute Solution

The **Static Case** now has the minimum amount of restraints and loads to **Compute** the **Static Case Solution.1**. The steps below show how to **Compute** the analysis.

Figure 3.19

8.1   **Compute** the analysis by selecting the **Compute**  [■] tool. The **Compute** window will appear; reference Figure 3.19.

8.2   Select the **pull down arrow** and select **All** from the list of options.

8.3   Select the **Preview** option.

8.4   Select the **OK** button.

8.5   The **Computation Resources Estimation** window will appear. The window appears because the **Preview** option in Step 8.3 was selected. If this was deselected, the window would not appear and the computation would begin after completing Step 8.4. This window is helpful because it estimates the time and memory that the computation will take. This is machine dependant and so the numbers could be different from Figure 3.20.

Figure 3.20

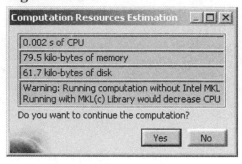

8.6   Select the **Yes** button.

9. Visualizing the Displacement

Figure 3.21

Upon successful computation, the image toolbar will be activated as shown in Figure 3.21. (Note: This tool may be hiding or not viewable. Verify that it is visible by selecting **View** and **Toolbars** and checking **Analysis Tools**). The **Load Arrows** symbol will turn from red to yellow. The restraint symbol will turn from red to blue. The symbol 🖼 in the **Specification Tree** will disappear. If the computation was not successful, a singularity error most likely occurred, which is generally due to a missing restraint.

Figure 3.22

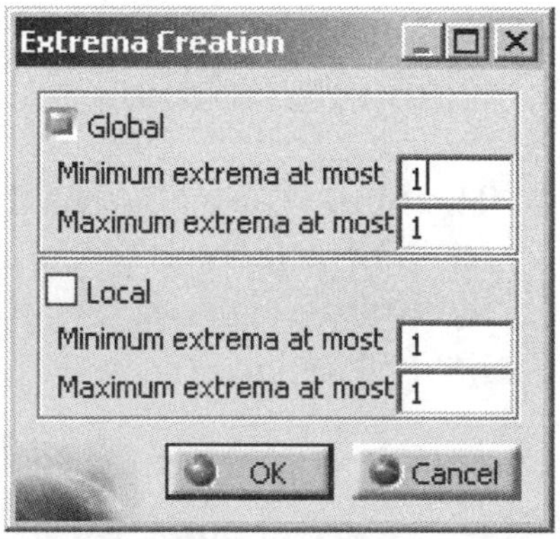

With the customize view set in Section 2 and a successful computation, you can now use the **Deformation**, **Von Mises Stress**, **Displacement**, **Principal Stress**, and **Precision** tools on the **Image** toolbar by selecting the corresponding tool. Look at the displacement view by following the steps below. Figure 3.22 is a reference for the following steps.

9.1   Select the **Displacement** 🔧 tool.

9.2   To determine the maximum and minimum displacement of the beam, select the **Image Extrema** 🔧 tool. The **Extrema Creation** window will appear.

9.3   Select the **Global** option.

9.4   Type "**1**" in the **Minimum extrema at most** field.

9.5   Type "**1**" in the **Maximum extrema at most** field.

9.6   Deselect the **Local** option.

9.7   Select the **OK** button.

9.8   Select the **Fit All In** ⊞ tool.

NOTE: The **Translational displacement vector Global Maximum.1** value in
Figure 3.23 is 0.205593 inches (yours may vary slightly from this value).

Figure 3.23

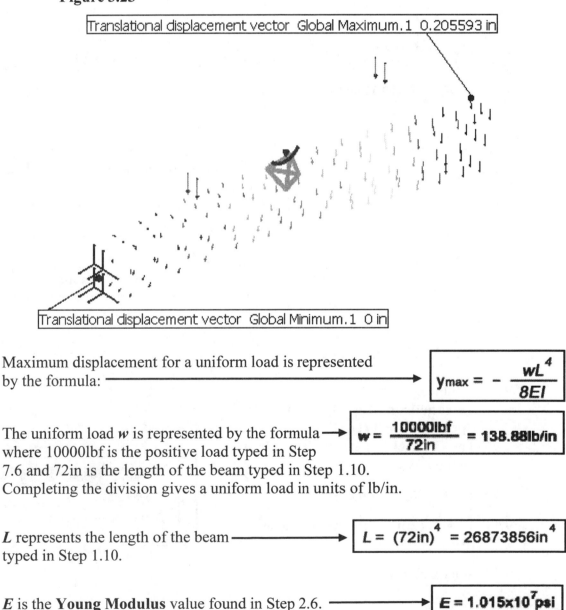

Maximum displacement for a uniform load is represented
by the formula: ────────────────────────────►

$$y_{max} = -\frac{wL^4}{8EI}$$

The uniform load *w* is represented by the formula ──►
where 10000lbf is the positive load typed in Step
7.6 and 72in is the length of the beam typed in Step 1.10.
Completing the division gives a uniform load in units of lb/in.

$$w = \frac{10000lbf}{72in} = 138.88lb/in$$

L represents the length of the beam ──────────────►
typed in Step 1.10.

$$L = (72in)^4 = 26873856in^4$$

E is the **Young Modulus** value found in Step 2.6. ───────►

$$E = 1.015 \times 10^7 psi$$

Figure 3.24

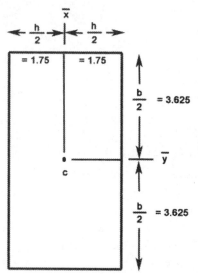

To view the values again simply double click on **Aluminum** in the **Specification Tree**. Then select the **Analysis** tab. Verify the value is 1.015×10^7 psi.

The moment of inertia, *I* for centroidal axis of the cross section **BeamAnalysis.CATAnalysis** is shown in Figure 3.24.

$$I\bar{y} = \frac{1}{12} b^3 h \qquad I\bar{y} = \frac{1}{12}(7.25in)^3(3.5in) = 111.14in^4$$

CATIA V5's displacement value of 0.205593 inches in Figure 3.23 is not the same answer from the displacement formula of 0.414 inches found below. This is close to a 50% error! To get a more accurate value decrease the mesh size and sag size. This takes longer to compute depending on how complex the part is.

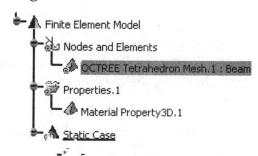

$$y_{max} = \frac{(138.88lb/in)(72in)^4}{8(1.015e+007psi)(111.14in^4)} = .414in$$

To change the **Mesh Size** and **Mesh Sag**:

9.9   Double click on **OCTREE Tetrahedron Mesh.1: Beam** in the **Specification Tree** (Figure 3.25). The **OCTREE Tetrahedron Mesh** window will appear.

9.10   Type "**.75in**" in the **Size** field.

9.11   Type "**.12in**" in the **Absolute Sag** field.

9.12   Select the **OK** button.

Figure 3.25

- Finite Element Model
  - Nodes and Elements
    - OCTREE Tetrahedron Mesh.1 : Beam
  - Properties.1
    - Material Property3D.1
  - Static Case

9.13 **Compute** the analysis another time by repeating Steps 8.1 through 8.6. If an error occurs, there is probably not enough memory; change the **mesh size** and **sag size** back to the default values of **4.5″** and **.72″** respectively.

9.14 Repeat Steps 9.1 through 9.8 to find the new maximum displacement extrema. This time you will notice many more displacement vectors.

NOTE: The **Translational displacement vector Global Maximum.1** value of 0.400487 (your value may vary slightly) inches is now much closer to the value of 0.414 inches from the conventional beam deflection formula. The error has been reduced to approximately 3% by decreasing the mesh size and sag size. Typically with a simple part dividing the default mesh size and sag sizes by 6 gives accuracy within 10%. If the computer took more than a minute to compute the result, change the **mesh size** and **sag size** back to the default value of **4.5″** and **.72″** respectively.

10. Visualizing the Von Mises Stress

Figure 3.26

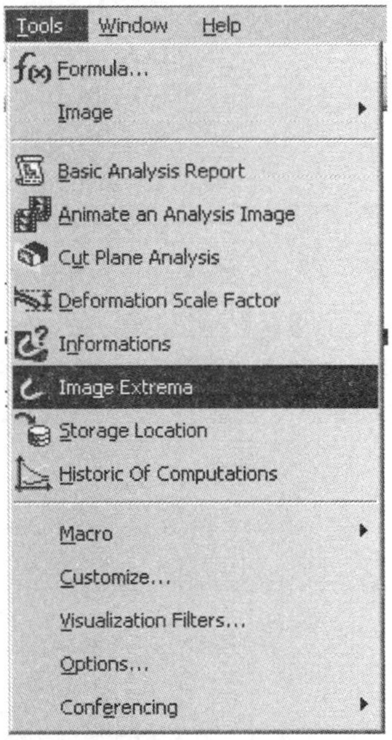

10.1 Select the **Von Mises Stress** tool to view the **Von Mises Stress** distribution and the **Von Mises Stress** distribution color palette (zoom in if needed).

10.2 Optional: Move the cursor over any area of the part and the values for the **Von Mises Stress** at each node will appear.

10.3 To determine the maximum and minimum **Von Mises Stress** select <u>**T**</u>**ools** and then the **Images Extrema** tool. Refer to Figure 3.26.

10.4 The **Extrema Creation** window will appear; see Figure 3.27.

10.5 Select the **Global** option.

10.6 Type "**1**" in the **Minimum Extrema at most** field.

Figure 3.27

10.7 Type "**1**" in the **Maximum Extrema at most** field.

10.8 Deselect the **Local** option.

10.9 Select the **OK** button.

10.10 Select the **Fit All In** tool.

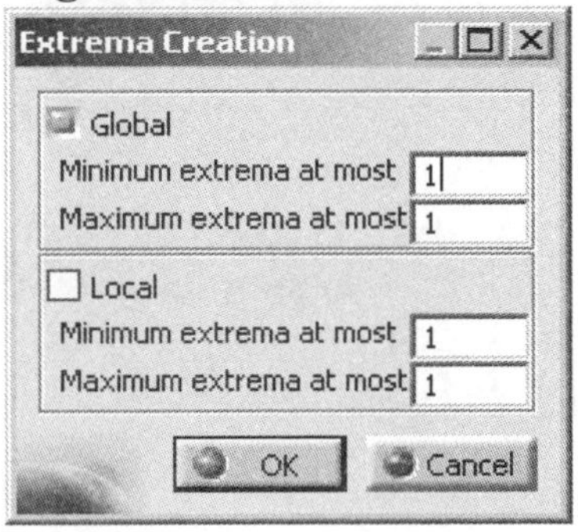

10.11 Take note of the **Von Mises Stress (nodal value) Global Maximum.1:** value in Figure 3.28 is 10877.6 psi.

Figure 3.28

Von Mises Stress (nodal value) Global Maximum.1: 10877.6 psi

The exact yield strength for the aluminum **BeamAnalysis.CATAnalysis** used in this computation is found by applying the following steps.

10.12 Select the **Von Mises Stress (nodal value)** on the **Specification Tree**. Refer to Figure 3.29.

10.13 Select the information ![tool] tool. The **Information** window will appear. (You may need to click once on **Von Mises Stress (nodal value)** if the window does not appear).

Figure 3.29

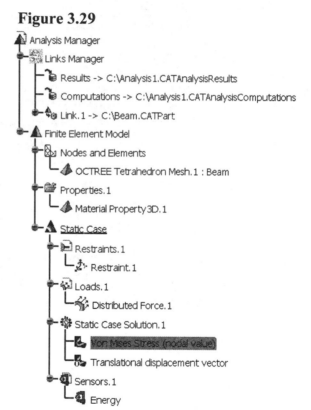

Figure 3.30

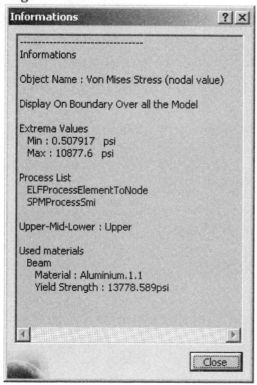

NOTE: Double clicking **Von Mises Stress (nodal value)** brings up the **Image Edition** window, which allows you to choose different options in viewing the image.

10.14 The **Yield Strength** for **Aluminum** is the last line in the window. Verify that the value is **13778.589psi**.

NOTE: The **Max Extrema Value** of **10877.6psi** found in Step 10.11 is also shown in the **Informations** window.

10.15 Select the **Close** button.

For many applications, you want to avoid permanent deformation after a load is removed. For ductile materials, such as aluminum or mild steel, a factor of safety (FS) against yielding is regularly used. The FS formula is defined as:

$$FS = \frac{\text{yield strength}}{\text{allowable stress}}$$

$$FS = \frac{13778.589\text{psi}}{10877.6\text{psi}} = 1.26$$

The **Factor of Safety** in the analysis is **1.26**. As long as the **Von Mises Stress Global Maximum.1** extrema value is below the **Yield Strength** of **Aluminum** the load applied to the cantilever should not deform the cantilever. This is only true for static loads, not for impact or repeated loads.

Warning: Allowable stresses and factors of safety for various materials are specified in numerous codes and should always be used to determine safe working loads. Keep in mind the analysis results depend on the mesh size and sag size.

11. Animating Views

Figure 3.31

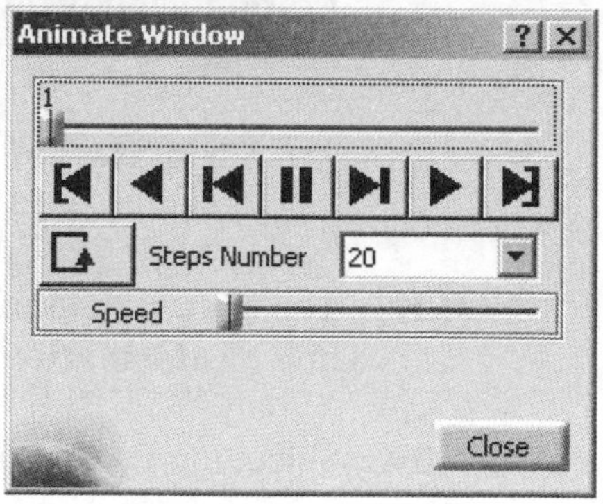

A very useful tool to help you visualize what is happening during an analysis is the **Animate** tool. This tool displays a series of views that follow one another and give the sense of movement. The **Animate** tool works with **Deformation, Von Mises Stress, Displacement**, and **Principle Stress** views but does not work with the **Precision** view. The **Animate** tool is useful with the **Deformation** view in detecting where a part needs restraints to eliminate a singularity error. You should still be in the **Von Mises Stress** view. Follow the steps below to animate this view and refer to Figure 3.31.

11.1   Select the **Animate**  tool. The **Animate Window** will appear.

11.2   If the animation has not begun select the **Play Forward** ▶ button.

11.3   Experiment with the other buttons, and scroll bars as desired.

11.4   Select the **Close** button.

12. Amplitude Modulation & Image Layout

The **Amplitude Modulation** tool helps scale the deformation amplitude. A large scaling factor will show a distorted view of the deformation. Like the **Animate** tool, the only view that does not work with this tool is the **Precision** view. In the **Von Mises Stress** view, scale the deformation by completing the following steps.

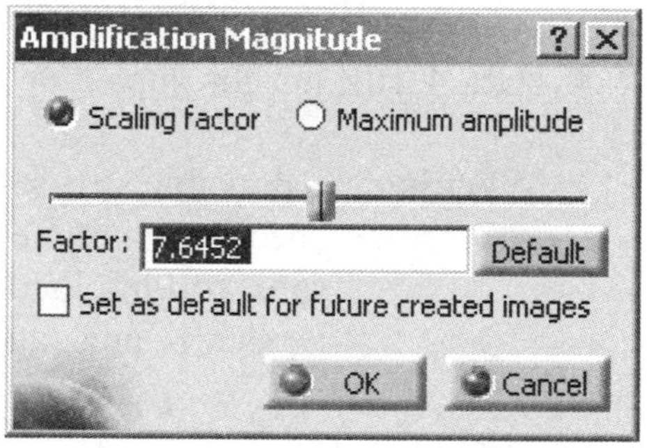

12.1   Select the **Amplification Magnitude**  tool. The **Amplification Magnitude** window will appear with default values as shown by the Figure 3.32.

12.2   Select **Maximum amplitude**. This will change the window as displayed in Figure 3.32a.

12.3   Change the **Length** field to "**60**" inches.

Figure 3.32

Figure 3.32a

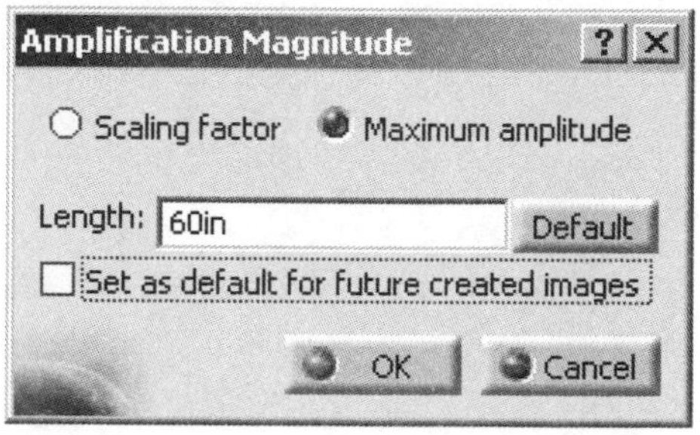

12.4   Select the **OK** button.

12.5   You should see a much distorted view of the beam.

12.6   Select the **Right View** 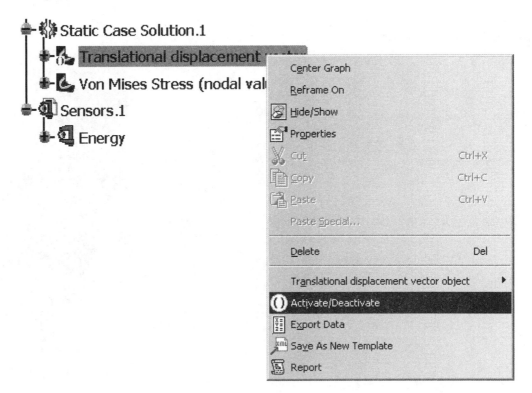 tool to get another view.

12.7   Select the **Fit All In** tool.

12.8   Select the **Amplification Magnitude** tool. The **Amplification Magnitude** window will appear.

12.9   Select **Maximum amplitude**.

12.10 Change the **Length** field to "**.414**" inches. This value is the value computed earlier using the displacement formula.

12.11 Select the **OK** button.

12.12 Select the **Isometric View** tool.

12.13 Select the **Fit All In** tool. This will give the most realistic view of the deformation.

Figure 3.33

You created a **Translational displacement vector** view and a **Von Mises Stress (nodal value)** view in the **Specification Tree**. This occurred when you selected the **Von Mises Stress** tool and the **Displacement** tool, for the first time. Arrange these views side by side with the **Image Layout** tool. The following steps explain how this is done.

12.14　Select the **Translational displacement vector** in the **Specification Tree** as shown in Figure 3.33 and right-click on the highlighted text.

12.15　Select the **Activate/DeActivate** text. This will activate the **Displacement** view and you will see both the **Displacement** view and the **Von Mises Stress** view. However the **Von Mises Stress** view will likely block the **Displacement** view.

12.16　Select the **Images Layout** tool.

12.17　The **Images Layout** window will appear as shown in Figure 3.34. Select **Along** the **Y** direction at a **Distance** of **10in**.

12.18　Select the **OK** button. You may have to rotate the part beam to get a clear view as shown by Figure 3.35.

Figure 3.34　　　　　　　　　　　**Figure 3.35**

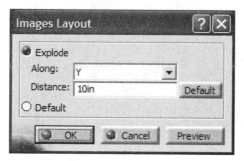

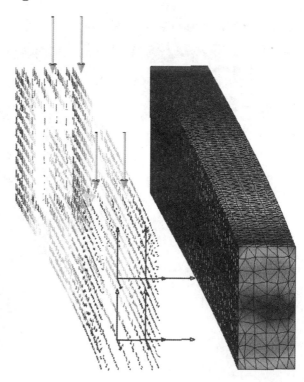

13. Cut Plane Analysis

The **Cut Plane Analysis** tool allows you to view the effect of a plane cutting through the analysis. To see how this tool works, complete the following.

12.19   Delete the **Translational Displacement vector** view in the **Specification Tree**.

Figure 3.36

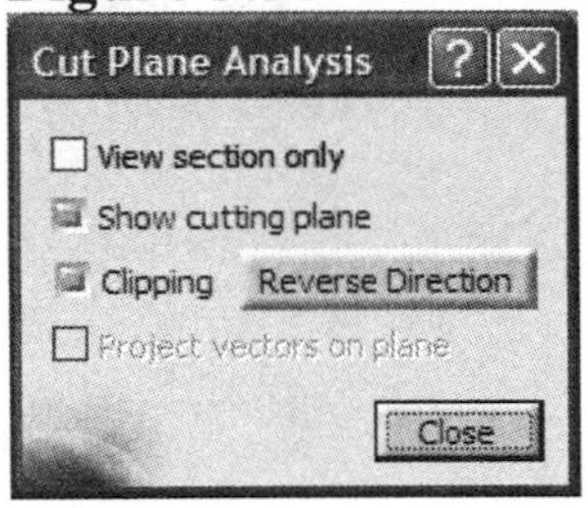

12.20   Select the **Cut Plane Analysis** tool. The **Cut Plane Analysis** window along with a cutting plane will appear as in Figure 3.36.

12.21   Select the **Fit All In** tool.

12.22   Manipulate the cutting plane by using the **Compass** tool. Try rotating and translating the compass. You should see something that resembles Figure 3.37 depending on the orientation of the compass tool.

Figure 3.38

Figure 3.37

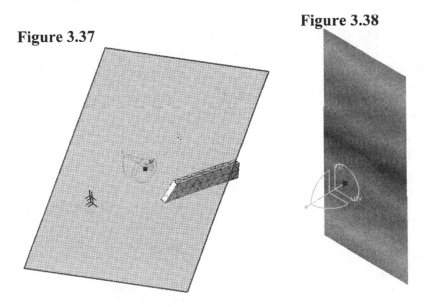

12.23   Select **View section only** option and deselect **Show cutting plane**. You should see something that resembles Figure 3.38. This depends on the orientation of the compass tool.

13.6   Select the **Close** button on the **Cut Plane Analysis** window.

It is up to you to experiment with the **Deformation**, **Precision**, and **Principal Stress** viewing tools. These views work much in the same way as the **Displacement** and **Von Mises Stress** views you have been working with.

14. Smooth Virtual Part

So far you have applied a load and a restraint where the resultant force of the load and the restraint were applied automatically to the centroid of the surface. A smooth virtual part will allow you to apply masses, loads, and restraints to other than the centroid. These are also referred to as supports. To do this you must specify a **Handler**. Create two points to be used as part handlers. Use the smooth virtual part because it will elastically deform the beam where it connects to the part handler whereas the rigid virtual part does not elastically deform the beam. Create two virtual parts with specified part handlers and two virtual parts with centroid part handlers by completing the following steps. It is possible to select multiple elements for supports (i.e., 3 edges and two surfaces).

14.1 Go into the **Part Design** workbench by double clicking on the **Beam** branch of the **Specification Tree**.

14.2 Insert a point by using the **Point** ▪ tool. The **Point Definition** window will appear.

NOTE: You may need to select **View**, **Toolbars** from the **Standard Window** toolbar. Then select the **Reference Elements (Extended)** toolbar to access the **Point** tool.

Figure 3.39

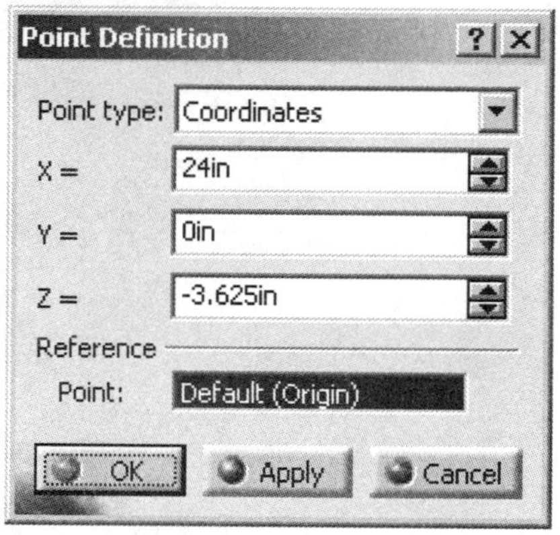

14.3 Select **Coordinates** from the **pull down arrow** for the **Point type** field.

14.4 Type in "**24in**" for the **X** = field, "**0in**" for the **Y** = field, and "**-3.625in**" for the **Z**= field.

14.5 Verify **Default (Origin)** is in the **Reference Point** field.

Figure 3.40

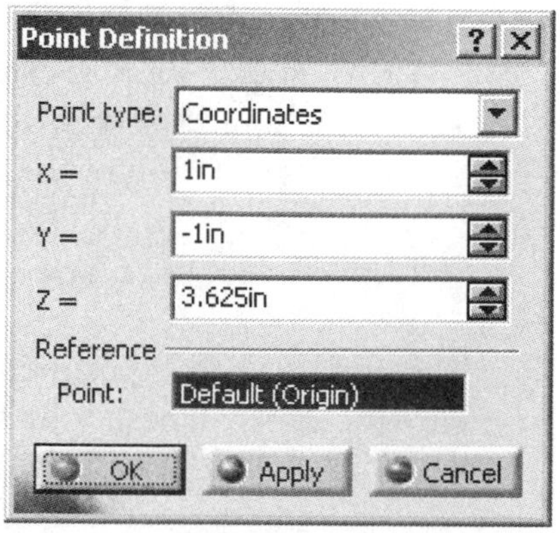

14.6 Verify the **Default(Absolute)** is the **Axis System**.

14.7 Select the **OK** button.

14.8 Insert another point by selecting the **Point** ▪ tool. The **Point Definition** window will appear.

14.9 Select **Coordinates** from the **pull down arrow** for the **Point type** field.

14.10 Type in "**1in**" for the **X =** field, "**-1in**" for the **Y =** field, and "**3.625in**" for the **Z=** field.

14.11 Verify **Default** values for both the Point and Axis System.

14.12 Select the **OK** button.

Figure 3.41

14.13 Enter the **Generative Structural Analysis** workbench.

14.14 Select the **Smooth Virtual Part** tool.

14.15 The **Smooth Virtual Part** window will appear as shown in Figure 3.41, with the **Supports** field highlighted in blue. Select the top surface of beam for the **Supports** field.

Figure 3.42

14.16 Select **No selection** in the **Handler** field. This will highlight the field blue as shown in Figure 3.42.

14.17 Select **Point.2** (coordinates 1, -1, 3.625) for the **Handler** either on the **Specification Tree** or on the beam.

14.18 The **Handler** field should now read **1 Point** as shown in Figure 3.43.

Figure 3.43

14.19 Select the **OK** button.

Figure 3.44

Select this point

Select this surface

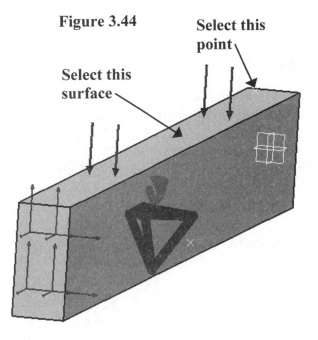

Figure 3.45

Smooth Virtual Part

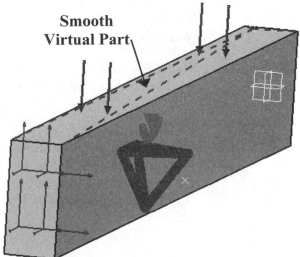

Figure 3.46

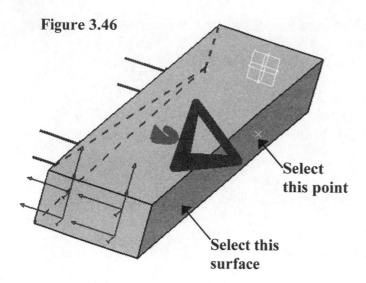

Select
this point

Select this
surface

Figure 3.47

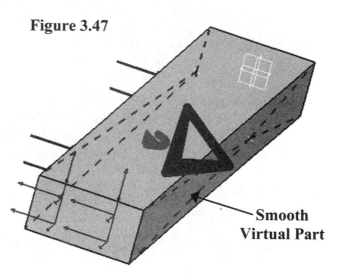

Smooth
Virtual Part

14.20   Select the **Smooth Virtual Part** tool.

14.21   The **Smooth Virtual Part** window will appear with the **Supports** field
        highlighted in blue. Select the bottom surface of beam. You may need to
        rotate the beam to select this surface.

14.22   Select the **No selection** in the **Handler** field. This will highlighted the
        field blue as shown in Figure 3.42.

14.23   Select **Point.1** (coordinates 24, 0, -3.625) for the **Handler**.

14.24   The **Handler** field should now read **1 Point**.

14.25   Select the **OK** button.

14.26 Delete **Restraint.1** from the front surface by selecting **Restraint.1** either in the **Specification Tree** or by selecting the **Restraint.1** symbol. Then right-click and select **Delete**. Refer to Figure 3.48.

14.27 Select the **Smooth Virtual Part** 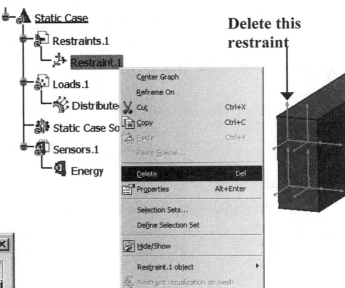 tool.

14.28 The **Smooth Virtual Part** window will appear with the **Supports** field highlighted in blue. Select the front surface of beam for the **Supports** field.

14.29 Select the **OK** button.

Figure 3.48

Delete this restraint

Figure 3.49

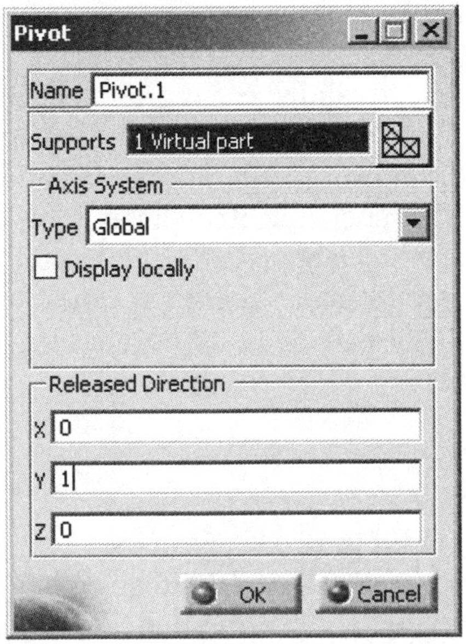

This creates a smooth virtual part called **Smooth Virtual Part.3** with the **Handler** as the centroid of the surface as shown in Figure 3.50.

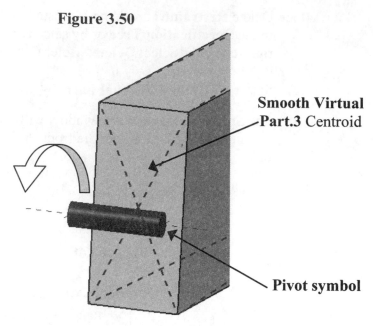

Figure 3.50

Smooth Virtual Part.3 Centroid

Pivot symbol

15. Mechanical Restraints

Now that you created virtual parts you can now use mechanical restraints. **Mechanical Restraints** are different types of connections that are associated with a virtual part. These restraints can imitate rollers, smooth surface supports, ball and sockets, single journal bearings, single journal bearings with a square shaft, single thrust bearings, single smooth pins, and single hinges. There are five types of **Mechanical Restraints**, the **Surface Slider** , **Slider** , **Sliding Pivot** , **Ball Joint** , and **Pivot** . The **Surface Slider** represents smooth surface supports, rollers or any mechanical device where the reaction is a force, which acts perpendicular to the surface at the point of contact. The **Slider** can represent a single journal bearing with a square shaft because it can slide but cannot pivot around an axis (it restrains two translations and three couple moments). The **Sliding Pivot** can represent a single journal bearing because it can pivot and slide along an axis (it restrains two translations and two couple moments which act perpendicular to the shaft). The **Ball Joint** restrains three translation components. The **Pivot** can represent a single thrust bearing, single smooth pin, or a single hinge because it restrains three translations and two couple moments.

15.1   Select the **Pivot** tool.

15.2   The **Pivot** window will appear as shown in Figure 3.49. With the **Supports** field highlighted, select **Smooth Virtual Part.3** either in the **Specification Tree** (you may have to expand the **Specification Tree** by selecting the + symbol to the left of **Properties.1**) or on the front surface of the beam.

15.3   The **Released Direction** frame with **X**, **Y**, and **Z** fields determine the pivot orientation relative to the axis system chosen in the **Type** box under the **pull down arrow**. For complicated geometries use the **Compass** tool to align the pivot orientation. Type "**0**" in for **X**, "**1**" in the **Y** field and "**0**" in the **Z** field.

15.4   Select the **OK** button.

15.5   Select the **Pivot** tool.

15.6   The **Pivot** window will appear with the **Supports** field highlighted. Select **Smooth Virtual Part.2** either in the **Specification Tree** or on the bottom surface of the beam.

15.7   In the **Released Direction** frame, type "**0**" in for **X**, "**1**" in the **Y** field and "**0**" in the **Z** field.

15.8   Select the **OK** button.

15.9   Change the **mesh size** and **sag size** back (if you haven't already) to the default size of **4.5in** and **.72in** since you are not concerned with accuracy as you are the concept of mechanical restraints. This will save computing time. Refer to steps 9.9 through 9.12.

15.10 **Compute** the result. Refer to Section 8 to review this procedure.

15.11 Select the **Von Mises Stress** tool.

Now apply a load at a specific point and direction on the top surface, not normal to that surface. Change the middle support pivot to a slider and notice the different behavior.

15.12 Select the **Distributed Force** tool.

15.13 The **Distributed Force** window will appear. For the **Supports** field select the **Smooth Virtual Part.1** either in on the **Specification Tree** or on the **Smooth Virtual Part.1** symbol located on the top surface of the beam.

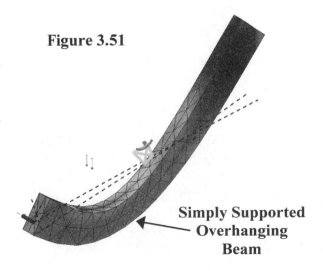

Figure 3.51

Simply Supported Overhanging Beam

15.14 Type "**10000lbf**" in the **Force Vector** field **X**, "**10000lbf**" in the field **Y**, and "**-10000lbf**" in the field **Z**.

NOTE: You may need to repeat Section 1.4 to reset your units if you have logged
out of your session at all.

15.15   Select the **OK** button. Zoom in on the arrow to see how it is vectored.

15.16   Delete **Pivot.2** be careful not to delete **Smooth Virtual Part.2**.

15.17   Select the **Slider** 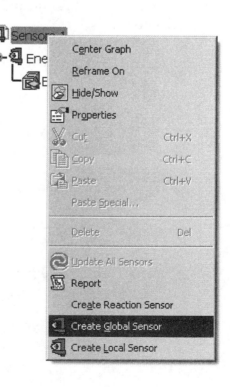 tool.

15.18   Select the **Smooth Virtual Part.2** for **Supports**.

15.19   Verify that "**0**" appears in the **X** field, "**1**" in the **Y** field, and "**0**" in the **Z**
field.

15.20   Select the **OK** button.

15.21   **Compute** the result. Refer to Section 8 to review this procedure.

15.22   Select the **Von Mises Stress** tool. Notice how the slider only allowed
the beam to slide in the **Y** direction.

16. Knowledge Advisor

Use **Knowledge Advisor** to warn you when you have exceeded the yield strength of
the **BeamAnalysis.CATAnalysis**. You will also modify the color palette to warn
you with the color red when the yield strength has been exceeded.

16.1   Create a **Sensor** so that you can use
it in **Knowledge Advisor**. Select
Sensors.1 on the **Specification
Tree**. Right-click and select **Create
Global Sensor**. (Figure 3.52)

Figure 3.52

16.2   The **Create Sensor** window will
appear (see Figure 3.53). Select
Maximum Von Mises.

16.3   Select the **OK** button.

16.4   Might have to change parameters in
options.

16.5   Go to the **Knowledge Advisor**
workbench.

16.6   Select the **Check** tool.

16.7   The **Check Editor** window will
appear. Select the **OK** button.

16.8   The **Check Editor:Check.1 Active** window will appear. (Figure 3.54) For the **Type of Check** select **Information** from the **pull down arrow**.

Figure 3.53

16.9   Type "**Exceeds Yield Strength**" in the **Message** field.

16.10 Select the **Maximum Von Mises Sensor** from the **Specification Tree** that was created in Step 16.3. This will retrieve all members of this sensor.

Figure 3.54

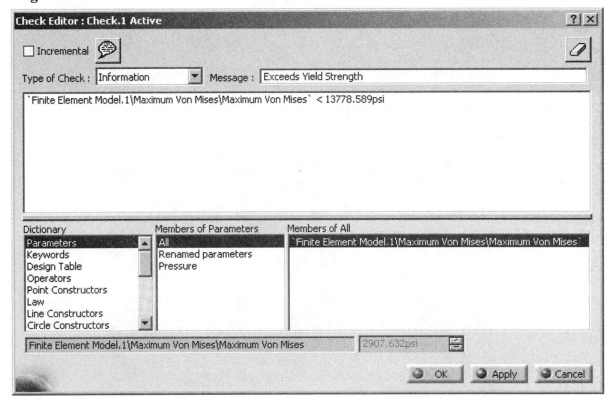

16.11 Double click on "**Finite Element Model.1\Maximum Von Mises\Maximum Von Mises**" in the **Members of All** section. This will place the text into the edition box. Reference Figure 3.54.

16.12 Now type in "**< 13778.589psi**" as shown in Figure 3.54.

16.13 Select the **OK** button.

16.14 The **Check.1** in the **Specification Tree** should have a green light.

The **Color Pallet** can also give an indication through the use of colors if a material exceeds its yield strength. The following steps show how to do this.

16.15 Enter into the **Generative Structural Analysis** workbench.

16.16 Double click on the **Color Pallet** as shown in Figure 3.55 (anywhere the regular cursor changes to the hand cursor).

NOTE: If you receive a **Warning** window stating the **ColorMap can't be edited because it is Xlocked**, right click on the **Color Pallet** and select **Unlock**.

16.17 The **Color Map Edition** window will appear. Select the **More>>** button. (Figure 3.56)

16.18 Select **Imposed Max** checkbox and type in the yield strength property of aluminum (**13778.589**) in its field.

Figure 3.55   <u>**Color Pallet**</u>

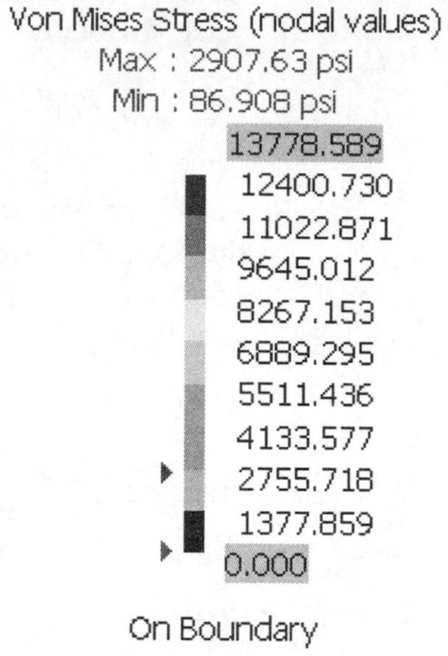

Von Mises Stress (nodal values)
Max : 2907.63 psi
Min : 86.908 psi

13778.589
12400.730
11022.871
9645.012
8267.153
6889.295
5511.436
4133.577
2755.718
1377.859
0.000

On Boundary

Figure 3.56

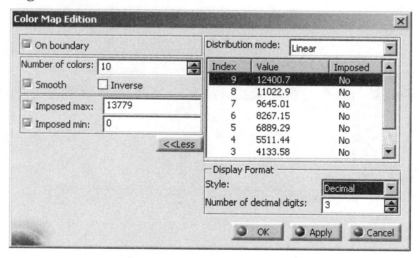

16.19 Select the **Imposed Min** checkbox and type "0" in its field.

16.20 Select the **pull down arrow** in the **Style** field and select **Decimal**. The **Number of decimal digits** is **3**.

16.21 Select the **OK** button.

The pallet displays the **Max** and **Min** values of the **Von Mises Stress** with its corresponding range, on the **Color Pallet**. It also displays the range in decimal values. Modify **Distributive Force.2** so that the beam exceeds its yield strength and see if **Check.1** gives a message.

16.22 Double click on **Distributive Force.2** in the **Specification Tree**. The **Distributive Force** window should appear. Modify the **Force Vector** field **X** to "**50000lbf**", the field **Y** to "**50000lbf**", and the field **Z** to "**-50000lbf**."

16.23 Select the **OK** button.

16.24 **Compute** the result. Refer to Section 8 to review this procedure.

Figure 3.57

16.25 The message box **Check.1** should appear that says **Exceeds Yield Strength** and the **Check.1** relations should have a red light symbol. Select the **OK** button on the **Check.1** message box.

Figure 3.58

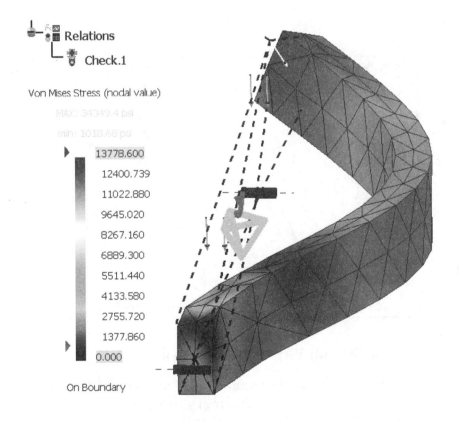

17. Insert a Buckling Case

In the previous sections we computed stress and deflection of the beam. CATIA V5 can also compute column instability or buckling. Column failure is influenced more by its geometrical configuration, modulus of elasticity and boundary connections than by its allowable compressive stress. Columns are normally thought of as long slender members that are loaded in axial compression. To insert a buckling case analysis to the beam, you will need to modify the previous **Finite Element Model** by following the steps below.

17.1   Delete **Distributed Force.1** and **Distributed Force.2**.

17.2   Delete **Pivot.1** and **Slider.1**.

17.3   Delete **Smooth Virtual Part.1, Smooth Virtual Part.2**, and **Smooth Virtual Part.3**.

Create loads and restraints on the **Beam.CATAnalysis** so that it mimics a **Pinned-Pinned** column shown in Figure 3.59.

Figure 3.59

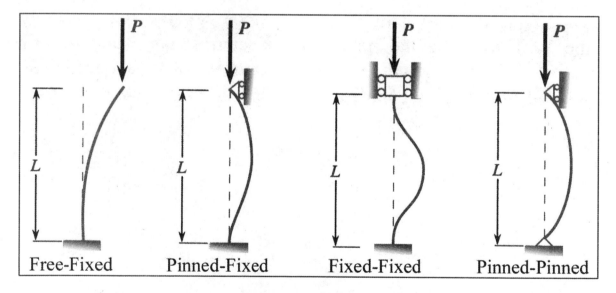

17.4   Select the **Smooth Virtual Part** tool.

17.5   The **Smooth Virtual Part** window will appear with the **Supports** field highlighted in blue. Select the front surface (same surface as Step 14.27) of **Beam.CATAnalysis** for the **Supports** field.

17.6   Select the **OK** button.

17.7   Select the **Pivot** tool.

17.8   The **Pivot** window will appear. With the **Supports** field highlighted select **Smooth Virtual Part.3** either in the **Specification Tree** or the **Smooth Virtual Part.3** symbol on the front surface of the beam.

17.9   In the **Released Direction** frame appears the **X, Y,** and **Z** fields. Type "**0**" in for **X,** "**0**" in for **Y,** and "**1**" in for **Z.**

17.10   Select the **OK** button.

17.11   Select the **Smooth Virtual Part** [symbol] tool.

17.12   The **Smooth Virtual Part** window will appear with the **Supports** field highlighted in blue. Select the back surface of **Beam.CATAnalysis** for the **Supports** field (you may have to rotate the **Beam.CATAnalysis** to select the back surface).

17.13   Select the **OK** button.

17.14   Select the **Advanced Restraint** [symbol] tool. The **Advanced Restraint** window will appear.

17.15   The **Supports** field should be highlighted in blue. Select the **Smooth Virtual Part.4** for the **Support.**

Notice that since the **Advanced Restraint** has a smooth virtual part for a support, the **Restrain Rotation 1**, **Restrain Rotation 2**, and **Restrain Rotation 3** are activated.

17.16   Verify that **Restrain Translation 2, Restrain Translation 3, Restrain Rotation 1,** and **Restrain Rotation 2** are selected and verify that **Restrain Translation 1,** and **Restrain Rotation 3** are deselected. This will allow the column to act as a pinned column at both ends, while the **Advanced Restraint** is able to translate in the **X** direction and rotate about the **Z** axis. Select **OK.**

17.17   Select the **Distributed Force** [symbol] tool.

17.18   The **Distributed Force** window will appear. For the **Supports** field select the **Smooth Virtual Part.4** either in on the **Specification Tree** or on the **Smooth Virtual Part.4** symbol located on the back surface of the beam.

17.19   Type "**1421000lbf**" in the **Force Vector** field **X,** "**0lbf**" in the field **Y,** and "**0lbf**" in the field **Z.**

17.20   Select the **OK** button.

After modifying the beam insert the **Buckling Case** by completing the following steps:

17.21 Select the **Compute** button. You have to compute a **Static Case** before you can insert a **Buckling Case**. If the **Check.1** message box appears, select the **OK** button.

17.22 Select **Insert** and then select **Buckling Case** on the **Standard Windows** toolbar. (Figure 3.60)

Figure 3.60

17.23 The **Buckling Case** window will appear. Select **Static Case Solution.1** from the **Specification Tree** for the **Reference** field. The **Hide existing analysis cases** option when selected hides all symbols applied to the beam from the **Static Case**.

17.24 Select the **OK** button.

The **Buckling Case** is now underlined in the **Specification Tree** and is now set as the current case. The **Buckling Case** consists of the **Static Case Solution.1**, **Buckling Case Solution.1**, and **Sensors.2** object sets. Notice most all tools are deactivated; this is because the **Static Case Solution.1** characterizes the **Buckling Case** solutions. This means to change, delete or add forces or restraints to the beam you must delete the entire **Buckling Case** on the **Specification Tree**. Then make the changes to the **Static Case**, re-compute the **Static Case** and then insert a new **Buckling Case**.

17.25 Select the **Compute** button to compute the **Buckling Case**.

17.26 Select the **Deformation** view tool.

17.27 In the **Specification Tree** under the current **Buckling Case**, double click on the **Deformed Mesh** to view the buckling factors with their associated modes (see Figure 3.61; the beam has been rotated to better show the effects).

Figure 3.61   Modes 1 Default Selected

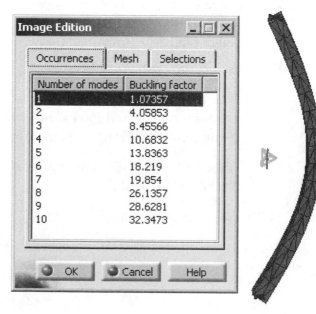

17.28   Select modes 2, 3, 4, … and so forth to show the beams **Deformation** view at those corresponding modes (reference Figure 3.62).

Figure 3.62   Modes 2 Selected

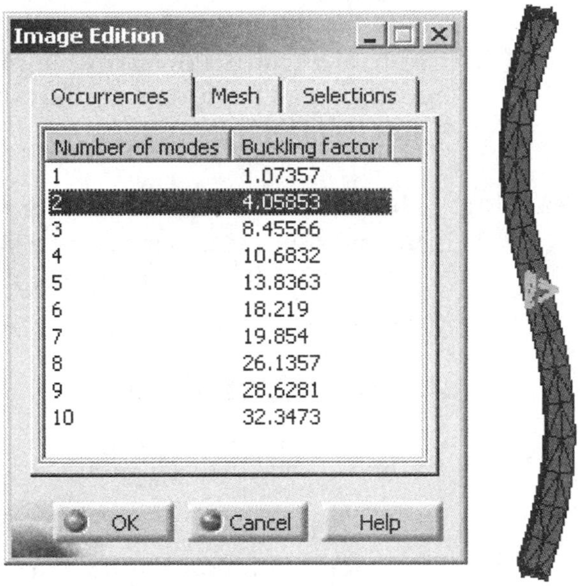

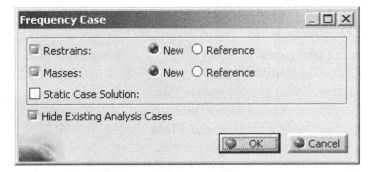

NOTE: The beam has been rotated to show the buckling effect.

17.29   Select the **OK** button.

18. Insert a Frequency Case

Whenever the natural frequency of vibration of a machine or structure matches the frequency of the external excitation, a phenomenon known as resonance takes place. This leads to excessive deflection and failure. CATIA V5 performs two types of frequency analysis called **Frequency Analysis** and **Free Frequency Analysis**. The difference is the **Free Frequency Analysis** does not allow any **Restraints** applied to the part. Insert a **Frequency Analysis** by completing the following steps.

18.1   Select **Insert** and then select **Frequency Case** on the **Standard Windows** toolbar. Unlike the **Buckling Case**, the **Frequency Case** does not need a reference from a **Static Case Solution** but offers that functionality.

Figure 3.63

18.2   The **Frequency Case** window will appear. Select the **Restrains** option and select the corresponding **New** option to the right.

18.3   Select the **Masses** option along with the corresponding **New** option to the right. Select the **Hide Existing Analysis Cases** option.

By selecting **New**, the **Frequency Case** will have nothing to do with the previous **Static Case** or **Buckling Case** analysis. It would be the same as choosing **Frequency Analysis** in Step 3.2 instead of **Static Case** (see Figure 3.8). Deselecting **Restrains**, and selecting **Masses** with its corresponding **New** option is like choosing **Free Frequency Analysis** in Step 3.2 instead of **Static Case** (see Figure 3.8).

Warning: Deselecting the **Hide Existing Analysis Cases** option, allows you to view the previous analysis case and symbols, but doing so with previous views activated will make it impossible to select beam surfaces and edges to apply new restraints and masses.

18.4 Select the **OK** button.

18.5 Select the **Pivot** tool.

18.6 The **Pivot** window will appear. With the **Supports** field highlighted, select **Smooth Virtual Part.3** either in the **Specification Tree** or on the **Smooth Virtual Part.3** symbol on the front surface of the beam.

18.7 In the **Released Direction** frame appears the **X**, **Y**, and **Z** fields. Type "**0**" in for **X**, "**1**" in for **Y**, and "**0**" in for **Z**.

18.8 Select the **OK** button.

18.9 Select the **Pivot** tool.

18.10 The **Pivot** window will appear. With the **Supports** field highlighted, select **Smooth Virtual Part.4** either in the **Specification Tree** or on the **Smooth Virtual Part.4** symbol on the back surface of the beam (You may need to rotate the part).

18.11 In the **Released Direction** frame, type "**0**" in for **X**, "**1**" in for **Y**, and "**0**" in for **Z**. Select **OK**.

Figure 3.64

18.12 Select the **Distributed Mass** tool. The **Distributed Mass** window will appear. With the **Supports** field highlighted, select the top surface of the beam. Type "**179lb**" in the **Mass** field. This will represent the mass of the beam, which is computed from the equation:

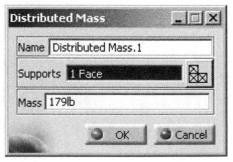

$$\text{Mass} = (\text{Density})*(\text{Volume})$$

$$179\text{lb} = (.098\text{lb/in}^3) \ (7.25\text{in})(3.5\text{in})(72\text{in})]$$

18.13 Select the **OK**
button

Figure 3.65

18.14 Select the
Compute tool.

18.15 Select the
Deformation
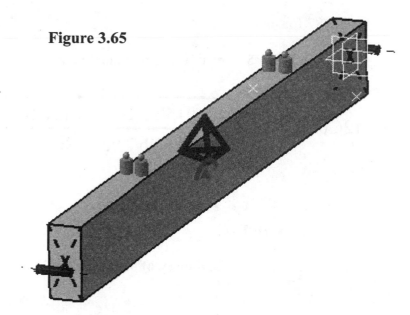 tool.

18.16 In the **Specification Tree** under the
current **Frequency Case** and
Frequency Case Solution.1, double
click on the **Deformed Mesh** to view
the frequencies with their associated
modes as seen in Figure 3.66.

Figure 3.66

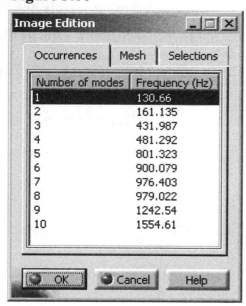

18.17 The default selection and view is the
first mode. The frequency for mode
1 of this uniform simply supported
beam is 130.66Hz (see Figure 3.66-
your answer may vary).

18.18 Select mode **2, 3, 4, …** and so forth
to show the **Deformation** view at
those frequencies.

18.19 Select the **OK** button.

Let's compare CATIA V5's result to a frequency equation. You can find the natural
frequency equation for a uniform beam; both ends simply supported from [Roark's
6th edition, Table 36, Case 1 description 1b.] The equation is

$$f_n = \frac{K_n}{2\Pi} \sqrt{\frac{EIg}{wl}}$$

Where K_n = constant where n refers to the mode of vibration; g = gravitational
acceleration (units consistent with length dimensions); E = modulus of elasticity;
I = is the moment of inertia.

$K_n = 9.87$ for mode 1

Notice CATIA V5's result is approximately equal to the formula.

$$126.65\text{Hz} = \frac{9.87}{2\pi}\sqrt{\frac{(1.015\text{E} \times 10^7\text{psi})(111.14\text{in}^4)(385\text{in/s}^2)}{(179\text{lb/72in})(72\text{in})^4}}$$

19. Creating Reports

19.1   To display a summary of the analysis, click on the **Basic Analysis Report** tool.

19.2   The **Reporting Options** window will appear. Select the **...** button to change the **Output directory**.

19.3   Change the **Title of the report** to "**BeamAnalysis**."

19.4   Multi-select **Static Case**, **Buckling Case**, and **Frequency Case** by holding down the Shift key.

19.5   Select the **OK** button.

19.6   The report will appear in html format with your default browser on your taskbar.

Summary

This lesson used a simple beam so it would be easier to compare the traditional method of analyzing a beam. Even though a basic beam was used, hopefully, you can see the application to more complex structures and how this workbench could make the analysis of more complex structures possible and a whole lot easier. By successfully completing this lesson, you are ready for more complex applications. If you struggled through the steps covered in this lesson, you should go back and work through them until you feel comfortable with each step. You can test your skill and understanding by answering the **Review Questions** and working through the **Practice Exercise** problems.

Review Questions

After completing this lesson, you should be able to answer the questions and explain the concepts listed below.

1. Before you enter **Generative Structural Analysis** workbench you should always.

   A. Give the part a name.
   B. Assign the part a material.
   C. Make sure the part is in the isometric view.
   D. Make sure the customized view is set to the proper selections.
   E. B and D

2. What are the five **Structural Properties** of the material that the workbench uses to **Compute** the analysis?

   _____   _____   _____

   _____   _____

3. What two tools can be used to find the **Extrema** values?

4. The **Animate** tool does not work with which view?

5. What tool allows you to look at a cross section of a part viewed in **Von Mises Stress**?

6. The **Load** symbols turn what color after computation?

7. The **Ball Joint** restrains three couple moments.

   A. True
   B. False

8. A **Slider** restraint acts like a hinge.

   A. True
   B. False

9. To apply a load to a surface other than the centroid of that surface, a virtual body must be created with the **Handler** being a point.

   A. True
   B. False

10. To obtain better accuracy of the analysis you should _____ the **mesh size** and **sag size**.

   A. Decrease
   B. Increase

11. What is the allowable stress for Structural (ASTM-A36) steel with a yield strength of 36ksi, and a factor of safety (FS) of 2.

   A. 72000psi
   B. 18000psi
   C. 18psi
   D. 10877psi

12. Restraints can be applied when inserting a **Free Frequency Analysis**?

   A. True
   B. False

13. A **Frequency Analysis** can be computed without first computing a static case?

   A. True
   B. False

14. The best practice in modifying a load, restraint, mass, pressure etc. while the current case is a buckling case, is to *delete* the buckling case altogether and make modifications in the static case that it corresponded to?

   A. True
   B. False

15. When inserting a **Frequency Analysis** and you need to select an edge or surface of the part, you should not select the **Hide existing analysis cases** option in the **Frequency Case** window?

   A. True
   B. False

16. What is the mass of a part with the structural property of density being equal to .161 lb/in^3 and a volume of 8640 in^3?

    A. 72 lb
    B. 695 lb
    C. 9 lb
    D. 1391 lb

17. What is the frequency mode 1 of the simply supported part at both ends, if Kn = 9.87 of a part with the structural property of density being equal to .161 lb/in^3 and E = 16530 ksi I = 1.25 in^4 g = 385 in/s^2 w = 19.31 lb/in l = 72 in?

    A. 36 Hz
    B. 18 Hz
    C. 6 Hz
    D. 72 Hz

18. The green symbol in Figure 3.67 represents a:

    A. Successfully computed force
    B. Un-computed mass
    C. Un-computed restraint
    D. Successfully computed mass

19. What 3 components does the **Finite Element Model** in the **Specification Tree** always have by default when entering the **Generative Structural Analysis** workbench?

    A. **Link.1**, **Results**, and **Computations**
    B. **Nodes and Elements**, **Properties.1**, and any case in D
    C. **Links Manager**, **Finite Element Model**, and **Analysis Manager**
    D. **Static Case**, **Free Frequency Case**, and **Frequency Case**

20. What 3 components does the **Links Manager** in the **Specification Tree** always have by default when entering the **Generative Structural Analysis** workbench?

    A. **Links Manager**, **Finite Element Model**, and **Analysis Manager**
    B. **Nodes and Elements**, **Properties.1**, and any case in D
    C. **Link.1**, **Results** link, and **Computations** link
    D. **Static Case**, **Free Frequency Case**, and **Frequency Case**

Practice Exercises

Apply and/or test your newfound knowledge.

1. Design cantilevered hollow tubing using the dimensions shown in the sketch. Make the beam **72″** long. Save the beam as **Lesson 3 Exercise 1**.

2. Apply a material type of **Titanium** and a load of **10000lbs** at the end of the beam. How much does the beam deflect? Save the beam as **Lesson 3 Exercise 2**.

3. Apply a material type of **Aluminum** and a load of **10000lbs** at the end of the beam. How much does the beam deflect? Save the beam as **Lesson 3 Exercise 3**.

4. Modify the beam to a solid beam and save it as **Lesson 3 Exercise 4**.

5. Apply a material type of **Titanium** and a load of **10000lbs** at the end of the beam. How much does the beam deflect? Save the beam as **Lesson 3 Exercise 5**.

6. Apply a material type of **Aluminum** and a load of **10000lbs** at the end of the beam. How much does the beam deflect? Save the beam as **Lesson 3 Exercise 6**.

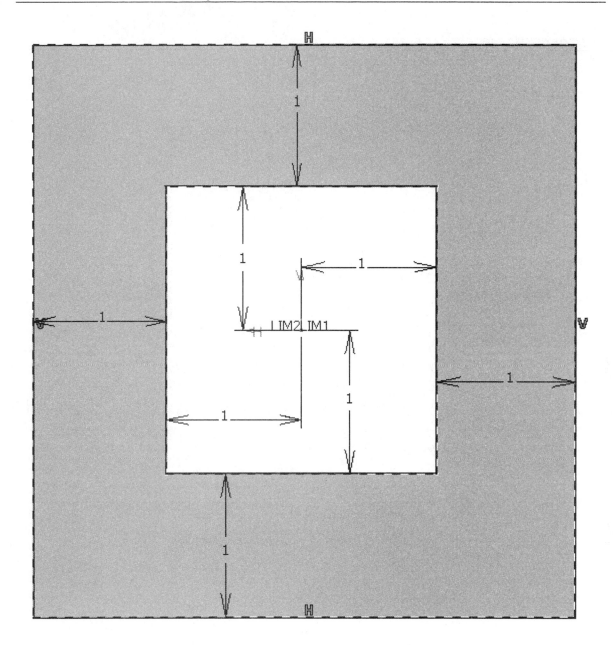

Notes:

Lesson 4
Sheet Metal Design

Introduction

This lesson describes step-by-step processes for creating and flattening sheet metal parts using both the **Generative Sheet Metal Design** and **Sheet Metal Design** workbenches. The first part of the lesson will cover the flattening of a sheet metal part that was created in the **Part Design** workbench. The second part of the lesson will cover the creation of **Sheet Metal Bracket.1** (see Figure 4.1). This lesson will cover the use of the most frequently used tools in the **Generative Sheet Metal Design** and **Sheet Metal Design** workbenches.

Figure 4.1

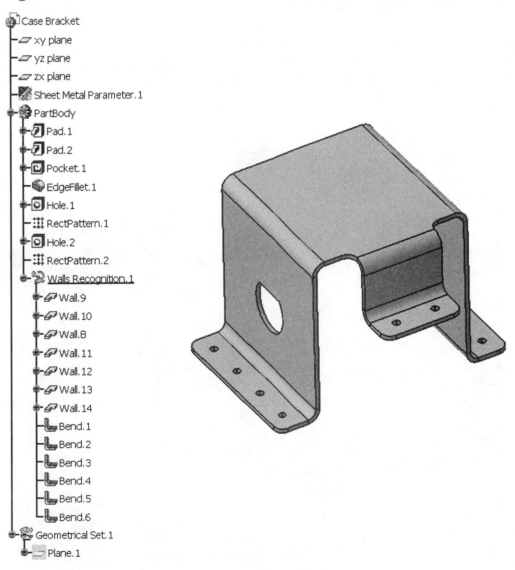

Objectives

This lesson will take you through the process of the creation of sheet metal parts, as shown in Figure 4.1. When you complete this lesson you should be able to do the following:

1. Select the **Generative Sheet Metal Design** and **Sheet Metal Design** workbenches.

2. Flatten a part created in the **Part Design** workbench.

3. Use the tools found in the **Generative Sheet Metal Design** and **Sheet Metal Design** workbenches.

4. Create flanges on a sheet metal part.

5. Create holes in sheet metal parts within the **Generative Sheet Metal Design** and **Sheet Metal Design** workbenches.

Figures 4.1 and 4.2 show examples of the sheet metal parts you will have created at the completion of this lesson. Figure 4.1 shows the **Case Bracket** along with its **Specification Tree**. Figure 4.2 shows the **Lower Bracket**.

Figure 4.2

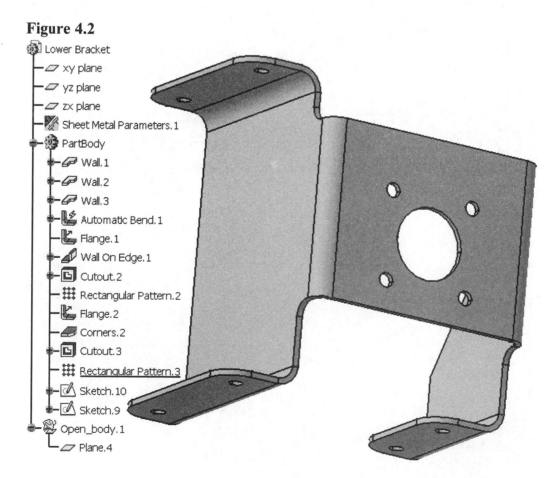

Tools and Toolbars

The following section lists the tools and toolbars with a brief explanation. This lesson does not use all of the tools listed in the workbenches.

NOTE: There are a lot of the same tools in both workbenches.

The <u>Sheet Metal</u> Toolbar

TOOLBAR	TOOL NAME	TOOL DEFINITION
	Sheet Metal Parameters	Information that drives the creation of walls and flanges. Includes the thickness of the default bend angle.
	Walls Recognition	Allows walls and bends to be recognized in the **Sheet Metal Design** workbench.
	Wall	Allows flanges to be created on a specified plane.
	Wall On Edge	Creates flanges on the edge of an existing wall.
	Extrusion	Allows for the creation of a sheet metal part or feature, by drawing a sketch and extruding the profile.
Bends Toolbar		
	Automatic Bends	Recognizes bends that have been created without a radius.
	Bend	Creates a bend between two touching walls.
	Conic Bend	Creates a varying angle bend.
	Bend From Flat	Creates a flange from a sketch and angles it depending on user specified inputs.

Swept Walls Toolbar

	Flange	Allows the user to specify the bend radius, bend angle and flange length to create a flange on the edge of a part.
	Hem	Creates a hem bend.
	Tear Drop	Creates a tear drop shaped bend.
	Swept Flange	Creates a flange using a profile and spline.

Unfold Toolbar

	Fold/Unfold	Folds and unfolds parts.
	Multi Viewer	Opens up a separate window with the part in a flattened view.

Pockets Container Toolbar

	Cutout	Creates holes, pockets, and cut flanges.

Stampings Toolbar

	Point Stamp	Creates stamped features on sheet metal parts.
	Extruded Hole	Creates a tapered hole.
	Curve Stamp	Creates a rounded stamp.
	Surface Stamp	Creates a stamped profile using a sketch profile.
	Bridge	Creates a stamped bridge.
	Louver	Creates a louver based on user specified constraints.
	Stiffening Rib	Creates a stiffening rib on a previously created bend.
	User Stamping	Allows for the defining of the stamp and dies used to create the sheet metal part.

Patterns Toolbar		
	Rectangular Pattern	Arrays features; holes and planes.
	Circular Pattern	Creates a circular hole pattern.
	User Pattern	Allows the user to define a customized hole pattern.
	Corner Relief	Define a corner relief locally on a set of supports.
Corner/Chamfer Toolbar		
	Corner	Creates a radius on the edge of a flange.
	Chamfer	Cut off, or fill in sharp edges of sheet metal parts.
	Fold/Unfold Points Or Curves	Allows the user to unfold points and curves.
	Save As DXF	Saves the flattened part as a **DXF** file so it can be opened up in the **Drafting** workbench.

The <u>Sketcher</u> Toolbar

TOOLBAR	TOOL NAME	TOOL DEFINITION
	Sketcher	Allows for the creation of profiles that may be used for walls, holes and pockets.
	Sketch With Absolute Axis Definition	Enables you to create a positioned sketch.

The <u>Constraints</u> Toolbar

TOOLBAR	TOOL NAME	TOOL DEFINITION
	Constraints Defined In A Dialog Box	Allows for the application of various constraints. i.e. angular, parallelism and perpendicularity.
	Constraint	Creates length and distance constraints.

Flattening a Part Created in the Part Design Workbench

The **Generative Sheet Metal Design** workbench in CATIA V5 allows users to flatten sheet metal parts that have been created in the **Part Design** workbench.

1.   Opening the Part

Open the **Case Bracket Part Design.CATPart** in the **Sheet Metal Design** Workbench. To accomplish this complete the following steps.

1.1   Go to www.schroff1.com and download the **Case Bracket Part Design** model from the Advanced CATIA V5 Workbook (Release 16) web page.

1.2   Open the part named **Case Bracket Part Design**. You may have to unzip the file before opening it in CATIA V5.

1.3   If you are not already in the **Generative Sheet Metal Design** workbench, you will need to switch to it. It is located in the <u>S</u>tart menu, **Mechanical Design**, and then **Generative Sheet Metal Design**.

1.4   Select the **Walls Recognition** tool. The command prompt will prompt you to "**Select the face for the reference wall**."

1.5   Select the face shown in Figure 4.3. Selecting the surface will bring up the **Recognition Definition** window. The selected face will become the **Reference Wall**. The **Reference Wall** determines which surface all the other bended surfaces will be flattened to.

Figure 4.3

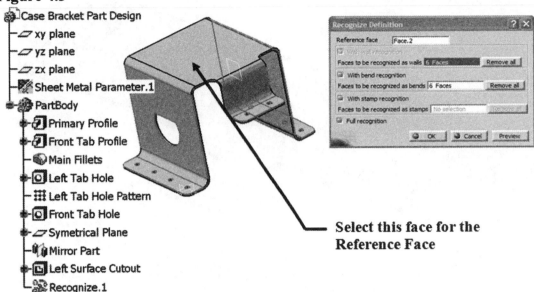

Select this face for the
Reference Face

1.6 Select the "**Faces to be recognized as walls**" box so that the box is highlighted. With the box highlighted select the remaining planar faces on the part. There are six remaining planar faces.

1.7 Select the "**Faces to be recognized as bends**" box. So the box is highlighted. With the box highlighted select all the filleted surfaces. There are six filleted surfaces.

1.8 Leave the Stamp recognition selection blank.

1.9 Select the "**Full recognition**" box at the bottom of the window.

1.10 Select the **OK** button to create the Sheet Metal Recognition. Notice the new branch that is added to the **Specification Tree** (reference Figure 4.3). Now all you have to do is flatten the part.

1.11 Select the **Fold/Unfold** tool. This will flatten the part to the specified surface. This is a toggle tool; to restore the part back to the folded condition re-select the tool. Reference Figure 4.4.

NOTE: Later on in the lesson the steps for saving the flattened part as a **DFX** file will be covered; for now, save it as a CATPart.

Figure 4.4

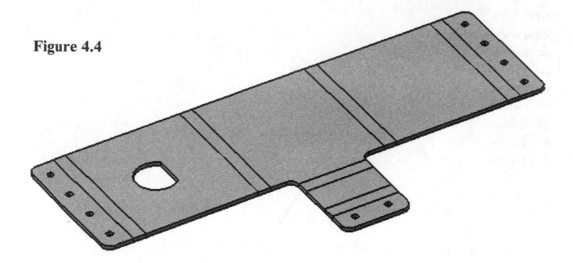

Creating a Sheet Metal Bracket Using the Sheet Metal Design Workbench

2. Select the Generative Sheet Metal Design Workbench

2.1 Start a new session.

2.2 Go to **File** and select **New**.

2.3 Select the **Generative Sheet Metal Design** workbench. If the **Generative Sheet Metal Design** workbench does not appear in the **New** window, you will have to select it from the **Start** pull down menu. Select **Start**, **Mechanical Design**, and then **Generative Sheet Metal Design** (see Figure 4.5).

2.4 Create a new part and name it **Lower Bracket**.

Figure 4.5

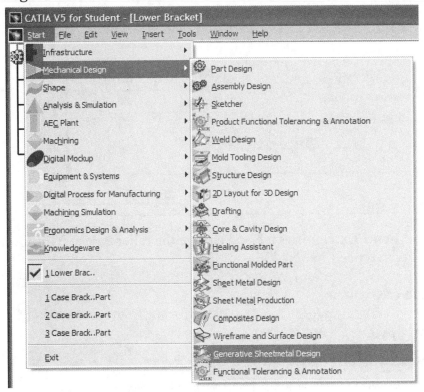

3. Setting the Sheet Metal Parameters

Before you are able to use most of the tools found in the **Generative Sheet Metal Design** workbench you must define the **Sheet Metal Parameters**. These parameters control the thickness of the material, default bend radius, corner relief, and bend allowance, along with other parameters that will not be covered in this lesson. To define the Sheet Metal Parameters complete the following steps.

3.1 Select the **Sheet Metal Parameters** 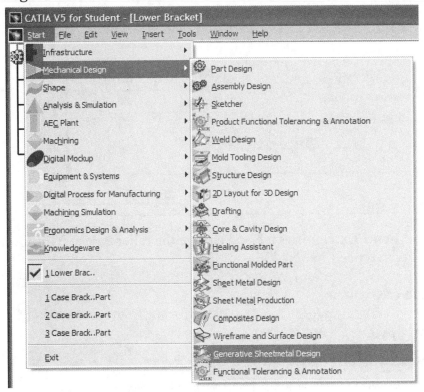 tool. This will bring up the **Sheet Metal Parameters** window as shown in Figure 4.6. Notice the four tabs; **Parameters**, **Bend Extremities**, **Bend Corner Relief** and **Bend Allowance**.

3.2 In the **Parameters** tab, change the **Thickness** to **.080**.

3.3 Change the **Default Bend radius** to **.190**.

Figure 4.6

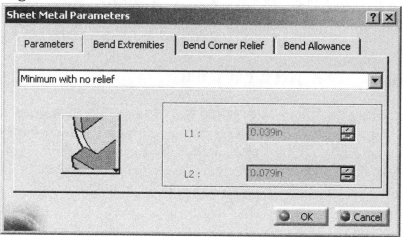

3.4 Select the **Bend Extremities** tab and change the relief type to **Minimum with no relief** (reference Figure 4.7).

3.5 Select the **OK** button.

Figure 4.7

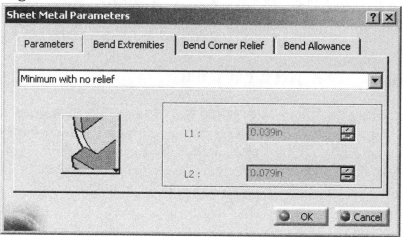

4. Creating the Primary Wall Using the Wall Tool

Different from previous CATIA V5 releases, Sheet Metal Parts must be created in the **Generative Sheet Metal Design** workbench and cannot be created in the **Sheet Metal Design** workbench.

4.1   Now that the parameters are set you can start creating your part.

4.2   Select the **Sketcher** tool and choose the **YZ** plane.

4.3   Create a sketch as shown in Figure 4.18.

Figure 4.8

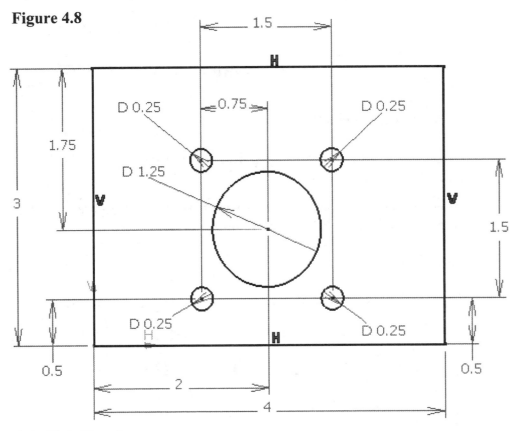

4.4   Exit **Sketcher**.

Figure 4.9

4.5   Select the **Wall** 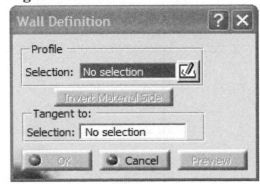 tool. This will bring up the **Wall Definition** window as shown in Figure 4.9.

4.6   For the **Profile** box select the sketch you just created. It may be a good idea to rename this sketch other than a generic label Sketch.1 so it has some meaning and will be easily recognized.

4.7   Select the **OK** button.
      The thickness of **Wall.1**
      and all flanges created
      within this part will
      reference the thickness
      that was entered into the
      **Sheet Metal
      Parameters**. You have
      just created the **Main
      Wall** (reference Figure
      4.10).

Figure 4.10

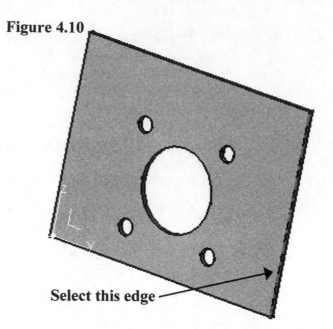

Select this edge

5. Creating Additional Walls

5.1   Select the **Wall** tool again. As before this will bring up the Wall Definition
      window.

5.2   Select the edge on the short side of **Wall.1** reference Figure 4.10. This will
      take you automatically into **Sketcher**.

Figure 4.11

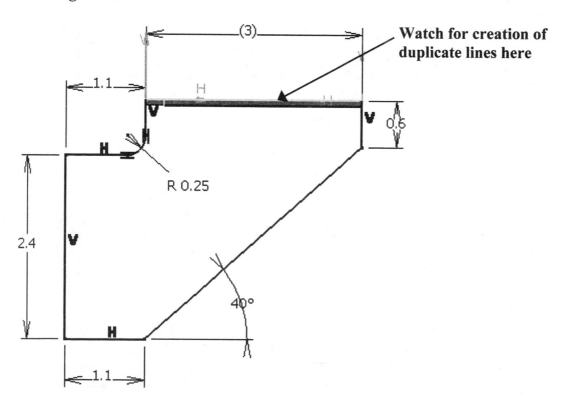

5.3   Create the sketch as illustrated in Figure 4.11. Note: Sketcher may create a generic wall sketch; you will have to modify it to make it similar to the sketch shown in Figure 4.11.

NOTE: CATIA V5 automatically generates a single yellow line for the edge you selected just before entering into **Sketcher**. You can use this line as part of your sketch. If you decide you want to draw your own line there as part of your sketch, you need to delete it the yellow one CATIA created so as not to create a duplicate. The yellow line signifies that it is linked to that specific edge created in the previous sketch. If the line in that sketch changes so will the yellow line in this sketch.

5.4   Exit **Sketcher**. The sketch will be extruded into a wall using the pre-defined properties.

5.5   Use the same process defined above to complete Wall.3. Select the edge on the side opposite the edge used for Wall.2.   Reference the dimensions provided in Figure 4.12.

Figure 4.12

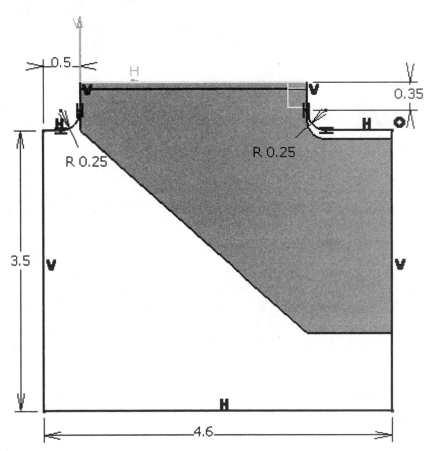

6. Generating Bends Using the Bend Tool

You are now going to generate your first bends by placing a radius joining the walls previously created. To do this, complete the following steps:

6.1   Select the **Bends** ⌐ tool. This will bring up the **Bend Definition** window as shown in Figure 4.13.

6.2   Select Wall.1 and Wall.2 for Support 1 and Support 2 respectively (as shown in Figure 4.13. CATIA V5 will provide a preview of the bend and the bend directions. To change the direction of the bend you can select the arrows displayed in the preview.

Figure 4.13

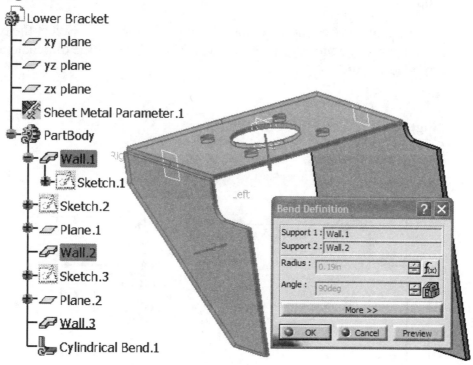

6.3   Select the **OK** button to create the bend. Notice the radius defined in the **Sheet Metal Parameters** is used to create the bends. The bend will appear in the **Specification Tree** under **Part Body/Cylindrical Bend.1**. If you wish to change the radius, you can click on the **Sheet Metal Parameters** tool found on the **Sheet Metal** toolbar or on the **Sheet Metal Parameters.1** found in your **Specification Tree**.

6.4   Using the same process (as described above), create a bend between Wall.1 and Wall.3.

7. Creating Flanges Using the Flange Tool

The Flange tool allows you to create additional walls (flanges) but using different information. The bend radius is automatically built between the walls. To create a flange using the Flange tool complete the following steps.

7.1   Select the edge of the smaller flange as shown in Figure 4.14.

Figure 4.14

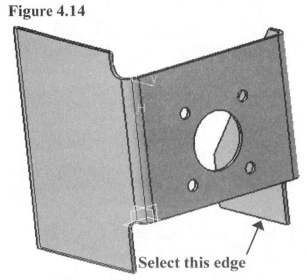

7.2   Then select the **Flange**  tool. This will bring up the **Flange Definition** window as shown in Figure 4.15.

7.3   Enter the information into the Flange Definition window as shown in Figure 4.15.

7.4   Select **OK**. Now you have a new flange. Reference the Specification Tree there is now a Flange.1 branch. The flange can be modified as any other entity in the Specification Tree.

Select this edge

Figure 4.15

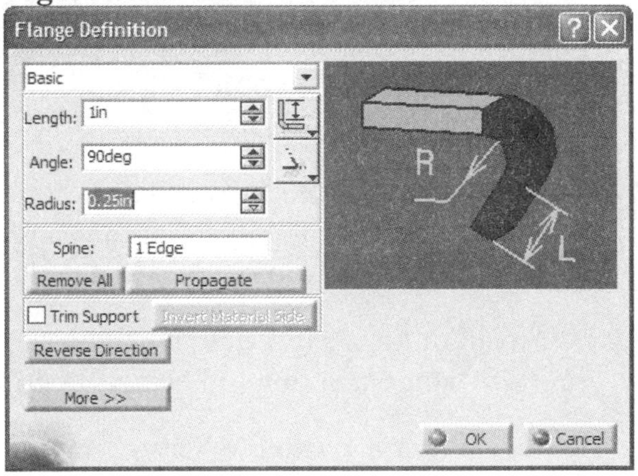

8. Creating Flanges Using the Wall on Edge Tool

The **Wall on Edge** tool allows you to create additional walls as the previous tools but uses different information to create the walls. To create a flange using the Wall on Edge tool, complete the following steps.

8.1   Select the edge as shown in Figure 4.16.

8.2   Select the **Wall on Edge**  tool. The direction of the flange will depend on the edge that is selected.

8.3 To change the direction, select the other edge. This will flip to the other side.

Figure 4.16

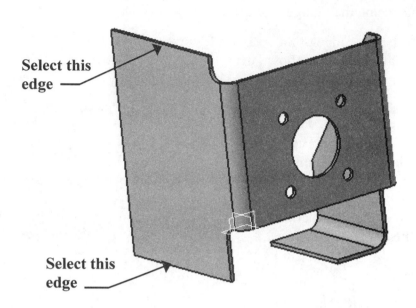

8.4 Adjusting toggles in the **Wall on Edge Definition** dialog box will also alter the position of the flange (reference Figure 4.17). If you click on the **Reverse Position** button, the flange will be rotated around the line that was originally selected.

8.5 Selecting the **Reverse Side** button or clicking on the red arrow will reverse the side of the line that the flange is on. Change these toggles back and forth a few times to see how the tools will alter the position of the flange.

8.6 For the **Reference** field, choose **Length**. This means that the length of the flange is going to be measured from the tangency point of the bend.

8.7 Enter a **1** into the **Value** field.

8.8 Leave the **Limits** values at **Zero** for now. They are used to adjust the width of the flange.

8.9 Notice that the **Clearance** value is grayed out. This value is referenced back to the radius value that was entered into the **Sheet Metal Parameters**.

8.10 The **Angle** of the bend will be **90deg**.

8.11 Check the **With Bend** toggle box. The bend will not show up and the flange will just be floating in space if you don't check this box.

8.12 Select the **OK** button to create the wall.

Figure 4.17

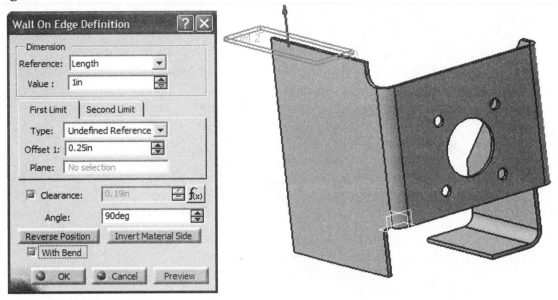

8.13 Repeat the previous steps to create the flange on the other edge as shown in Figure 4.16. Use the same values as shown in Figure 4.17.

9. Creating Corner Radii and Holes in the Sheet Metal Design Workbench

9.1 Us the **Corner** tool to create a **.5″** radius on each of the corners of **Flange.1**, **Wall on Edge.1** and **Wall on Edge.2**. Reference Figure 4.18.

9.2 Use the **Hole** tool to create a holes on **Wall on Edge.1** and **2** as shown in Figure 4.18. The **Hole** tool works almost identically to the **Hole** tool in the **Part Design** workbench.

9.3 Use the **Rectangular Pattern** tool to create the second hole in the flange.

9.4 Repeat the steps for creating the holes to place two holes in each of the other flanges, **.25″** from the edge; see Figure 4.18.

Figure 4.18

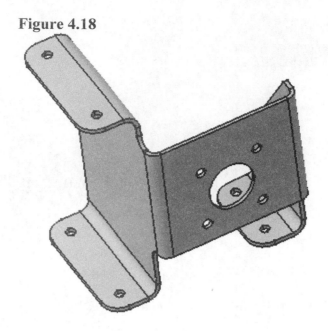

10. Flattening the Bracket Using the Fold/Unfold Tool

You can use the **Fold/Unfold** tool at any and every point of creation. It allows you to preview how the part is going to look in an unfolded condition. You need to check your part periodically in the unfolded condition to verify that the features that have been created are going to show up.

To flatten the part, select the **Fold/Unfold** tool. The part will automatically flatten (unfold). The flanges will all be flattened to the same plane as the main wall, i.e. the first wall that was created. See Figure 4.19.

Figure 4.19

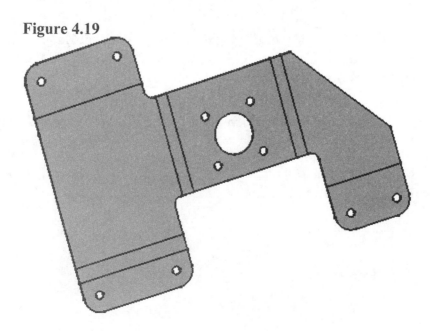

11. Saving the Unfolded Part as a DXF File and Opening It in the Drawing Workbench

If you need to export this flat pattern to another format for production purposes or to create a drawing you can create a **DXF** file. This enables the view of the flattened part to be opened up in the **Drawing** workbench. When the part is saved as a **DXF** file, it doesn't matter if the part is in the folded or unfolded condition; it will always show up flattened in the **DXF**. To create a DXF file complete the following steps.

11.1   Select the **Save as DXF** tool and save the part as **Lower Bracket.DXF**.

11.2   Now open the **Lower Bracket.DXF**. Go to **File** and then **Open**. Go to the folder where you saved your **DXF** file, select it, and click on **Open**.

11.3   This will open the flat pattern part in the **Drawing** workbench. Reference Figure 4.20.

Summary

You have now learned the basics of the **Generative Sheet Metal Design** workbench and should be able to use this new found knowledge as a basis for the exploration of additional sheet metal applications. There are many tools that have not been given attention in this current lesson edition that are useful for the rapid development of sheet metal parts. As you are working through the following exercises, try out some of the tools that were not covered. It would be beneficial to go through the various dialog boxes throughout the creation of the following parts and adjust the different settings to see how they affect the parts. To truly master this workbench and all its tools, you will need to invest a lot more time exploring additional tools.

Figure 4.20

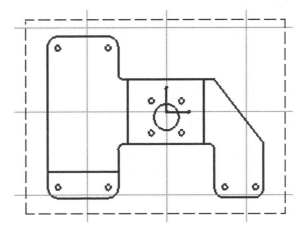

Review Questions

After completing this lesson, you should be able to answer the questions and explain the concepts listed below.

1. The tool that allows flanges to be created on a specified plane is:

   A. Extrusion
   B. Wall
   C. Sheet Metal Parameters
   D. Walls Recognition

2. No matter how parts are created, all features will show up and appear the same in the flattened view.

   A. True
   B. False

3. The number of options available within the wall creation field on the **Walls Recognition Definition** dialog box is what?

   A. 1
   B. 2
   C. 3
   D. 4

4. When creating a flange using the **Wall On Edge Definition** dialog box, the **With Bends** box must be checked or else the bend will not show up and the flange will just be floating out in space.

   A. True
   B. False

5. The **Sheet Metal Parameters** must be defined before you are able to use most of the tools found in the **Sheet Metal Design** and **Generative Sheet metal Design** workbenches.

   A. True
   B. False

6. Saving a part as a **DXF** file:

   A. Enables the view of the flattened part to be opened up in the **Drawing** workbench.
   B. Doesn't guarantee that the part will show up flattened.
   C. Allows the part to be in a folded or unfolded condition
   D. A and C
   E. All of the above

7. When the **Reverse Position** button in the **Wall On Edge Definition** dialog box is clicked:

   A. It will reverse the side of the line that the flange is on.
   B. The flange will be rotated around the line that was originally selected.
   C. The flange will be measured starting from the tangency point of the bend.
   D. A and B
   E. All of the above

8. There is not a **Hole-Creation** tool in the **Sheet Metal Design** workbench.

   A. True
   B. False

9. The four different tabs on the **Sheet Metal Parameters** dialog box are:

   A. Parameters, Bend Corner Relief, Thickness of the Material, and Default Bend Radius.
   B. Bend Extremities, Bend Corner Relief, Bend Radius, and Bend Allowance.
   C. Parameters, Bend Extremities, Bend Corner Relief, and Bend Allowance.
   D. Bend Corner Relief, Thickness of the Material, Bend Radius, and Bend Allowance.

10. When creating a bend using the **Bend tool**, the radius of the bend is defined at that time.

    A. True
    B. False

Practice Exercises

Now that your **Sheet Metal Design** tool box has some tools in it, put them to use on the following practice exercises.

1. This part should be straightforward. Save the part as **Lesson 4 Exercise 1.CATPart**. Don't worry so much about having all the dimensions exactly correct, but more about getting use to how and which tools are best to use for different situations.

    a. Create the following bracket as shown using the **Wall** and **Wall On Edge** tools.
    b. All angles are **90** deg.
    c. The holes are to be placed **.25"** from the edges.
    d. All bend radii are **.15"**.
    e. The material is **.075"** thick.

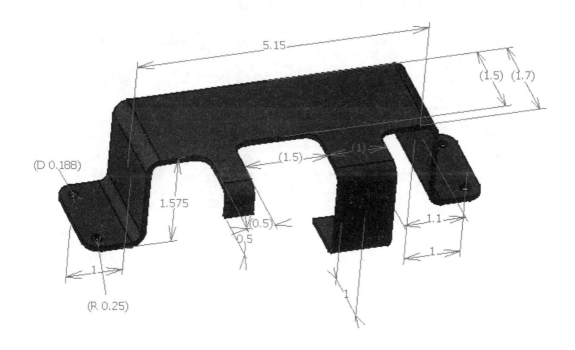

HINT: You must first establish your sheet metal parameters before you can start creating the walls.

2. This part should be straightforward. Save the part as **Lesson 4 Exercise 2.CATPart**. Don't worry so much about having all the dimensions exactly correct, but more about getting comfortable with how and which tools are best to use for different situations.

    a. Create the following bracket as shown using the **Wall** and **Wall on Edge** tools.

    b. The holes are to be placed **.25″** from the edges and have a diameter of **.125** inch.

    c. All bend radii are **.2″** and angles **90** degs unless otherwise specified.

    d. The material is **.1″** thick.

    e. Create the initial wall as a **4″ × 4″** as shown in the sketch below.

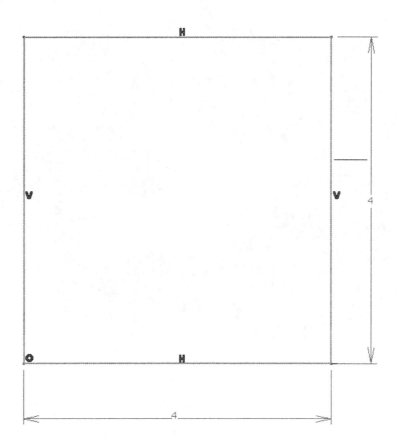

    f. The back side and the two inner-side flanges are to be created using the **Wall on Edge** tool. The back side flange has a bend angle of **70** degs and is **2.5″** long. The inner-side flanges are **1.5″** tall. To create these flanges use the limit function. The 1st limit is **0** and the 2nd limit is **1.5″** for both flanges.

g.   The top wall will be created using the **Flange** tool. The angle is **110** degs and the length is **3.237″**.

h.   The outer-side flanges that come down from the top wall are to be created using the **Flange** tool. They will have a radius of **.3″** and a length of **1.8″**. These two flanges will be **Relimited**, instead of the default **Basic** flange type. In order to use the relimited function you need to create two boundaries or limits. To do this, create a plane on each side of one of the inner-side flanges.

i.   Create the rest of the part as illustrated below.

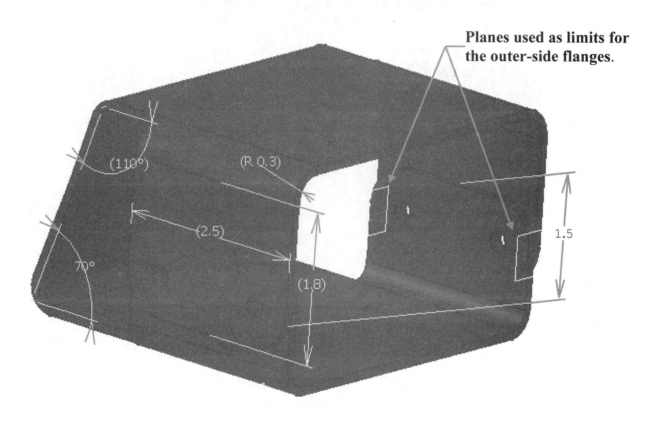

Planes used as limits for the outer-side flanges.

Lesson 5

Prismatic Machining

Introduction

In this lesson, you will go through each step of setting up and milling a prismatic part. Prismatic milling is the most common and least difficult type of machining that involves planar levels and boundaries. This lesson covers only a few of the many features available and is not necessarily the best or most efficient way to machine this part. Feel free to experiment with as many other methods as you would like.

Objectives

After completing this lesson, you should be able to do the following:

1. Set up a machining operation.

2. Apply several different types of machining operations to a solid.

3. Create and/or select required tools.

4. Apply tools to the machining operation.

5. Modify the machining operations.

6. Verify the machining operations.

7. Create a post process file.

Workbench Tools and Toolbars

The following section lists the tools and toolbars with a brief explanation. This lesson does not use all of the tools listed in the workbenches, nor does it show all of the toolbars available.

The <u>Manufacturing Program</u> Toolbar

TOOL ICON	TOOL NAME	TOOL DEFINITION
	Part Operation	Establish machine, axis, and visualization parameters for the operation.
	Manufacturing Program	Contains one or more manufacturing operations for the part operation.

The <u>Prismatic Operations</u> Toolbar

TOOL ICON	TOOL NAME	TOOL DEFINITION
Axial Machining Operations Toolbar		
	Drilling	Drill cycle, feed in, rapid out, and standard drill geometry.
	Spot Drilling	Same function as drill cycle, spotting tool geometry.
	Drilling Dwell Delay	Drill cycle with dwell.
	Drilling Deep Hole	Drill cycle for drilling with full retract between pecks.
	Drilling Break Chips	Drill cycle for drilling with partial retracts between pecks.
	Tapping	Tap cycle for right hand thread.

		Reverse Threading	Tap cycle for left hand thread.
		Thread without Tap Head	Thread with single point tool.
		Boring	Boring cycle, feed in and feed out.
		Boring and Chamfering	Bore with dwell at bottom, special tool.
		Boring Spindle Stop	Bore with stop at bottom for retract.
		Reaming	Reaming cycle, feed in and feed out.
		Counter Boring	Cycle, feed in, dwell at bottom, and feed out.
		Counter Sinking	Cycle, feed in, dwell and rapid out.
		Chamfering 2 Sides	Cycle, feed down distance, rapid thru, feed up distance, rapid out and special tooling.
		Back Boring	Cycle, stop spindle, rapid thru hole, start spindle, feed up distance, stop spindle, rapid out and special tooling.
		T-Slotting	Cycle, rapid to depth, transverse feed in, mill, transverse rapid out, rapid out and special tooling.
		Circular Milling	Cycle, mill out a circular area.
		Thread Milling	Mill a thread with special thread milling tool.
		Pocketing	Mill material from an irregular shaped closed or open pocket with or without islands.
		Facing	Mill off the flat surface or face of the part.
		Profile Contouring	Mill by defining a contour and depth for a path.
		Curve Following	Insert a curve following operation in the program.
		Groove Milling	Insert a groove milling operation in the program.

| | Point to Point | Mill by defining a series of endpoints for the path. |
| | Prismatic Roughing | Allows you to quickly rough machine a part in a single operation. |

The <u>Auxiliary Operations</u> Toolbar

TOOL ICON	TOOL NAME	TOOL DEFINITION
Tool Change Toolbar		
	Drill Tool Change	Define a tool change to this type of tool: drill.
	Tap Tool Change	Define a tool change to this type of tool: tap.
	Thread Mill Tool Change	Define a tool change to this type of tool: thread mill.
	Countersink Tool Change	Define a tool change to this type of tool: countersink.
	Reamer Tool Change	Define a tool change to this type of tool: reamer.
	Spot Drill Tool Change	Define a tool change to this type of tool: spot drill.
	Center Drill Tool Change	Define a tool change to this type of tool: center drill.
	Multi-Diameter Drill Tool Change	Define a tool change to this type of tool: step drill.
	Boring and Chamfering Tool Change	Define a tool change to this type of tool: bore & chamfer.
	Two Sides Chamfering Tool Change	Define a tool change to this type of tool: two sided chamfer.
	Boring Bar Tool Change	Define a tool change to this type of tool: boring bar.

	Counterbore Mill Tool Change	Define a tool change to this type of tool: counterbore tool or spot face.
	End Mill Tool Change	Define a tool change to this type of tool: end mill.
	Face Mill Tool Change	Define a tool change to this type of tool: face mill.
	Conical Mill Tool Change	Define a tool change to this type of tool: conical mill.
	T-Slotter Tool Change	Define a tool change to this type of tool: T-slot cutter.
	Machine Rotation	Causes rotation of a rotary table or indexer.
	Machining Axis Change	Define a new origin for a part operation.
	Post-Processor Instruction	Add an instruction directly to the post processor, machine specific.

Transformation Management Toolbar

	COPY Operator Instruction	Apply a COPY Operator to operations in the program.
	TRACUT Operator Instruction	Apply a TRACUT Operator to operations in the program.
	Copy Transformation Instruction	Transform an operation to a different location.
	Opposite Hand Machining Options	Define the complete manufacturing program of a symmetrical work piece.

The <u>NC Output Management</u> Toolbar

TOOL ICON	TOOL NAME	TOOL DEFINITION
	Tool Path Replay	Display a graphic representation of the tool path.
NC Output Generations Toolbar		
	Generate NC Code in Batch Mode	Post process using selectable processors and parameters.
	Generate NC Code Interactively	Post process to an apt file only.
	Manage Batch Queue	Sets up a queue list for multiple post processing.
	Generate Documentation	Create program documentation "setup sheet."
	Screen Capture	Capture a portion of the screen graphic to be saved to a JPEG file.

The <u>Machining Features</u> Toolbar

TOOL ICON	TOOL NAME	TOOL DEFINITION
Pattern MAS Container Toolbar		
	Machining Pattern	Define a series of points as a pattern.
	Machining Axis System	Define a new machining axis system.

The <u>Machining Process</u> Toolbar

TOOL ICON	TOOL NAME	TOOL DEFINITION
	Machining Process View	List of current machining processes.
	Machining Process	Define a machining process.

1. Creating the Models Required for this Lesson

For this lesson you will need to create two simple models. The first one is the part to be machined and the second one is the raw material or "stock" part.

   1.1 Create the Housing1.CATPart as shown in Figure 5.1. Save the part as
       Housiung1.CATPart.   Make a note where the document is saved.

Figure 5.1

Housing1

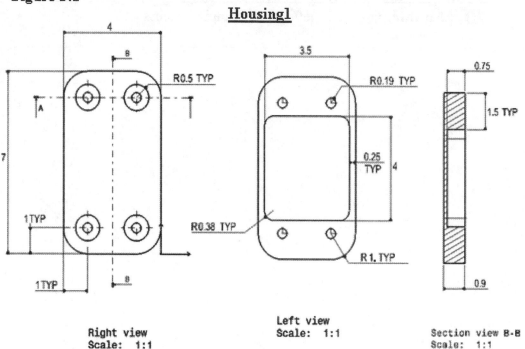

Right view
Scale: 1:1

Left view
Scale: 1:1

Section view B-B
Scale: 1:1

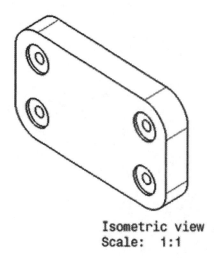

Isometric view
Scale: 1:1

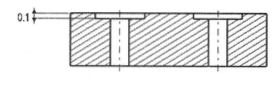

Section view A-A
Scale: 2:1

1.2 Create the Stock1.CATPart as shown in Figure 5.2. Save the part as Stock1.CATPart. Make a note where the document is saved. The **Stock1.CATPart** is a rectangular block that encompasses the volume of the part, and a little excess if desired (4.25 × 7.25). It can be included in the **Housing1.CATPart** as a second body. Set your **Stock** pad up as shown in Figure 5.2 so you have excess material on the top and bottom of the part to be milled.

Figure 5.2

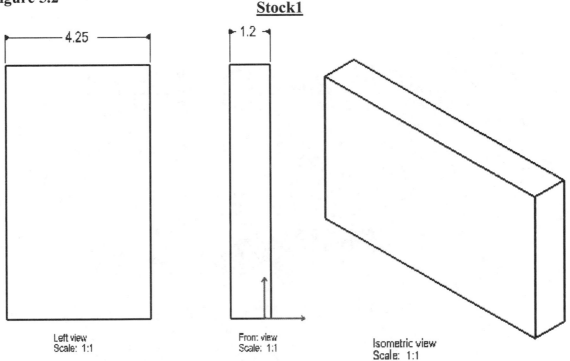

Stock1

1.3 Open the **Product Structure** workbench.

1.4 Insert both the **Housing1** and **Stock1** parts by select the **Existing Component** tool. Remember to select the **Product1** in the **Specification Tree** so CATIA V5 will know where the component is going to be inserted. The **File Selection** window will appear.

1.5 Hold the <CTL> key down, while selecting the **Housing1** and **Stock1** parts.

1.6 Select the **OK** button. This will insert the **Housing1** and **Stock1** parts into the **Product1** document.

1.7 Right click on **Product1** in the **Specification Tree** this will bring up a pop up window.

1.8 Select the **Properties** option.

1.9 Type "**Housing.1**" into the **Part Number** box to rename it.

1.10 Save the document.

1.11 Close the product window; this will give you a blank CATIA V5 screen.

2. Getting Started with the NC Processing

2.1   Select **Start**, **Machining**, and **Prismatic Machining** as shown in Figure 5.3.

Figure 5.3

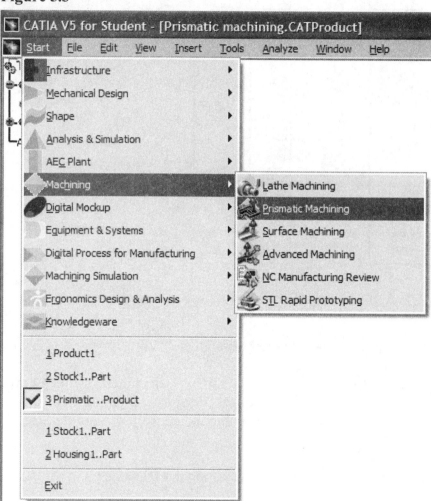

3. Set Defaults to Inch Mode

This is a critical step because there are a lot of parameters to define in creating tool paths. If you have mixed or incorrect units you could easily scrap parts or worse yet damage the milling machine and tools. To set the units complete the following steps.

3.1   Go to **Tools, Options, Parameters And Measures**, and then the **Units** tab.

3.2   Set **Length** to **Inch(in)**.

3.3   Set **Linear feed rate** to **Inch per minute(in-mn)**.

3.4   Set **Angular feedrate** to
       Inch per turn(in_turn).

3.5   Set **Linear spindle speed** to **Foot per minute(ft_mn)**.

3.6   Select **OK** to complete setting the units.

4. Load the Product Assembly for NC

4.1   Double click on **Part Operation.1** branch of the Specification Tree as
       shown in Figure 5.4. This will bring up the **Part Operation** window as
       shown in 5.5.

Figure 5.5

Figure 5.4

**Double
click here**

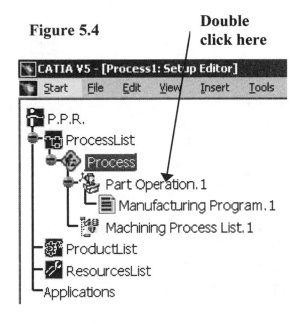

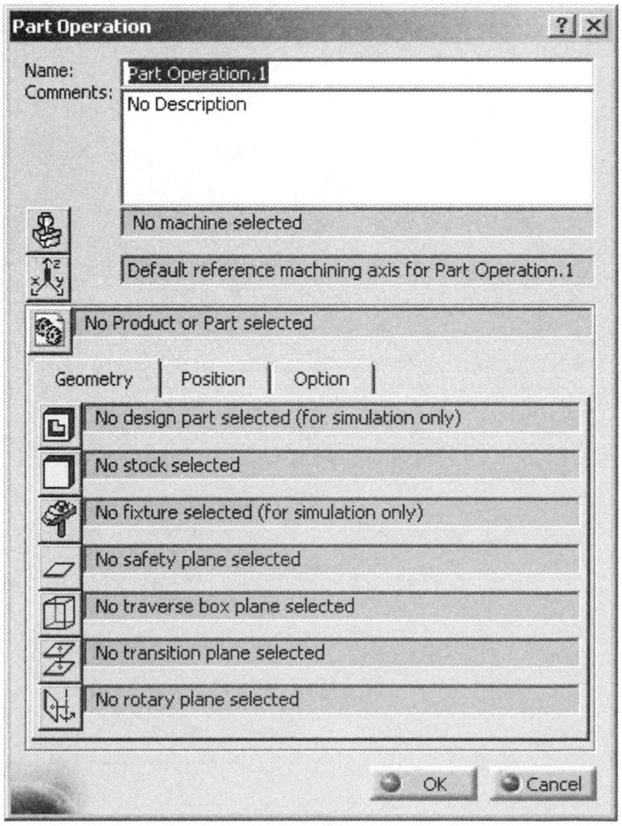

4.2   Rename Operation.1 to something that is more descriptive and means more to you. Notice that you also have a **Comments** box to place any comments and/or notes in. This is a great communication tool.

4.3   Select the **Product or Part** 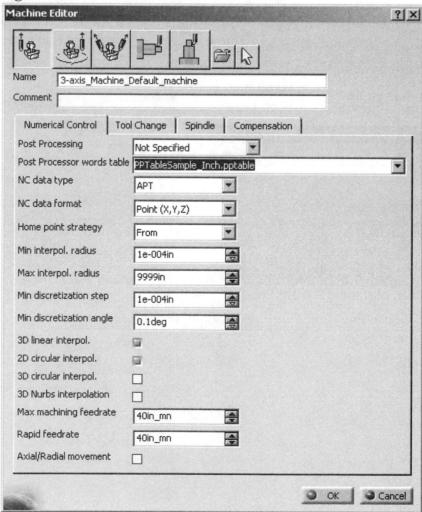 tool. This will bring up the **File Selection** window. This allows you to select NC product that was created earlier (if one exists). Select **Housing1.CATProduct**; this is the Product (assembly) you created and saved in the previous steps.

4.4   Select the **Open** button to load the product. The parts will appear on the screen and in the **Specification Tree**.

5. Setting the Machine Parameters

5.1   Select the **Machine Editor** tool (one of the first tools in the **Part Operation** window). This will bring up the **Machine Editor** window as shown in Figure 5.6.

Figure 5.6

5.2   You can rename the machine to something that you have in your shop if desired.

5.3   Select the arrow in the **Post Processor words table** list box and select **PTableSample_Inch.pptable**. This sets your posting to inch mode. These tables can be modified to fit specific machines exactly but will not be covered in this lesson.

5.4   Open the list box for **NC data type**: and select **APT**.

5.5   **Interpol radius** is the min and max radius your machine can cut.

5.6   **Discretization** values describe the machine resolution or the smallest step increment it can make.

5.7   Under the **Tool Change** tab, you can specify a standard tool load that you might have set up already in the machine and whether or not your machine can support radius compensation.

5.8   Under the **Spindle** tab specify a tool change point if you manually change tools.

5.9   The **Orientation** values will not change unless your spindle is not in line with the "**Z**" axis.

5.10   Select the **OK** button to close the window.

6. Set Up a Machining Axis

6.1   The **Reference machining axis system** tool allows you to relocate and rename the axis system if you desire.

6.2   Select the tool to open the **Default reference machining axis for Part Operation.1** dialog box. Select the **red dot** at the center of the axis system as shown in Figure 5.7. The window will close allowing you to select a point on the part to place the axis.

6.3   Select the corner of the stock as shown. The new axis system will have the same alignment as the current one. The sensitive areas will turn green to indicate that the axis system is defined as shown in Figure 5.8. You can also rename the axis if needed.

6.4   If you need to reverse any of the elements, you simply select one of the **black arrow** sensitive icons, and then select a corresponding geometry element.

6.5   Select the **OK** button to complete this step.

Figure 5.7

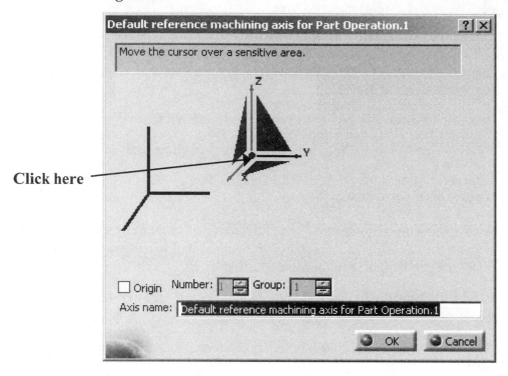

Click here

Figure 5.8

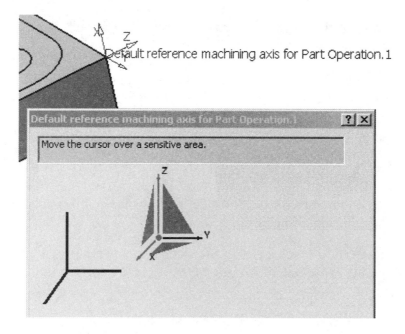

7. Set the Visualization Elements and Other Parameters

7.1 In the geometry tab (of the Part Operation window), select the 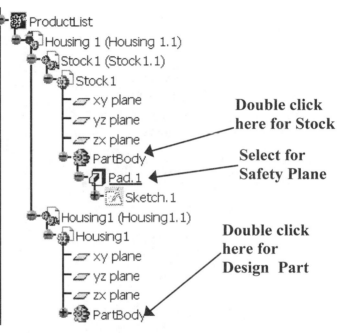 **Design part for simulation** tool. The window will close to allow you to select the design part from the screen. The design part is sharing the same space as the **Housing1** part so you can not see the **Housing1** through the **Stock1** part. Select the **Housing1** from the **PartBody** branch of the **Specification Tree**.

7.2 Repeat the process for the **Stock**, except select the **Stock1** part. Reference Figure 5.8.

7.3 Select the **Safety Plane** tool. The window will disappear and the prompt zone will prompt you to select a "...**planar face or point to define the safty plane**". Select **Pad.1** of the **Stock** as shown in Figure 5.10. Notice that a **Safety Plane** will be created.

Figure 5.9

7.4 Right click on the newly created **Safety Plane** and select **Offset** from the pop-up as shown in Figure 5.10.

7.5 Enter an offset of **1″**. You now have a Safety Plane one inch above the surface of the stock.

7.6 In the Part Operation window select the **Position** tab. You can enter a tool change point for this program if you want to override the machine default. You will not use the center setup in this lesson.

Figure 5.10

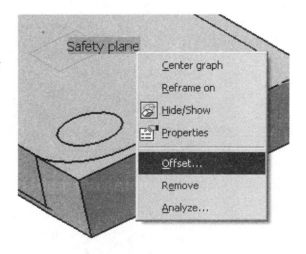

7.7   The **Option** tab allows you to set up optional code output parameters.

7.8   Select the **OK** button to close the **Part Operation** window.

8. Defining the Geometry

8.1   Select the **Manufacturing Program.1** branch of the **Specification Tree** to make it active. Reference Figure 5.11.

Figure 5.11

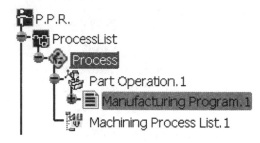

8.2   Select the 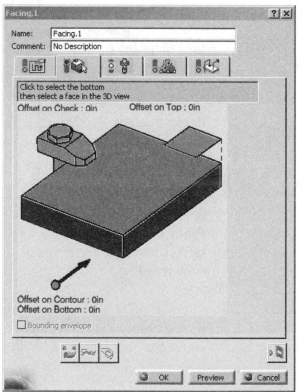 **Facing** tool on the **Machining Operations** toolbar. This will bring up the **Facing.1** window as shown in Figure 5.12. Selecting this tool also created two new items to the **Specification Tree.** A default tool was added under **Manufacturing Program.1** branch. A facing operation was added also.

Figure 5.12

8.3   The **Facing.1** window has five tabs as shown in Figure 5.12. Each tab contains different machining parameters. Each tab has a **Status Indicator** . This tool indicates how complete the parameters are set for each tab. A **red light** indicates that more information is required before the process is complete. A **yellow light** indicates that the operation is not verified, and a **green light** indicates that all required data is present for processing.

8.4   You can modify the name of the operation if you like.

8.5   Notice that the data entry tab is selected by default because the required data to complete the operation is missing. You can pre-select data to be processed but that will be covered later

8.6   As you pass the mouse pointer over the graphic in the window areas of the graphic will change color indicating that they can be selected.   In addition, a hint will appear in the message box just below the tabs.

8.7   Select the top surface of the graphic. The message box located above the graphic will prompt you to "**Click to select the bottom, then select a face in the 3D view**". The window will close to allow you to select the corresponding face on the part.

8.8   Select the top surface of the part. In order to select the part surfaces through the stock, place the mouse cursor over the part and press the **Up Arrow** key on your keyboard. A **Selector** tool will appear which allows you to select entities beneath the surface. The selector has a center circle and four arrow heads on it as shown in Figure 5.13. Clicking repeatedly on the top arrow will cycle through the entity selections. When the one you want becomes highlighted, click on the center of the circle to accept it. An alternate method would be to 🖼 **Hide/Show** the stock temporarily.

Figure 5.13

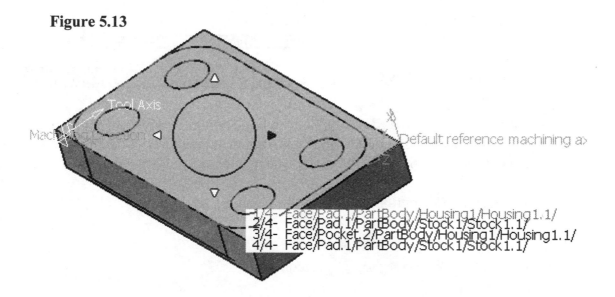

8.9   Selecting the face will bring the **Facing.1** window back up. Notice now the graphic and **Status Indicator** are now green. This means that there is enough information for this tab.

8.10 Your current selection will face off the surface, only you will need to face the entire top of the part. To accomplish this you will need to set up a border. Right click on the border of the **graphic** in the **Facing.1** window as shown in Figure 5.14. A **Context** window will open allowing you to choose some different ways of selecting the boundary. Select **By Boundary of Faces**. The window will close momentarily.

Figure 5.14   ┌─ **Right click here**

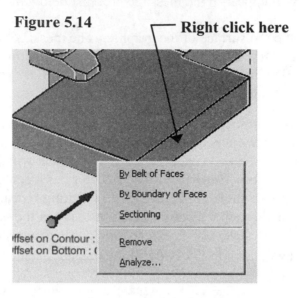

8.11 Notice the **Edge Selection** toolbar appears shown in Figure 5.15. This toolbar comes up differently for the different selection options.

Figure 5.15

8.12 Select the top face of the **Stock** and the top border will highlight. In addition, the choices in the **Face Selection** toolbar will become active. Select the **Preview the Contour** tool to see the projection of the face to the cutting surface.

8.13 Select the **OK** button to return to the **Facing.1** window.

8.14 Click on the **Top** ▭ tool.

8.15 Select the top of the **Stock** to establish the top surface.

8.16 Notice the other sensitive areas in the **Facing.1** window. You can set offset values for all of your faces and pick start and end points. You can also pick check surfaces or objects. Picking the black arrow allows you to change the machining direction. You will not need any of these for your project yet.

9. Setting Up the Strategy Tab

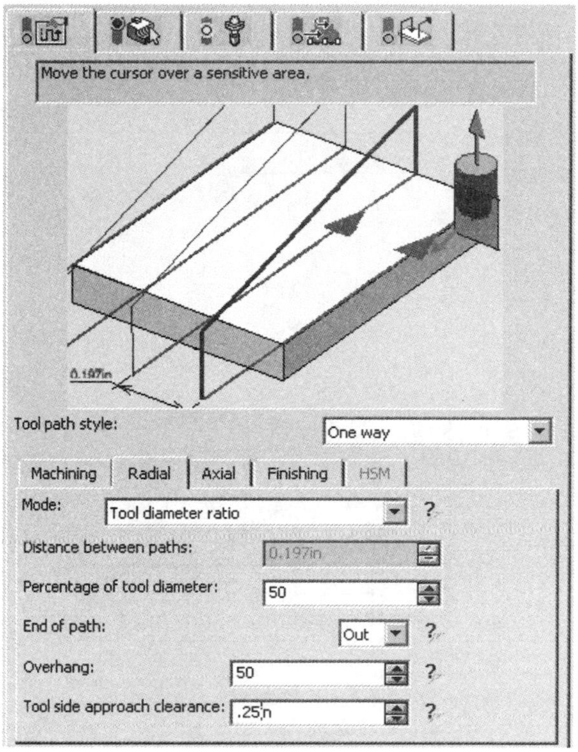

9.1 The first tab in the row is the ⊟ **Strategy** tab. Here you can set up the type of cut path to use and some of the path characteristics. The graphic just below the message box is a representation of the tool path style you chose from the list box below it.

9.2 Select on the **Tool path style** list box arrow.

9.3 Select **One way**. Notice that the graphic changes to reflect the new path style reference Figure 5.16.

9.4 In the **Radial** tab, beneath the **Tool path style**, select **Out** in the **End of path** list box and type in **.25** in the **Tool side approach clearance** roll box. Reference Figure 5.16.

Figure 5.16

10. Setting Up the Tool

10.1 The third tab in the **Facing.1** window is the ⊟ **Tool Selection** tab. This is where you can select and/or define the tool you want to use. The tool defaults to a standard endmill, but you will want a face mill instead.

10.2 Just below the row of tabs is a row of possible tool types. Select the **Face Mill** 🔲 tool.

10.3 The graphic will change to the selected tool type and allow you to modify the dimensions of the tool. Notice that the dimensions of the tool graphic are **sensitive areas** that change color as the mouse pointer passes over them. Double click on the sensitive area to open an **Edit Parameter** box. Enter a new value and the graphic will update. Change the values to match those shown in Figure 5.17 and 5.18.

Figure 5.17

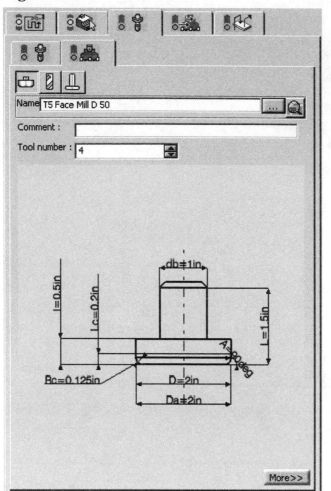

Figure 5.18

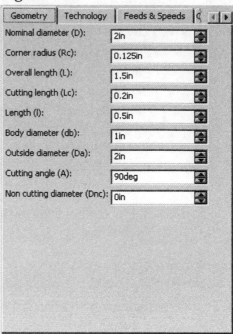

10.4   You can change the name, add a comment, and assign a tool number as needed. The ⟨...⟩ icon allows you to re-select an old tool, and the ⟨🔍⟩ icon allows you to select one from a library file.

10.5   Selecting the ⟨More>>⟩ tab expands the window allowing you to see additional parameters. Leave these as they and click the ⟨<<Less⟩ button to reduce the window back again. See Figure 5.17 and 5.18.

11. Setting Feeds and Speeds

11.1   The fourth tab 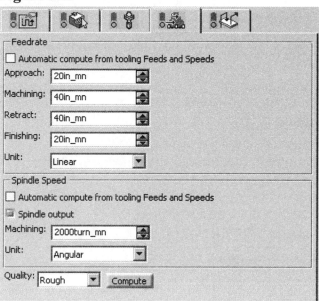 allows you to set the feeds and speeds of the cutter. Right clicking on the roll boxes will open a menu of parameters you can use to adjust the defaults. Refer to the Figure 5.19 for values to enter.

Figure 5.19

12. Setting Up Macros

CATIA uses macros, which are like small sub-routines, to define entry and exit moves, clearance plane moves, and just about any kind of motion that is supplemental to the basic tool path. You can even use them to define drill cycles and control post processor commands. The macros in this lesson will be relatively simple.

12.1   In the following steps, you will set up an **Approach** macro, a **Retract** macro and a **Return** macro. The **Return** macro is necessary when using a "one way" strategy.

12.2   Select the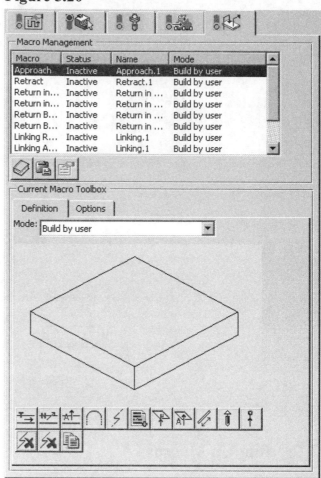
        Macro Definition tab
        as shown in Figure
        5.20.

12.3   Select the **Approach**
        macro in the **Macro
        Management** box as
        shown in Figure 5.20.

12.4   The row of tools at the
        bottom of the tab
        allows you to choose
        from a number of
        different motions.
        These motions can be
        "stacked up" as
        needed.

12.5   Select the
        Remove all motions
        tool to clear the graphic
        of any existing
        motions. This will
        give you a "clean
        slate."

12.6   Select the **Add
        Axial motion up to a
        plane** tool. The graphic
        will change to display a
        visual description of the
        motion to be added as
        seen in Figure 5.21.

12.7   If you do not select a
        plane to approach from,
        the default clearance
        plane you selected earlier
        will be used. For this
        lesson the default will
        suffice.

Figure 5.20

Figure 5.21

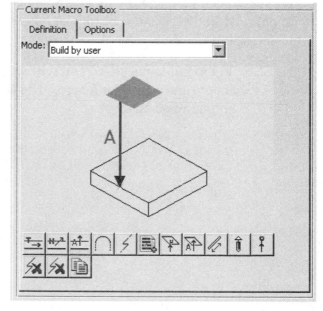

12.8 Right click on the **Vertical purple yellow line** in the graphic. This will bring up a **Contextual** menu allowing you to select a feed rate as shown in Figure 5.22.

Figure 5.22

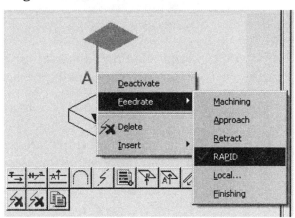

12.9 Select the **Feedrate**, then select **RAPID** from the drop down window. Notice that **the purple yellow line** turned **red** to indicate **Rapid**.

12.10 Select the **Copy approach Macro on all approach motions of the other macros** tool. This will keep all of your macro settings for the rest of the operation,

12.11 Repeat the above steps for the **Retract** macro found in the **Macro Management** box.

12.12 Repeat these steps again for the **Return in a Level Retract** and **Return in a Level Approach** macros.

13. Replaying the Operation

13.1 At the bottom of the **Facing.1** window there is a **Tool Path Replay** tool. This allows you to process and view the operation you just created.

13.2 Select the tool. This will bring up a control box as shown in Figure 5.23.

Figure 5.23

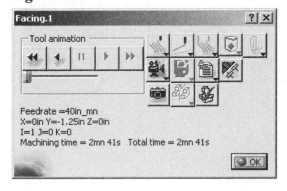

Figure 5.24

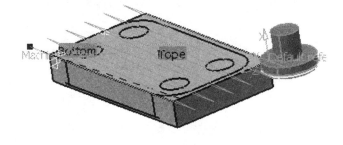

13.3   To replay the path, press the ◀◀ icon, then press the ▶ icon located in the **Tool Animation** frame.

13.4   Notice that the lower left part of the window displays a continuous status report as the tool path progresses.

Figure 5.25

13.5   Off to the right are more tools for setting various display modes (reference Figure 5.25). Some tools have **Drop down** arrows indicating that there are more options under each tool. Take a few minutes to explore them.

13.6   Select the 🎥 **Video** tool to start the display of solid verification. The **Zip Mill** window opens up with the **Stock** that you selected earlier. If you did not specify any stock, this will default to a stock size that roughly covers the machining area. The same control window as before is present to control the display.

Figure 5.26

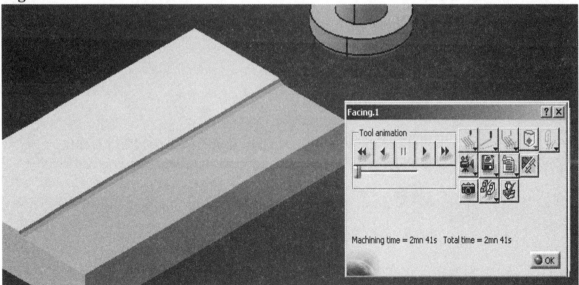

13.7   You can exit the **Zip Mill** window by closing it with the ⊠ in the upper right corner. This will return you to the preview screen, or you can select ● OK in the control box to return to the **Facing.1** window.

13.8   Select ● OK in the **Facing.1** window to complete the facing operation.

14. Spot Drilling the Holes

14.1   The next operation will be to spot drill the four holes in the top of the part.

14.2   You do not really need to see the stock anymore so now is a good time to put it into **Hide/Show**. This will make entity selection a bit easier.

Figure 5.27

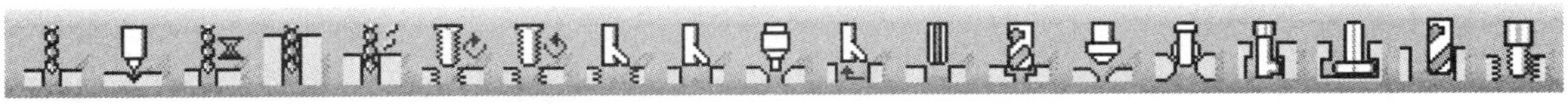

14.3   Notice that the  ⊣⊢ **Drilling** tool has a small arrow in it. Select the arrow to see the different drilling choices that are available. Reference Figure 5.27). Place the mouse pointer over each tool for a brief description. Select the **Spot Drilling** tool. Select on **Manufacturing Program.1** in the **Specification Tree** to open the **Spot Drilling.1** window.

14.4   In the graphic area select the **Red sensitive** area as shown in Figure 5.28.

14.5   Select the four holes to spot drill. The holes can be selected by selecting on the edges of the holes.

Figure 5.28

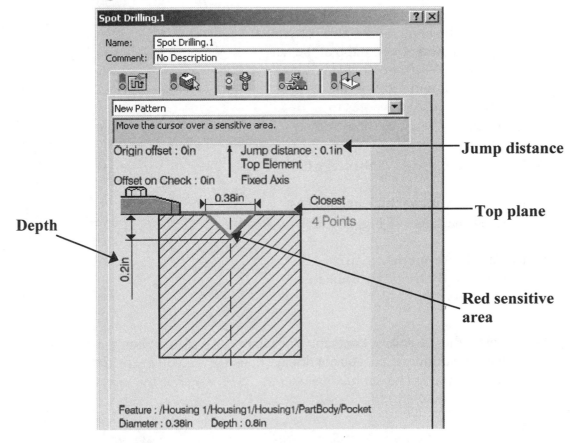

14.6   Double click in a blank area to return to the definition window. The **Status indicator** is green and the **add position** indicator shows **4 Points** selected. Notice that the hole's diameter is automatically set. You can override this value if needed.

14.7   Double click on the **Depth** sensitive area labeled in Figure 5.28.

14.8   Enter a value of **.2**.

14.9   Double click on the **Jump distance** sensitive area and enter a value of **.1**. A value entered here will override any default values established elsewhere.

Figure 5.29

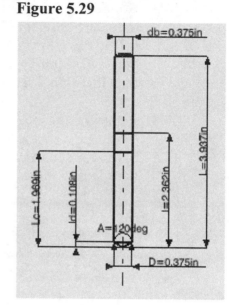

14.10   Select the **Top Plane** sensitive area.

14.11   Select the top of the part.

14.12   Select the **OK** button in the **Face Selection** toolbar.

14.13   If the directional arrows on the part do not point up, you will need to reverse them with the **Black arrow** sensitive tool.

14.14   Notice the name of the hole pattern **Spot Drilling.1** at the top of the tab window. You can rename it if you like. You will recall it later when you drill the holes to depth.

Figure 5.30

14.15   Select the ⬛ Strategy tab.

14.16   Set the **Approach clearance (A)** to **.3″** as shown in Figure 5.30.

14.17   The **Depth mode** has two choices: **By tip** or **By diameter**; select **By tip**.

Approach clearance (A) :	0.3in
Depth mode :	By tip (Dt)
Plunge mode :	None
Dwell mode :	None
First compensation :	1
Automatic ROTABL :	☐
Output CYCLE syntax :	☐

14.18   Select the ⬛ **Tool** tab. The tab opens with a default tool that fits the type of operation you are doing. It also gives you the next sequential tool number. The default diameter of **.591″** which is too big. Change it to **.375″** as shown in Figure 5.29.

14.19 Change the **Shank** dia. to **.375″**.

Figure 5.31

14.20 Select the 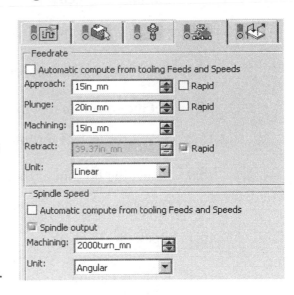 **Feeds** tab and set the values as shown in Figure 5.31.

14.21 Select the **Macro** tab and set up the **Approach** and **Retract** macros to the default plane. This is the same procedure used on the previous step.

14.22 **Replay** the path. If the tool path is acceptable select the **OK** button to accept the path.

15. Drilling the Holes to Size

In the previous step you set up a **hole pattern** for spot drilling. Now you will recall the same pattern and apply another operation. To do this complete the following steps.

15.1 Select the arrow in the drilling tool.

Figure 5.32

15.2 Select the **Drilling Deep Hole** tool.

15.3 Double click on **Spot Drilling.1** in the **Specification Tree**. The **Drilling Deep Hol.1** window for the **Deep Hole** cycle will open. At the top of the **Geometry** tab is a drop down list containing previously defined patterns. Select the down arrow to open the list. Select the one used in the spot drill operation (**Machining Pattern.1**). A **copy** of that pattern will be inserted into the operation. You still need to set the various parameters in the geometry tab.

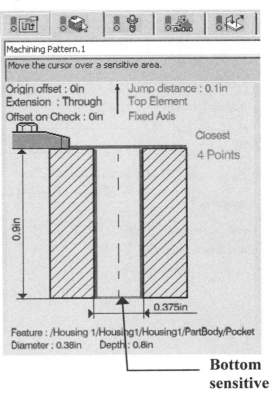

15.4   Notice that the diameter is retrieved from the model. You are still able to modify it if needed.

15.5   Set a **Depth** as before.

15.6   Select the **Extension** sensitive tool.

15.7   Set the selection to **Through**.

15.8   Select the **Select bottom** sensitive tool.

15.9   Select the bottom of the part as shown in Figure 5.32.

15.10 In the strategy tab, set the values as shown in Figure 5.33.

15.11 Open the **Tool** tab and select the **Drill** tool.

15.12 Edit the parameters to those of a **3/8″** drill.

15.13 In the **Feeds** tab, set the values as shown in Figure 5.34.

15.14 Set up the **Approach** and **Retract** macros to the default plane (same as before).

15.15 **Replay** the path. If it is acceptable, select the **OK** button to complete.

Figure 5.33   **Figure 5.34**

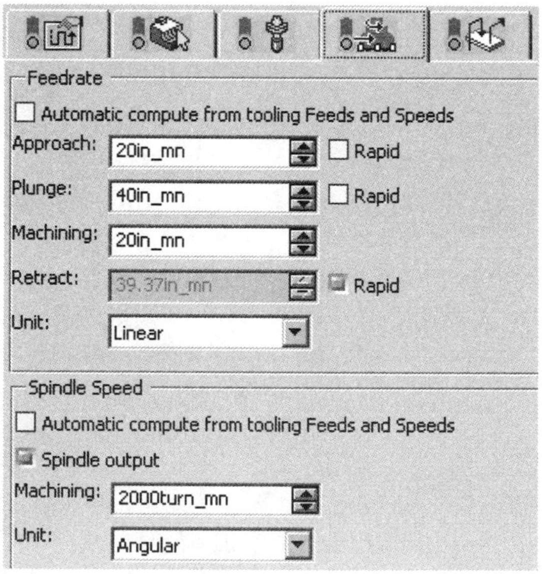

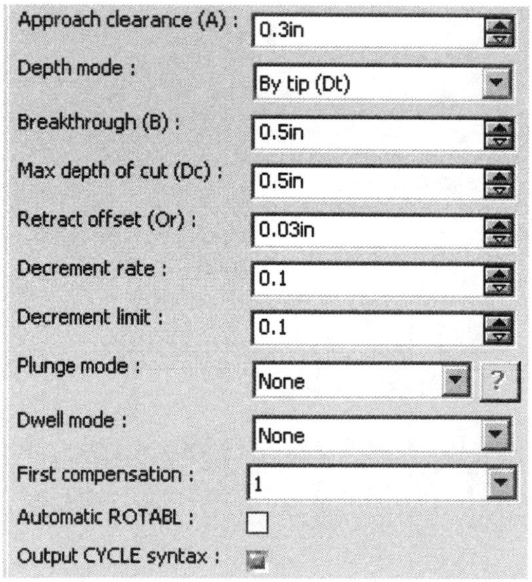 Approach clearance (A) :	0.3in
Depth mode :	By tip (Dt)
Breakthrough (B) :	0.5in
Max depth of cut (Dc) :	0.5in
Retract offset (Or) :	0.03in
Decrement rate :	0.1
Decrement limit :	0.1
Plunge mode :	None
Dwell mode :	None
First compensation :	1
Automatic ROTABL :	☐
Output CYCLE syntax :	☑

Feedrate
☐ Automatic compute from tooling Feeds and Speeds
Approach: 20in_mn   ☐ Rapid
Plunge: 40in_mn   ☐ Rapid
Machining: 20in_mn
Retract: 39.37in_mn   ☐ Rapid
Unit: Linear

Spindle Speed
☐ Automatic compute from tooling Feeds and Speeds
☑ Spindle output
Machining: 2000turn_mn
Unit: Angular

16. Milling the Counterbores

The next step is to mill the counter bores using a canned cycle. To do this complete the following steps.

16.1 Expand the ⊥ **Drilling** tool.

16.2 Select the **Circular Milling** tool from the list.

16.3 Even though the pattern is the same as the holes it is easiest to re-select the pattern. This time select on the top edge of the counter bores. This will allow the correct default dimensions to be filled in.

16.4 Fill in the remaining data as shown in Figure 5.35, including the top and bottom surfaces.

Figure 5.35

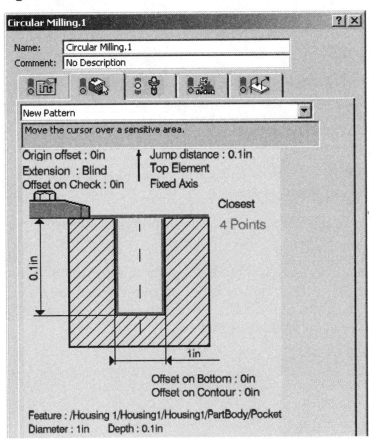

16.5 There are quite a few parameters in the **Strategy** tab but most of them will be **OK** as defaults. Set the values as shown in Figure 5.36 and continue on to the **Tool** tab.

Figure 5.36

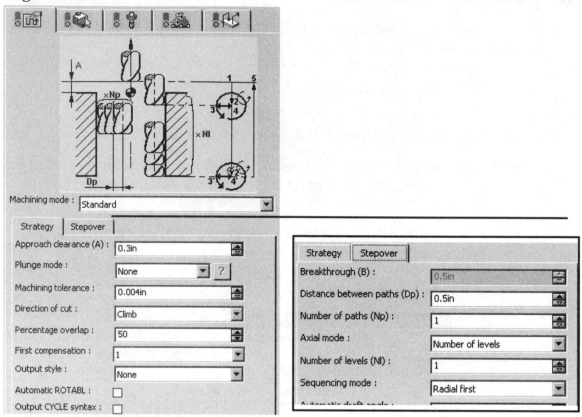

16.6   Select the **Tool** tab.

16.7   Modify the tool name and the values to give you a ½" standard end mill with no corner radius.

16.8   Select the **Feeds** tab and enter appropriate values for the tool.

16.9   The **Macro** tab is a bit different for this operation. Most of the macros are turned on as defaults with an arc entrance and exit. You will notice that all of the areas of the paths are sensitive icons and can be modified as needed. Accept the defaults as they are.

16.10 The macros in this operation will automatically provide a smooth transition into and out of the cut path. Replaying the path should produce results similar to the example in Figure 5.37.

Figure 5.37

16.11 Press **OK** to accept the path and save the operation.

17. Mill the Opposite Side of the Part

Now that you have successfully completed the first side of the part, roll the part image over on the screen to get ready to do the bottom of the part. The following steps will take you through milling the O.D. of the part and the pocket. Although clamping hardware is not included in the model, assume that four screws in the previously drilled holes are holding down the part. Retrieve the **Stock** model from **Hide/Show** since you will need it for your new **Machining Axis System**.

17.1 Select the ▨ **Part Operation** tool in the **Manufacturing Program** toolbar.

17.2 Select the **Part Operation.1** in the **Specification Tree**. A second operation will appear under **Part Operation.1** branch.

17.3 Double click on **Part Operation.2** in the **Specification Tree**. The **Part Operation** window will open as before. Set up all of the parameters as before including the **Machining Axis System**.

17.4 Select the corner of the part as shown in Figure 5.38 for placement of the axis. The axis will have the same orientation as the current axis, but you will need to flip it over for this operation. After the **Axis** dialog box returns, click on the "**X**" axis sensitive graphic. This will open up the context box. Click the **Reverse Direction** check box to flip the axis system over. Be sure to fill in the **Design for simulation part**, **Stock** and **Safety Plane** details similar to what you did in the previous part operation.

17.5 Click **OK** to accept the operation parameters.

Figure 5.38

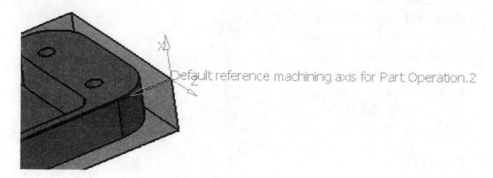

18. Milling the O.D.

In this step you will mill the O.D. of the part. To complete this operation complete the following steps.

18.1   Since you no longer need to see the **Stock** hide it using the **Hide/Show** 🖻 tool.

18.2   Select the **Manufacturing Program** 📄 tool.

18.3   Select the **Part Operation.2** branch from the **Specification Tree**. This will create the next program operation.

18.4   Make sure that **Part Operation.2** is highlighted then select the 🖉 **Profile Contouring** operation button in the **Prismatic Operations** toolbar. This will bring up the Profile Contouring.1 window as shown in Figure 5.39.

Figure 5.39

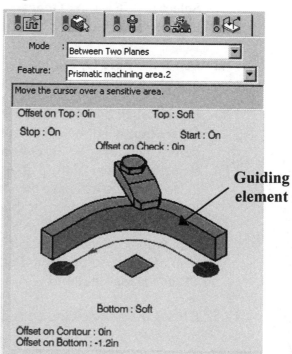

18.5   Select the little down arrow on the right side of the Mode: box. Reference Figure 5.39. This will display all the options under the Mode box. Select the **Between two planes** option.

18.6 Select the **Bottom** sensitive option in the graphic window. This toggles back and forth between a soft and hard bottom.

18.7 Double click on the **Offset on Bottom** in the bottom of the graphic window. Enter a value of **-1.2″**.

18.8 Select the **Select the Bottom** in the graphic area. You will now be prompted to select the bottom of the part. Select the bottom of the part.

18.9 To define all the needed parameters select the **Guiding Element** in the graphic area. For this prompt select an upper edge of the part. The **Edge Selection** toolbar will appear as seen in Figure 5.40. Rather than selecting each edge individually select the **Navigate on Belt of Edges** tool. This tool will allow you to select all the edges around the part automatically.

Figure 5.40

18.10 Be sure the ⬛Guide **Arrow** points to the outside of the part. If it doesn't select on the arrow to change directions.

18.11 Select the **OK** ⬤ OK button to accept.

18.12 Right click on the **Start** and **Stop** buttons to turn both of them **On**.

18.13 This completes the 🔲 **Geometry** tab. Select the 🔲 **Strategy** tab.

18.14 Set up the operation to take two passes on the face to get a smooth finish. Set the **Tool path style** to **One way**.

18.15 Under the **Stepover** tab set the **Number of paths** and **Number of levels** both to **1**.

18.16 Under the **Finishing** tab, set the **Mode** to **Side finish last level** and set the **Side finish thickness** to **.02**.

18.17 Select the 🔲 **Tool** tab.

18.18 Select the  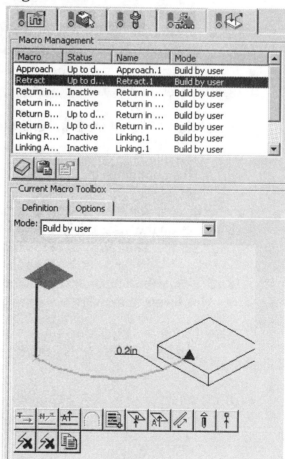 **End Mill** tool. Set the cutter up to be a **1″** flat end mill as seen in Figure 5.41.

Figure 5.41

18.19 Select the  **Feeds** tab. Set the values for the feeds and speeds as shown in Figure 5.42.

18.20 Select the  **Macro** tab. The **Approach** macro is highlighted by default, as seen in Figure 5.43. The suggested path is displayed.

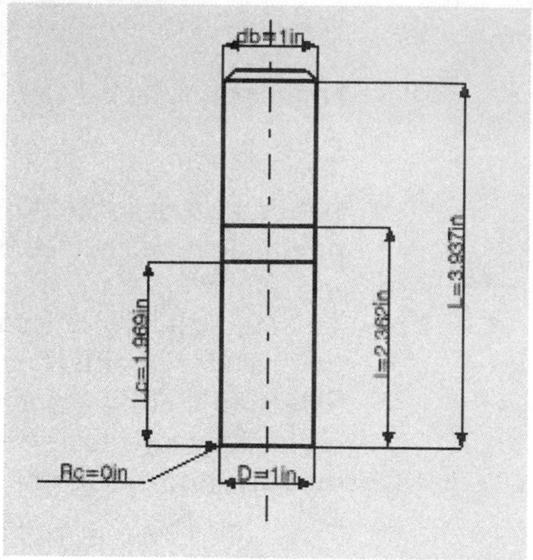

Figure 5.42

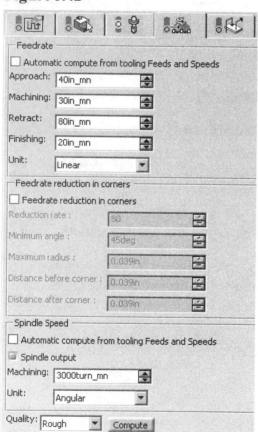

Figure 5.43

18.21 Select the  **Copy approach macro . . . macros** tool.

18.22 Select the **Retract** macro in the list and repeat the above selection.

18.23 The **Finish path** macros will inherit their parameters from the **Approach** and **Retract** macros. Set the **Feedrates** for the **Return Finish Path Retract** and **Return Finish Path Approach** macros to **RAPID** as before.

18.24 The Preview button will let you know if any required parameters are missing.

18.25 Select **Replay** to verify your work. If everything looks acceptable select the **OK** OK button to complete the operation.

19. Milling the Pocket

The next operation will be to mill out the pocket. To complete the pocket complete the following steps.

19.1 Select the last operation so it is highlighted.

19.2 Select the **Pocketing** tool in the **Prismatic Operations** toolbar. This will open the **Pocketing.1** window.

19.3 Select the Closed Pocket found in the bottom of the graphic area as shown in Figure 5.44. Notice that it will toggle between **Open** and **Closed** pocket options. Toggle it to the **Closed Pocket** mode.

Figure 5.44

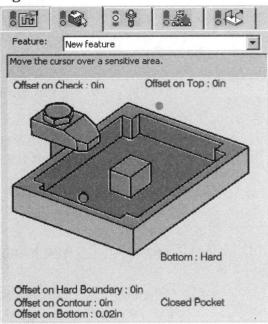

19.4 Make sure the **Bottom** parameter is toggled to **Hard**.

19.5 The easiest way to pick the pocket parameters in this case is to select on the **Select the bottom** in the graphic area. Select the floor of the pocket. This will automatically select the walls and island (if present) of the pocket as boundaries.

19.6 In the **Strategy** tab set the values to those shown in Figure 5.45.

Figure 5.45

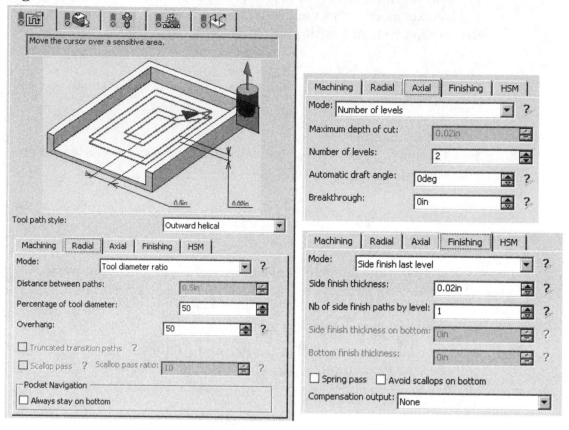

19.7   In the **Tool** tab you are going to re-use a tool so click on the ![...] **Select a tool in document** tool. Select the ½″ **End Mill** cutter from the list.

19.8   Set the **Feedrate** and **Spindle Speed** values as shown in Figure 5.46.

19.9   Select the ![icon] **Macro** tab and select the **Approach** macro from the **Macro Management** list.

19.10   Select the ![icon] **Remove all motions** tool to start from scratch.

19.11   Select the ![icon] **Add Ramping motion** tool.

19.12   Select the ![icon] **Add Axial motion up to a plane** tool. The plane motion will be added to the spiral. Double click on the **Spiral infeed** sensitive tool, reference Figure 5.47.

19.13   Set the **Clearance** parameter to **.5**. This value is actually the distance from the start of the spiral to the bottom of the pocket level that it will cut on.

Figure 5.46

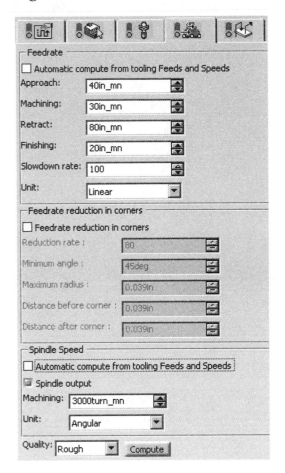

Figure 5.47

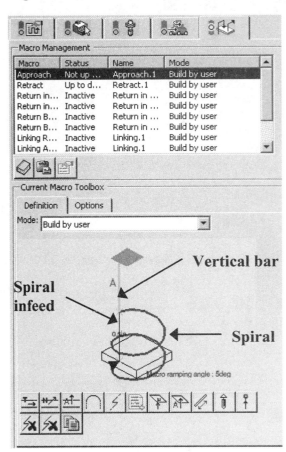

19.14 Right click on the **Spiral** option. This will bring up the **Context** box where you can set parameters for the spiral.

19.15 Set the **Feedrate** parameter to **Machining**.

19.16 Double click on the **Spiral** and a window will appear as seen in Figure 5.48. Set the **Horizontal safety distance** and the **Vertical safety distance** to **.5** and the **Ramping angle** to **5** deg.

19.17 Right click on the **Vertical bar** below the plane to set **Feedrate** values for the approach. The default plane will be used unless you specify a new one.

19.18 Select the 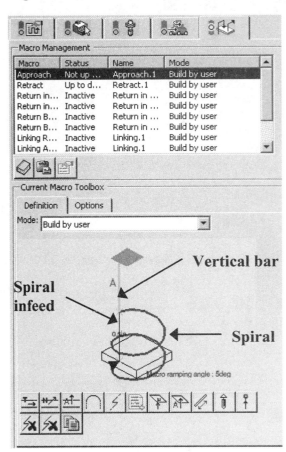 **Copy approach macro . . . macros** tool so that any additional macros we pick will be set up the same way.

Figure 5.48

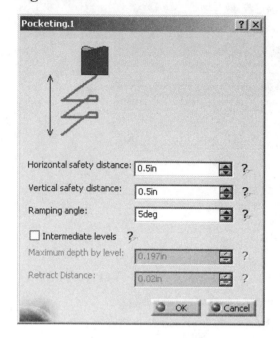

Figure 5.49

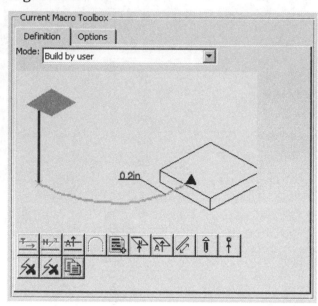

19.19 Select the **Retract** macro.

19.20 Select the 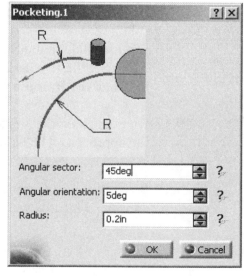 **Remove all motions** tool to start from scratch again. On this retract you will arc away from the drive surface for a smooth cut.

19.21 Select the **Add Circular motion** tool.

19.22 Select the **Add motion perpendicular to a plane** tool. Right click on the arc shaped segment as shown in Figure 5.49. This will open the **context** window.

Figure 5.50

19.23 Set the **Feedrate** to **Machining**.

19.24 Double click on the arc. This will bring up the window similar to the one shown in Figure 5.50.

19.25 Set the parameters to **Angular sector = 45**, **Angular orientation = 5**, and **Radius = .2**. This will lift the tool off the surface as it arcs away from the wall.

19.26 Set the **Feedrate** up to the plane to **RAPID**.   Select the **Copy retract macro . . . macros** tools.

19.27 Highlight and then right click on **Return Between Levels Retract**. This will allow you to **Activate** both the **Retract** and **Approach** macros as shown in Figure 5.51. All of the parameters will be passed from the **Approach** and **Retract** macros you just set up. Do the same for the **Return Finish Path Retract** macro. You will need to change the approach for the **Finish path** since it should be an arc approach instead of a spiral.

Figure 5.51

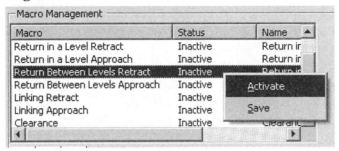

19.28 Highlight the **Return Finish Path Approach** macro. Select the **Remove all motions** tools.

19.29 Select the **Add Circular motion** tool.

19.30 Select the **Add motion perpendicular to a plane** tool. Right click on the arc segment icon and set the parameters the same as the **Retract** macro in Figure 5.50.

19.31 Select the [Preview] button to see if you missed anything.

19.32 Select the **Replay** tool to process the path.

19.33 Select the **OK** [OK] button to accept the path.

20. Post Processing

To complete the machining process you need to post process it.

20.1 Highlight the **Manufacturing Program** you would like to process.

Figure 5.52

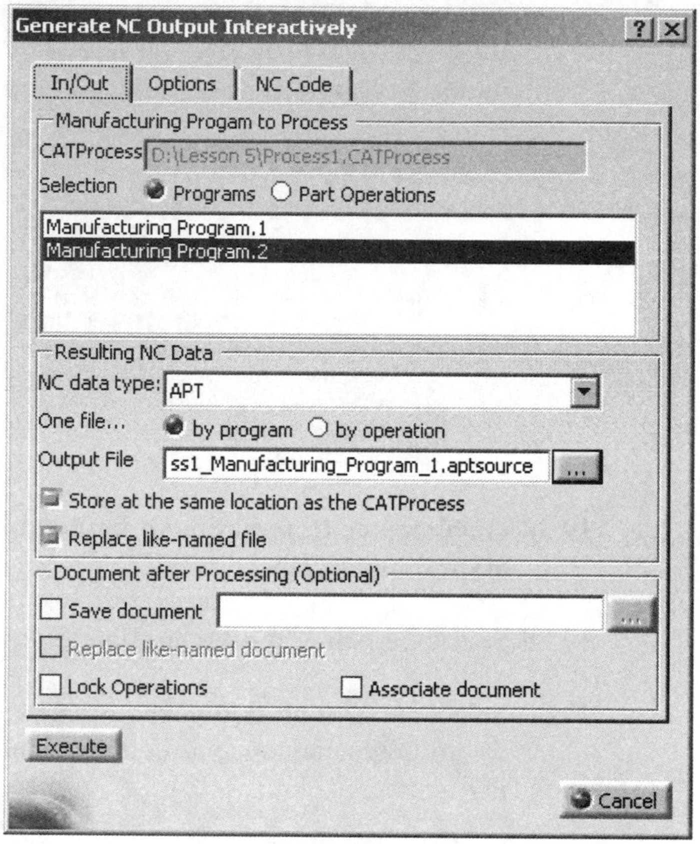

20.2 Select the  **Generate NC Code Interactively** tool in the **NC Output Generations** sub toolbar. This tool is in the **Tool Path Management** toolbar. This will bring up a window similar to the one shown in Figure 5.52. At this point you can enter the name and directory of the posted document.

20.3 Select **Store at the same location as the CATProcess**.

20.4 Select the **Execute** tool to save the **APT** document. You can review the APT document using any of the word processor programs.

Summary

CATIA V5 **Prismatic Machining** workbench has done wonders in simplifying the machining process without giving up any of the expected CATIA NC power. There are many tools (icons) to get used to, but the surface selection process is easy yet powerful. This is a brief introduction to its real power. You need to continue to work and explore and experience the in depth power the **Prismatic Machining** workbench really has.

Review Questions

This lesson was intended to provide a step-by-step example of the creation of a simple part program. You should now have the knowledge to continue exploring the **Prismatic Machining** workbench.

1. How many toolbars are available in the **Prismatic Machining** workbench?

2. What kind of items would you include in a **Product Assembly** file?

3. What kind of information is entered into the **Part Operation** window?

4. Why would you want to set up a **Reference Axis** system?

5. What is the purpose of the **Visualization** elements? What happens if you do not provide any?

6. How many items are generated in the **Specification Tree** when a **Machining Operation** is selected?

7. Explain the purpose and function of the **Status Lights** in the **Operation Definition** window.

8. What effect does the mouse pointer have in the **Operation Definition** window?

9. If an entity were hidden inside of another entity such as a solid stock, how would you go about selecting the hidden entity? Is there more than one way to do this?

10. How is the **Face Selection** window used?

11. Name the five tabs in the **Operation Definition** window and explain the functions of each one.

12. Describe the different ways that a tool can be selected or defined in the **Tool** tab.

13. What is the purpose of the **Macro** function in **Prismatic Machining**?

14. What icon would you use to access the **Zip-Mill** window?

Practice Exercises

For milling exercises, log on to http://www.schroff1.com and click on the link for the Advanced CATIA V5 Workbook. Download the following file:
L5_Milling_exercises.zip.

Terms & Definitions

The terms and definitions below are not your regular dictionary definitions. The definitions are based on how they are used in this workbook. The workbook definitions are included to help lessons to clearly communicate the meaning to the reader.

Assembly: A CATIA V5 session or file (document) that has multiple CATParts assembled together. The file/document would be saved using the CATProduct extension.

Blue Compass: A CATIA V5 tool used in the **Drafting Workbench** to orient the orthographic layout of a part.

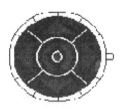

Body: A profile that has been extruded, revolved or swept to create a single solid. Body can be used in the place of solid. In the **Part Design Workbench** a part (**CATPart**) can have multiple bodies.

Boolean: Solids that share space. If you have two separate solids and they overlap (share some space in 3D) the shared space can be subtracted out (Boolean math).

CATDrawing: This is CATIA V5's file extension for files created in the **Drafting Workbench**. The different file types (extensions) that CATIA V5 creates can be and are linked together. A **CATDrawing** is usually linked to a **CATPart** file or **CATProduct** file. **CATDrawing**s are referred to as documents.

CATIA V5: Computer Aided Three-Dimensional Interactive Application, Version 5. CATIA V5 is a product of Dassault Systemes and marketed by IBM.

CATPart: This is a CATIA V5 file extension. **CATPart** files are created in the **Sketcher** and **Part Design Workbenches**. This workbook at times refers to the part and/or file as a **CATPart**. **CATPart** files are referred to as documents

CATProduct: This is CATIA V5's file extension for files created in the **Assembly Design Workbench**. The different file types (extensions) that CATIA V5 creates can be and are linked together. **CATPart** files assembled together are saved as a **CATProduct** file. **CATProduct** files are referred to as documents.

Compass: A tool CATIA V5 uses to help move and/or manipulate the orientation of CATIA V5 parts. The location of the compass is by default the top right of the working screen.

Component: In generic terms it is used the same as entity, a sub set of the whole. A component is sometimes referred to as a simple part. The **Product Structure** and **Assembly Design Workbenches** use component in specific terms, "**Insert New Component**" and "**Insert Existing Component**".

Constraints: A method of applying parameters to a profile sketch, part entity or assembly. The parameter determines the relationship of one entity to another entity, or a particular property of just one entity. A constraint looks and acts much like two and/or three-dimensional dimension. There are **Geometrical Constraints** and **Dimensional Constraints. Dimensional Constraints** can be determined by a formula as well as a numerical value.

Document: Any type of file containing data. The type of data contained is usually designated by the file extension. For example, a CATPart, CATProduct and CATDrawing are all CATIA Document. Files, models and/or parts are often referred to as documents.

DMU: Digital Mock Up.

Dress Up Features: Features used to dress up (modify) an extruded, revolved or swept solid. The features are created using dress up tools such chamfer, corner and break.

Entity: Any kind of single, two or three-dimensional CATIA V5 creation. Entity is sometimes used interchangeably with element, geometry and/or component. Some examples of entities are; a line, an edges, a surface and even a constraint.

Extrude: A 2D profile/periphery created in the **Sketcher Workbench** that is made into a 3D solid. This is accomplished in the **Part Design Workbench** using the **Pad** tool. Lesson 1 and 2 talk about extruding the part or profile sketch, but they are referring to the **Pad** tool.

File: This is what the CATIA V5 creation is saved in, also referred to as a document. The type of file CATIA V5 creates depends on the workbench it was created in. There are **CATPart** files, **CATDrawing** files and **CATProduct** files. CATIA V5 has more types of files, but this workbook only covers the three listed. CATIA V5 refers to a file as a document.

Formula: Math formulas can be used to drive the constraint values.

Geometry: Any kind of single or multiple, two or three-dimensional CATIA V5 creation. Geometry is sometimes used interchangeably with the word "element" and/or "entity."

Hide/Show: A toggle tool that places selected entities in a workspace that is not visible from the typical workspace. The selected geometry is not deleted but just place out of view for later reference. Entities placed in the **Hide/Show** will be dimmed on the **Specification Tree**. You can use the **Swap** tool to view **Hide** workspace.

Highlight: Highlight an element by moving the cursor onto the element and clicking the left mouse button so the element is turned red which is the default color. The element must be selected to highlight, so the word "select" is sometimes used interchangeably with highlight.

Icon: Represents the tool. To start a process the tool must be selected, you select the icon that represents the tool.

Insert Existing Component: A tool found in the **Product Structure** and **Assembly Design Workbench** that allows you to insert an exiting document, this tool is basically the same as inserting a **CATPart.** Reference the Menu 2 (**Specification Tree**) in the Introduction.

Insert New Component: A tool found in the **Product Structure** and **Assembly Design Workbench** that allows you to create a part that is exclusive to that product, it does not stand alone as a its own document. What this really means is you can not use the newly created component in another **CATProduct** document. Reference the Menu 2 (**Specification Tree**) in the Introduction.

Instance: In the **Assembly Design Workbench** the same existing entity (usually **CATPart** or **CATProduct**) can be inserted into the assembly an unlimited amount of times. The instance keeps track of how many times the part was inserted into the assembly. The instance shows up in the **Specification Tree**. In this example **Part2** was inserted 3 times. If **Part2** is modified, the modification will be propagated in all instances.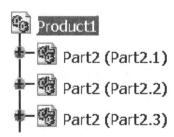

Knowledgeware: A design and application process implementing industry knowledge and standards. Physically it is a toolbar containing tools that allow you to create and manipulate knowledge based information, creates relational design. There are numerous knowledgeware tools throughout CATIA V5. The tools used in this workbook are **Formula** and **Design Table**.

L Shaped Extrusion: The name of a specific part created in Lesson 1. It is also referred to and includes its file extension, "**L Shaped Extrusion.CATPart.**"

Normal: Perpendicular, 90 degrees to the reference element.

Open Body: A branch that is created under the **PartBody** branch of the **Specification Tree**. Wireframe and surfaces entities are found in this branch (**Generative Shape Design Workbench**).

Parametric: Geometric entities that contain intelligence. For example a line has a start and end point and is defined by a slope. A parametric line contains the length, location and its relationship to other entities such as parallel and tangent. So, as the entity is modified all the related entities automatically adjust depending on the predefined relationship.

Parent/Child Relationships: This is directly related to the **Specification Tree**. A **Parent** is at the base branch of the tree. The **Child** components are everything on the lower (smaller) branches. Multiple **Child** components define the **Parent** component. Deleting the child component can create problems with the **Parent** component.

Part: The term "part" is synonymous with CATPart. Part is used to refer to a specific CATPart such as "**L Shaped Extrusion.CATPart.**" For example in the workbook the "**L Shaped Extrusion**" could be referred to as "the solid" or "the part."

Periphery: The outside edge and/or surface of a part. Periphery is at times used interchangeably with the word profile.

Plane: A graphical entity CATIA V5 uses to represent a defined two-dimensional slice of the CATIA V5 three-dimensional working space.

Profile: The profile is the cross sectional outline of a part. Profile is at times used interchangeably with the word periphery. Profile and periphery are used to define a sketch that is ready to be extruded, revolved or swept.

Prompt Zone: The bottom left of the CATIA V5 screen that has changing text, depending on the tool being used. You select a particular tool and CATIA V5 will prompt you on what selection and/or input is required.

Select an object or a command

Reference: The original **CATPart** that instances are linked to. Reference the Menu 2 (**Specification Tree**) in the Introduction.

Relational Design: Relational design could refer to one individual part but is usually used in reference to an assembly. An assembly consisting of parametrically designed parts. The individual parts share predefined relationships usually in the form of constraints, formulas and design tables. Correctly predefining the relationships could result in quick and easy modifications to the assembly. This is opposed to being required to individually modify each part and part entity to the new requirement.

Select: Move the cursor over the entity and click the left mouse button. The result of selecting an entity is the entity being highlighted or a process being started.

Sketch: A two dimensional drawing consisting of lines, points, arcs, etc. A sketch is created in the **Sketcher Workbench** and/or the **Drafting Workbench**.

Sketch Features: 3D geometrical entities based on a 2D sketch (**Sketcher Workbench**). Solids are created from sketch features by extrusion (Pad tool), rotation or sweeping. If a body is created using a tool shown in the Sketched-Based Features toolbar.

Sketcher: Short reference for **Sketcher Workbench**.

Solid: A type of part. A 3D entity that a material type can be applied to such as a CATPart. A solid can also be an imported solid using STEP or other solids translator. In the workbook a specific part such as the "**L Shaped Extrusion.CATPart**" is referred to as a solid.

Specification Tree: An organized history of everything required to create the part /product. Every step to creating a part is documented in a tree structure. There are icons that represent different branches to the tree such as Partbody, Product, Openbody and Sketch. Lesson 2 shows how to use replay to review the design process.

Surface: An entity that describes a boundary in space but has no thickness. A surface can be stretched over a wireframe or extracted from a solid. A surface can look very similar to a solid. A surface can be shaded and enclosed to create a solid. A document containing a surface/surfaces has a **CATPart** or **CATProduct** extension.

Tool: The operation that accomplishes a particular task and/or process, such as the **Pad** tool. Tools are represented by icons. One or more tools that share a similar task/process are grouped together to make a **Toolbar**.

Toolbar: A designated bar containing one or more individual tools. The toolbar will be labeled according to the functions of the tools it contains; for example, the Sketch Based Feature toolbar.

T Shaped Extrusion: The name of a specific part you create in Lesson 2. It is also called out with its file extension, "**T Shaped Extrusion.CATPart**." The "**T Shaped Extrusion**" is sometimes referred to as the "part" during the particular lesson. The "**T Shaped Extrusion.CATPart**" is also referred to as a document.

Wireframe: A combination of three-dimensional **Open Body** elements. Usually consists of points, lines and arcs. A wireframe cannot be shaded. The workbook will capitalize and bold the word wireframe when it is referencing a tool and/or a specific wireframe.

Workbench: A specific set of CATIA V5 toolbars packaged together to accomplish a particular task for example the Part Design Workbench has tools to create individual parts where the Drafting Workbench supplies tools specific to drafting and creating production drawings. Workbenches have their own screen layout, default tools bars/tools and files extension (document). Usually the workbench name signifies what its particular task is.